SPIRAL GUIDES

Travel With Someone You Trust ®

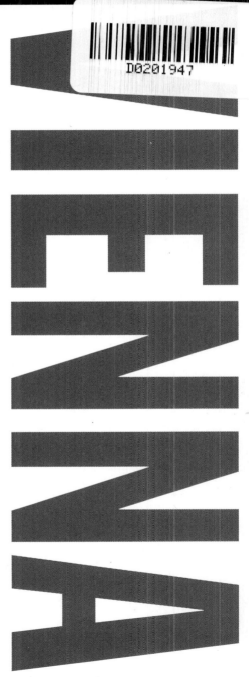

Contents

the magazine 5

Finding Your Feet 35

Medieval Vienna 47

The Imperial City 69

The Western Ringstrasse 93

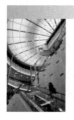

Written by Hanne Egghardt and Katharina Kunz
Copy edited by Katrin Wampula
Picture research by Gabriele Forst
Page layout by Cyclus · Visuelle Kommunikation
Translated by Christopher Wightwick and Sylvia Goulding
English text copy edited by Silva Editions Ltd
Updated by Neal Bedford
American editor Tracy Larson

Published in the United States by AAA Publishing,
1000 AAA Drive, Heathrow, Florida 32746
Published in the United Kingdom by AA Publishing

ISBN 978-1-59508-278-7

Cover design and binding style by permission of AA Publishing

Color separation by Leo Reprographics
Printed and bound in China
by Leo Paper Products

10 9 8 7 6 5 4 3 2 1

A03439
Transport map © Communicarta Ltd, UK

the magazine

A few years ago Austrian opinion was sharply divided over a character in the TV series *A echter Wiener geht net unter* (Your true Viennese will never be beaten). There were indignant cries of "We're really not as vulgar as that!", while others thought it "really great, a slice of life". However you take it, though, you can learn a lot about the Viennese from the TV series.

The character, Mundl Sackbauer, is a loud-mouthed primitive, never without a bottle of beer in his hand and fond of letting go with strong language. He is a lovable, ungainly rogue who always manages to avoid giving offence despite his dubious

the past, stereotyping has centred on three traits above all. The first was quibbling: very rarely, it was said, can you get it right for the Viennese – they find fault with

A true Viennese ...

dealings. So he is on a par with Helmut Qualtinger's legendary Herr Karl, a character taken straight from the malicious world of lower-middle-class Vienna, who became the image of the archetypal Viennese opportunist and malcontent.

A "true Viennese"?
Does a "true Viennese" exist? Go and find out for yourself that there's no such thing. In

everything. The second was more positive: they have a "golden heart", especially for animals, it was believed. The third and last was their predilection for "Viennese *Schmäh*", a unique sort of sarcastic humour.

These three age-old stereotypes no longer hold true today – if, indeed, they ever did. The young people of today, especially, are modern-thinking and open to the world. Perhaps the only thing you will genuinely come across is the Viennese Schmäh, since many places

Page 5: The Pallas Athene fountain in front of the Parliament building

Above left: Cabbies at their favourite pastime

Above right: Occasionally you can scale the Rathaus-platz walls have their own and local sense of humour – if you can understand the dialect, that is. Ask about the building works in Vienna or any other universal topic for complaints, and you'll hear the typical mixture of "*Schmäh*" and grumbles. Talk about the hotly disputed "poo-bags", which in July 2004

Multiethnic Vienna

The fact is, of course, that there is no such thing as a "true Viennese" and probably never has been. From its earliest days through to its rise as a city at the end of the 19th

won't be beaten

century, people of the most varied origins have lived in this city on the fault-line between East and West. Even around 1900 it was still a requirement that higher-grade civil servants should speak six to eight languages. And if you look in the Vienna telephone book you'll see that names like Swoboda and Cerny, Kovacs and Arslan fill

were imposed on cab-horses, to catch droppings even before they have a chance to foul the streets, and you'll hear a passionate plea for the dignity of the horse. But is that "*Schmäh*" so different from what you would hear in other cities?

Above left:
A quiet moment in the café

Above centre:
Business doesn't stop for shopping

Above right:
Naughty but nice – the ice-cream parlour

What is "Viennese Schmäh"?

Scholarly dissertations have been written on the subject of what "Viennese *Schmäh*" really is, but there is still no precise explanation. Whatever its definition, it is certainly composed of a number of elements: a curious sort of humour, a trenchant way of talking and a dash of bragging. Its home base is above all at cafés, in wine bars with their earthy locals, and late at night by the Wiener sausage stall, where the chat, and with it the *Schmäh*, flows so freely that the Viennese say "*Schmäh*'s on the run".

UN Headquarters

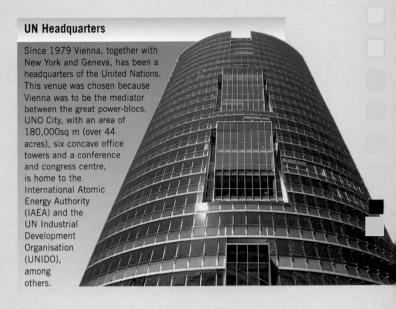

Since 1979 Vienna, together with New York and Geneva, has been a headquarters of the United Nations. This venue was chosen because Vienna was to be the mediator between the great power-blocs. UNO City, with an area of 180,000sq m (over 44 acres), six concave office towers and a conference and congress centre, is home to the International Atomic Energy Authority (IAEA) and the UN Industrial Development Organisation (UNIDO), among others.

many columns. In fact, immigrants have always shaped Vienna with their cultures, their cuisines and their lifestyles. Long before the idea of multiculturalism was common currency, people from every corner of the empire were drawn to the city on the Danube, which became a melting pot for the multi-ethnic state. And later, when Vienna was the over-large head of a shrunken realm, the influx continued. Thousands came pouring in from Hungary after 1956, joined from the 1970s on by people from what was then Yugoslavia and from Turkey, who were known as "guest-workers".

A taste of the Caribbean on the Danube

Immigrants created Vienna's unique atmosphere for the city's cultural

Facts and Figures

Vienna, with an area of 415sq km (160sq miles) and a perimeter of 133km (82 miles), has 1.6 million inhabitants, of whom 18% are foreigners. In population terms, Vienna is the seventh largest European capital.

development. Around 1900 this fertile background allowed the sciences, architecture, decorative and fine arts, as well as music to flourish. Writers such as Arthur Schnitzler and Robert Musil, Heimito von Doderer and Hermann Broch, Alfred Polgar and Egon Friedell drew their creative inspiration from the diversity of Vienna's roots.

In recent years Vienna has begun to rediscover its old strength and creativity. There's a strong sense of urban revival, the city is full of a vibrant life seldom felt before. "Your true Viennese will never be beat." How true...

Multicultural music in Stephansplatz

Vienna and the Danube

To say that Vienna lies "on the beautiful blue Danube", as the text of the Strauss waltz has it, is pure nonsense. The Danube is murky and grey, and always has been. The 280m (305-yard) wide river was certainly always important as a transport artery, but its flooding posed equally great dangers. In the 1970s the construction of the New Danube, an additional river channel 20km (12.5 miles) long, brought some relief. It also created the Donauinsel (Danube Island), a vast recreation area (► 153).

HIGHLIGHTS AT A GLANCE

Once Round the Ringstrasse

It's not the most luxurious form of transport, but taking trams D or 2 round the Ringstrasse is the simplest and cheapest way to see the elegant buildings either side of Vienna's famous boulevard close up. You can start your circular route wherever you want, at Schwedenplatz, by the Staatsoper or at Schottentor, and then stay put until you arrive back at your starting point. The Ring isn't just a name, it really is a ring.

The Most Exciting Musical Experiences

Nothing beats a visit to the Staatsoper (➤ 98). But performances of classical music in the Konzerthaus (➤ 136) or the Musikverein (➤ 131) come a close second. Recently Vienna has also caught up with the world of jazz. Joe Zawinul's Birdland (➤ 158) in the newly refurbished Hilton Hotel is truly sensational, and Porgy and Bess (➤ 68) also ranks high.

The Most Exciting Museums

"Art and enjoyment" is the motto of the new Viennese museums. In the museum district (➤ 103), art and urban

Background: The traffic jam at Schottentor

Above: From the terrace of the Haas-Haus you can almost touch the Stephansdom

Left: The Staatsoper, Vienna's most famous temple of music

Right: A sweet place to go: Demel's café in Kohlmarkt

flair can be enjoyed in many venues. The lavishly renovated Albertina (► 82) is an imposing temple to the arts, and the splendid Palais Liechtenstein (► 26) really is a "place of baroque joie de vivre". But it would be a mistake if these marvellous new museums led you to neglect the Kunsthistorisches and Naturhistorisches museums (Museum of Art History and Museum of Natural History), not only because of their fascinating exhibits but also because of the fine architecture of both buildings.

Leisure in the Open Air

In summer the opera and film festival at Rathausplatz (► 18) is a favourite free open-air event of the Viennese. Other popular shows for cool entertainment on hot summer nights include Copa Cagrana on the Danube Island, the Summer Stage by the Danube Canal, and the University Campus in the inner courtyards of the old AKH (► 19). The Schweizerhaus in the Prater (► 155) is also great fun.

The Finest Views

- The north tower of Stephansdom (► 52)
- The terrace of the Gloriette (► 134)
- The cafeteria in Leiner's furnishing store (► 105)
- The great Ferris wheel (► 146)

The Best Torten

The very best Viennese *Torten* – gâteaux, flans, cakes – are to be had at Demel's, the court confectioner's on Kohlmarkt

(► 90), but you're also guaranteed top quality in the world-famous café Sacher (► 110) and many other patisseries such as Kurkonditorei Oberlaa (► 111), café Landtmann (► 111) and Slukas (► 111).

The Finest Viennese Coffee-houses

Sperl's (► 134) is the most romantic of all Viennese coffee-houses, Landtmann's (► 111) the liveliest and the Bräunerhof (► 89) the most traditional. In any case: don't just take a look, but set aside at least an hour to enjoy the ambience.

The Best Places for Children

- Ride bumper-cars in the Wurstelprater (► 150)
- Admire butterflies in the Palmenhaus (► 86)
- Watch the animals in the Schönbrunn zoo (► 121)

Right: Splendid butterflies feel at home in the butterfly house

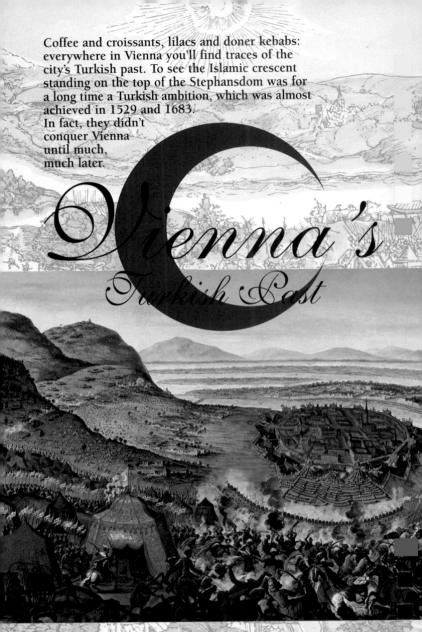

Coffee and croissants, lilacs and doner kebabs: everywhere in Vienna you'll find traces of the city's Turkish past. To see the Islamic crescent standing on the top of the Stephansdom was for a long time a Turkish ambition, which was almost achieved in 1529 and 1683.
In fact, they didn't conquer Vienna until much, much later.

Vienna's Turkish Past

Sultan Suleiman II the Magnificent, sultan of the Ottoman Empire, had the ambition to extend his realm and set his sights on Vienna. In 1529 he laid siege to the city with 150,000 troops, while 20,000 camels brought reinforcements and supplies. At that time Vienna was not well fortified, and the defending general, Count Niklas Salm, had only 20,000 troops. Virtually at the eleventh

Background:
The First Turkish Siege, 1529

Above: The Second Turkish Siege, 1683–99

hour, though, the city was saved, winter arrived earlier than usual at the beginning of October, and the invaders were forced to withdraw.

In 1566 Sultan Suleiman II was again marching against Vienna. He besieged the town of Szigetvár in Hungary and put it to the torch on the night of 5 September. On the same night he died of a heart attack, so he never got his second look at Vienna. All the same, he gave something to the city's image. It was he who presented an emissary of the emperor, Ogier Ghislain de Busbecq, with a few tulip and hyacinth bulbs, and some lilac plants. Since then Vienna has been at its most beautiful each year in May, when the lilacs bloom all over the city.

The Kipferl – a Giant Crescent

In 1683 the Turkish forces besieged Vienna a second time. Once again the situation was desperate. Within the city dysentery was rife, and supplies were running low. To prove that they had enough flour, the Viennese are said to have baked a *kipferl*, a pastry shaped like a giant crescent and hoisted it in defiance above the city walls. Vienna's fate was on a knife-edge, but the relief army under Polish king Jan Sobieski came to the rescue. The attackers were put to flight – they even left their coffee-making gear behind (► 28)!

Peaceful Conquest

By the 18th century Turkey posed no further threat – in fact all things Turkish became fashionable. Painters and composers produced works "alla turca", and people wore oriental-inspired clothing and used harems as the backdrop to operas, as in Mozart's *Die Entführung aus dem Serail*. Few contemporary composers could do without instruments such as cymbals, triangles and glockenspiels.

At the end of the 1950s the first Turkish immigrant workers arrived in Vienna. Since then 52,000 of them have settled in the city. Sometimes they joke that "now we have conquered the city after all". And in the meanwhile the Viennese themselves have taken to doner kebabs and heatedly discuss the pros and cons of Turkey's entry into the European Union.

► 28

Turkish Footsteps

- **Wien 1, Am Hof 11:** a gilded Turkish cannon-ball
- **Esterházykeller, Wien 1, Haarhof:** a plaque commemorates the fact that during the Turkish siege of 1683 the city's defenders took wine at this cellar.

Zur Zeit der Belagerung Wiens durch die Türken im Jahre 1683 tranken hier in diesem Keller schon die Verteidiger der Stadt den vom Fürsten Esterházy verabreichten Humpen frei Wein.

- **Neustädterhof, Wien 1, Sterngasse 3:** the largest Turkish cannon-ball in the district.
- **Galerie des Michaelertors, Wien 1, Michaelerplatz:** Turkish trophies

Top: An actress in Mozart's opera *Die Entführung aus dem Serail* – all very Turkish

In places as diverse as Schönbrunn, Hofburg and Kapuzinergruft you find traces of Maria Theresa. That's hardly surprising, as the Empress is the ancestral mother of Austria. During her reign (1740–80) the state was reorganised.

The Baroque
Empress

The second day of May, 1750, was a fateful day. It was when Empress Maria Theresa made a radical change to the constitution, bringing together the hereditary provinces of Austria and the lands of the Bohemian kingdom to form a single state. This act made the capital, Vienna, the centre of an empire, and in consequence the city needed an appropriate royal residence. And so Maria Theresa had the palace of Schönbrunn enlarged.

"Thou, happy Austria, marry!"

Although Maria Theresa fought and lost wars, she married off her 16 children to all points of the compass, following the motto "Bella gerant alii, tu, felix Austria, nube" (Let others wage war, thou, happy Austria, marry). Marie Antoinette had the worst luck. At the tender age of 15 years, she was married to the French King Louis XVI and ended up on the scaffold in the French Revolution.

Maria Theresa, Holy Roman Empress and Queen of Hungary and Bohemia

Maria-Theresien-Platz

Since 1888 "Europe's mother-in-law" has gazed from her place of honour between the Kunsthistorisches Museum and the Naturhistorisches Museum towards the city centre. At the empress's feet stand the men who came to fame during her reign. Among the 16 high-relief figures you can find Mozart, Haydn and Gluck.

Everywhere in Vienna you feel the imperial splendour and the elegance of the "k.u.k." era, short for "kaiserlich und königlich" (imperial and royal) and nostalgia for the "good old days". The great symbol of that time was Franz Joseph I. The emperor with the paternal look and the long sideburns ruled for 68 years and he oversaw Vienna's transition to an important city.

"It was very beautiful ...

Franz Joseph ascended the imperial throne in 1848, the year of revolutions, at the age of only 18. Always true to the advice of his counsellors and his mother, Sophie, whose cool and unbending nature he had inherited, he remained conscientious and dogmatic throughout his rule. In 1854, in Vienna's Augustinerkirche,

he married the very young Elisabeth, known as "Sisi". She soon began to suffer from the distant manner of the emperor and his mother. The emperor found solace with his soulmate, the actress Katharina Schratt.

"It was very beautiful, we were very pleased": this was one of the courteous, but

The emperor's ascent to the throne, 2 December, 1848

... we were very pleased"

meaningless phrases which the emperor liked to use. A more appropriate phrase might have been "I have been spared nothing", for he had to endure a series of blows. In 1867 his brother Maximilian was executed in Mexico; in 1889 his son, Crown Prince Rudolf, committed suicide in Mayerling (➤ 166); in 1898 his wife Elisabeth was the victim of an assassination; and in 1914 the heir to the throne, Archduke Franz Ferdinand, and his wife were murdered.

The Construction of the Ringstrasse

When Emperor Franz Joseph came to the throne, Vienna was still encircled by broad ramparts and fortifications, which had long lost their function and were in practice just a tight corset hemming in the city. The proposal

to raze them provoked violent protest – anyone with the time and leisure to read the *Wiener Zeitung* for Christmas Day 1857 would have been astonished. With the words, "It is my will", the emperor gave the official order to start the demolition of the fortifications and construction of the Ringstrasse, and thus an era of urban expansion. Vienna developed from its idyllic Biedermeier period (early 19th century) into a cosmopolitan city, a metropolis whose architecture was designed to show

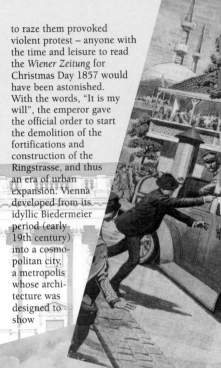

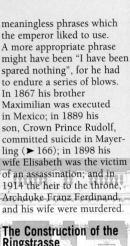

In Franz Joseph's day the imperial army was a significant force

with precious objects, but lived in a modest, even spartan manner in Schönbrunn. Grown cautious as a result of various political mistakes, he increasingly became the symbol of political inactivity and opposed any innovations or reforms, also refusing to abdicate in favour of his nephew Franz Ferdinand. In 1914, at the age of 84, he signed, in Bad Ischl, the declaration of war on Serbia, and so began World War I. The Austro-Hungarian empire collapsed under the strain of war, but the emperor was spared seeing it happen: he died in 1916, two years before the end of the war.

its domi-nance over every town in the kingdom (▶ 93).

Heyday and decline

Under Franz Joseph's rule cultural and intellectual life flourished, though the emperor himself had little interest in the fine arts. He did not surround himself

Poor Unhappy Sisi

What had begun as a great romance ended in loneliness and sorrow. The young empress (1837–98) suffered under the ceremonial protocol of the Hofburg and the strict regime of her mother-in-law, Sophie. She took refuge in illness, isolation and extensive travel. Her beauty became an obsession. She spent hours each day tending her ankle-length hair, rode, exercised and followed strict diet regimes – on some days she ate only a few oranges. Fate was unkind to the empress: in 1857 her two-year-old daughter Sophie died and her soulmate and good friend King Ludwig II of Bavaria drowned in mysterious circumstances in Starnberger See. When in 1889 her son Rudolf and his lover Mary Vetsera committed suicide, her melancholy deepened. "Would that death would surprise me," she wrote in her journal. Her wish was fulfilled when she was assassinated in Geneva by the Italian anarchist Luigi Luccheni, who stabbed her with a file.

Totally Cool:
The Outdoor

Gone are the days when the Viennese spent summer and winter entirely in smoke-filled coffeehouses. Outdoor living is now all the rage: streetlife, ethnic food in the fresh air, cinema beneath a starry sky and impromptu parties. A fresh wind is blowing through the streets of Vienna, and not only in summer.

Vienna's open-air cinemas

- **Arena**, Wien 3, Baumgasse 80, tel: (01) 798 85 95, www.arena.co.at
- **Filmarchiv** (Austrian avant-garde), Wien 2, Obere Augartenstrasse 1, tel: (01) 216 13 00, www.filmarchiv.at
- **Kino unter Sternen** (classics original version), Wien 2/ 20, Augarten-Schlüssel-wiese, tel: (0800) 644040, www.kinountersternen.at
- **Rathausplatz** (opera and classical music films), Wien 1, Rathausplatz, tel: (01) 4000-81 00, www.wien-event.at
- **Schloss Neugebäude** (box office hits, entertainment), Wien 11, Meidlgasse, tel: (01) 74 03 41 11 18, www.schlosskino.at
- **Tribüne Krieau** (cult, classics and music), Wien 2, Nordportalstrasse 247, no phone, www.krieau.com
- **Volxkino** (repertory and box office hits), Wanderkino, tel: (01) 219 85 45, www.volxkino.at

Life

"Schani, get the garden ready" – as soon as the boss spoke these words, Schani the apprentice waiter knew that spring had arrived. On the first warm sunny days he carried tables and chairs outside – and the "Schani-garden" was ready. That's how it used to be.

Nowadays Vienna has been totally transformed. Practically the entire city centre is one huge Schani-garden. From Graben to Kohlmarkt, Lugeck to the inner courtyard of the MuseumsQuartier, it's one café and restaurant after another. Almost every week new bars and meeting places open: these chic and modern spots have all the flair and freshness of up-to-the-minute gastro-culture.

The Whole of Vienna in Party Mood

Throughout the summer a party mood reigns in the numerous Copa Cagrana bars on the Danube Island (► 158) and at Summer Stage at the Rossauer wharf on the Danube Canal. Here fashionable bars set up "open-air branches", with live music and amusements such as trampolining. The university campus pubs in the inner courtyards of the old AKH (the former general hospital) are also always crammed full (Wien 9, Spitalgasse2). So the question is: who in Vienna really spends the evenings in front of the television? There are obviously not many couch potatoes who want to miss the open-air party.

The outdoor life, however, isn't just a summer thing. In the run up to Christmas, streams of people go to the Advent markets, and the mulled wine stalls are the coolest place to meet your friends. Austrians celebrate New Year in a big way and party on the street all night. And if it's a really icy winter, Rathausplatz becomes a skating rink.

Above left: There's always a lively scene in Stephansplatz

Centre: Summer Stage holds many events

Left: MQ is a favourite meeting place

Above right: Riverside bars are great for hot nights

Right: Nina Proll on the Danube Island

Death must be

To say that Vienna has a special relationship with death is a cliché, but there is some truth in it. Traces of the liaison are everywhere. It extends from the reverence paid to memorials and tombs, last resting places and grave-yards, which is almost a cult, to the Viennese songs sung at the wine harvest: sad, melancholic and beautiful.

The Viennese and death go back a long way: to the 17th century, when "der liebe Augustin" (dear Augustin), a famous minstrel, was accidentally thrown into a mass grave for plague victims. Even there he did not lose his sense of humour, but went on clowning around to the tune of his bagpipes, to keep his courage up. And so he survived, among all the plague-riddled corpses.

The story culminates in the notion that a "fine corpse" (a splendid funeral) is the highpoint of life. And there is a scholarly side to this preoccupation with death: in Vienna, Sigmund Freud (1856–1939) researched the death wish; Erwin Ringel (known in the trade as Mr

The Bestattungsmuseum (Funerary Museum) is one of Vienna's curiosities. Six hundred exhibits document every imaginable product of the cult of death. Mourning clothes, sashes and grave-diggers' equipment are on display beside the most varied examples of urns, coffins and hearses, including the late 19th-century economy coffin, with a lid which allowed it to be re-used. (Wien 4, Goldegggasse 19, tel: 501 95, Mon–Fri noon–3, Bus No 13A, Tram D Belvederegasse, visits need to be booked and are free as part of a 45-minute guided tour)

a Viennese

The plague column at the Graben is a reminder of horror and death

Suicide) founded Europe's first crisis intervention centre in 1948; and in Vienna Professor Tomáš Masaryk (1850–1937), who was later to become the President of Czechoslovakia, wrote his doctoral thesis on the topic of suicide.

Europe's Largest Cemetery

The Zentralfriedhof (Central Cemetery), which the Austrian multimedia artist André Heller called the "aphrodisiac for necrophiles", is at 2.4sq km (about one square mile) the largest cemetery in Europe. The custodian at the main gate has a guide to the last resting-places of great personalities: here lie the musicians Johannes Brahms, Johann Strauss father and son, Wolfgang Amadeus Mozart (memorial) and Franz Schubert; and the actors Curd Jürgens and Helmut Qualtinger, who coined the marvellous words: "In Vienna you have to die before they'll say 'Long live ...!', but then you'll live for aeons."

Melancholy and Happiness

The waltz kings Johann Strauss father and son, themselves often shaken by fear of death, wrote music whose surface gaiety is always tinged with a touch of melancholy and pain. That goes also for the Heurigen (wine taverns) music. When the waves of gaiety are at their peak, enter Death. Not inspiring fear, though, but as a friend. "When it's all over, with music and wine ..." – that's a reminder of death, easy to sing ...

The 400-year-old Jewish cemetery is hidden in an idyllic spot in a residential area of Vienna. The entrance to the cemetery is through a retirement home. (Wien 9, Seegasse 9–11, Mon–Fri 8–3, Tram D Seegasse)

Street performers won't play the "Blue Danube" waltz in the U-bahn, but you'll still notice that Vienna is the world capital of music. The cornerstones of this elite art are the Staatsoper (▶ 98), Philharmoniker, Konzerthaus (▶ 136) and Musikverein (▶ 131).

Vienna Plays First

Vienna has been home to more musicians than any other city in the world. On the "Walk of Fame" between Naschmarkt and the Stephansdom the 70 marble stars commemorate great musicians of the world (see above left for Haydn's). Most of them did not have an easy life in the city though. The cabaret artist Georg Kreisler once put it thus: "Vienna has always been hostile to

W A Mozart

Mozart has often been treated badly in Vienna. The Mozarthaus was a disgrace until renovation finally started in 2004. Steffl's department store now stands on the site of Mozart's last residence, and the room he died in is commemorated by a bust and a plaque sitting among toys, children's clothing and antique furniture. And "Mozart's grave" in the Friedhof St Marx (▶ 179) is empty: the greatest musical genius of all time was buried in a mass grave, no one knows where.

The House of Music

To hear, see and feel music – the Haus der Musik (House of Music), a super-modern musical theme park with seven separate experience zones, makes it all possible. You can even take the baton yourself and conduct the Philharmoniker (Wien 1, Seilerstätte 30, tel: 01/516 48, www.hdm.at).

Fiddle

music, doing its best to frighten off any significant musician." In many cases it succeeded. Franz Schubert was destitute. Hugo Wolf starved. Anton Bruckner was valued as a teacher and organist, but never as composer. Gustav Mahler had to get himself baptized before he could become director of the opera, and Webern, Schönberg and Berg were simply ignored. And as for the fact that Haydn, Beethoven and Gluck, whom Vienna likes to boast about, were not even born here – well, nobody mentions that.

The Vienna Waltz Conquered the World

All the same, no one can deny that musical history has been written in Vienna. Twice, in the classical era and at the end of the 19th century, more pioneering musicians were working in Vienna than in any other city. And from the banks of the Danube the strains of the Strauss family's waltzes travelled around the world.

Nowadays, Vienna is equally famous for its musicians and instrument-makers as for its first-class centres of training and performance. The Wiener Sängerknaben (Vienna Boys' Choir), Philharmoniker and Bösendorfer grand pianos are synonymous with the highest standards in the whole world.

The New Year Concert

Many people love Viennese music as a vibrant and cheerful start to the year. The New Year Concert from the Golden Hall of the Musikverein is broadcast around the world and watched by millions.

Background: Violins are on sale in markets as well as music stores

Above: Bliss in three-four time – the Vienna waltz

Left: Mozart spent his best years in the Mozarthaus Wien (► 60)

Far left: The three "Viennese" stars: Haydn, Beethoven and Mozart

VIENNESE JUGENDSTIL

Viennese Jugendstil (art nouveau) is more than an architectural style. A way of life, it combines graphic design, architecture, commercial art and traditional crafts into one great and very elegant synthesis.

It all began with a youthful rebellion. In 1897 Gustav Klimt and his comrades-at-arms left the "Genossenschaft", the artists' association, and founded a new artists' group, the "Secession", a name which was later applied to the style itself. The artists Josef Hoffmann, Joseph Maria Olbrich, Koloman Moser, Otto Wagner and Adolf Loos now had one main aim: to protest against meaning-less ornamentation, such as that used to excess on the buildings of the Ringstrasse.

The Secession Style
The floral art nouveau style, which flourished at that time in other countries, foundered in Vienna on the conservative attitude of the emperor. And when (eventually) the new style finally reached the city it developed its own identity

Above: "A golden titbit" is what the Viennese call the Secession movement

Where to See Jugendstil
• **Majolikahaus** Otto Wagner's house with decorative iron balconies and a façade of majolica tiles (Wien 5, Wienzeile 40), and next to it the apartment block at Linke Wienzeile No 38.
• **Postsparkasse** (Post Office Savings Bank) Otto Wagner's milestone in architectural history (Wien 1, Georg-Coch-Platz 2)
• **MAK** (Museum of Applied Arts). Craftwork from Gustav Klimt's Stoclet frieze design to Thonet's bentwood furniture and work from Viennese workshops (Wien 1, Stubenring 5, www.mak.at)
• **Backhausen-Wiener-Werkstätte-Museum**, the Backhausen Vienna Workshop Museum holds 3,500 original designs (from the period 1860–1950) from the textile firm Joh. Backhausen & Söhne (Wien 1, Schwarzenbergstrasse 10, www.backhausen.at)

A FLIGHT OF FANCY

marked by clear, severe forms. Viennese Jugendstil was characterised by a retreat from curves and

movement. And in the Sanatorium Purkersdorf, which has a flat roof and glass walls, Josef Hoffmann explored new directions towards functionalism.

a return to straight lines, from organic to geometric forms. Vienna Jugendstil's favourite shape was the square; verticals were also important to them. Ornamentation was used sparingly and always set against large empty surfaces. Vienna Jugendstil should be seen as a late phase of the art nouveau movement, which anticipated the Bauhaus style of the 1920s.

On the Way to Modern Architecture

Top: Otto Wagner's urban railway stations have been renovated

Right: Generous and functional: the Post Office Savings Bank

From this point of view, the Jugendstil works of Otto Wagner, such as the Stadtbahn (Urban Railway) and its stations (► 125) and the Postsparkasse (Post Office Savings Bank), are truly pioneering achievements. With the Secession (► 126), the exhibition hall of the new artists' association, Joseph Maria Olbrich created another Viennese emblem which also gave its name to the

Decorative Art

The Secessionists did not stay together for long. In 1905 Klimt, Wagner, Hoffmann and Moser left the group. Art, they declared, must penetrate into every arena. With this in mind, Hoffmann and Moser took over the direction of the craft association "Wiener Werkstätte" (Vienna Workshops), in order to devote themselves to the reform of domestic culture and to bring their aesthetic standards to bear on every aspect of daily life. They created fabrics, furniture, clothes and other everyday items; typically handmade and of immense beauty their aesthetic quality still fascinates today.

Museum-Mad Vienna

If the whole city seems to you like one giant accumulation of museums then you've got the right impression. Vienna has almost twice as many museums as, for example, Munich. And more keep opening every year. The amazing thing is that each new museum is even more spectacular than the last.

Until a few years ago the city of Vienna was proud of having almost 100 museums with exhibits from every era. But recent developments have almost put the past to shame.

Palais Liechtenstein. This "place of baroque joie de vivre" presents life and art as a great, sumptuous artistic unity, with music, literature and dance forming the framework to exhibitions of

MQ became an exciting place for urban encounters

Since the mid-1990s Vienna has caught what can only be described as museum-fever, with one gigantic museum boasting vast exhibition areas after another.

The construction of the MuseumsQuartier (Museum District) had already given Vienna more exhibition space than any other city, but this was followed by the Albertina and, in spring 2004, by the

the Princes' collections, brought from Vaduz, the capital of Liechtenstein, to Vienna to be spectacularly displayed.

The museum boom has altered the city as greatly as the construction of the Ringstrasse 150 years ago. This time the city has created an urban district devoted to art and palaces refurbished to a high standard with no

Above left: The Kunsthistorisches Museum is a gigantic treasure chest

Above right: In the MQ you can also eat, drink and listen to jazz

The most exciting museums

expense spared, making the entire cultural district accessible to everyone.

A New Life in the Museums

However, just showing valuable pictures in galleries or exhibiting some precious, interesting or unusual objects in glass cases is no longer considered enough. Moreover, visitors are no longer to be enticed into a quick visit, taking in works of art at the double, "ticking off" the latest trend as they go. Instead they are invited to surrender to a completely new cultural attitude. "Life and enjoyment" is the motto for Vienna's cultural area. And that's not overstating it.

In the new temples of art visitors leisurely stroll around in pleasant surroundings, meet their friends and eat and drink, chat and linger.

The atmosphere suits the visitors' urban lifestyle in the early 21st century. Its charm lies for the most part in the highly successful combination of old and new, the symbiosis of valuable historic masonry with modern architecture.

Although neither visitors to the city nor the Viennese themselves can spend their whole time in museums, bigger and brighter exhibitions are staged to woo visitors. The competition for custom is immense – enlivening each visit as well as the spirit and hopefully also boosting trade.

The Albertina is the latest highlight in the Viennese museum landscape

Die aufregendsten Museen

- MuseumsQuartier (▶ 103)
- The Albertina (▶ 82)
- Liechtenstein Museum (Wien 9, Fürstengasse 1, tel: 01/319 57 67 252, Fri–Mon 10–5, Tram D, Bus 40A Bauernfeldplatz, admission: expensive, www. liechtensteinmuseum.at)

The journalist Alfred Polgar thought the Viennese coffee-house was a place for people who wanted to be alone but needed company to feel alone. It has long fulfilled this function. This delicate blend of myth and "*Schmäh*" goes back to 1685, when the Polish commercial traveller Kolschitzky obtained a licence to serve the public "kahve, the Turkish Drink".

The Viennese Coffee Houses

Legend has it that for a long time the Viennese did not know what to do with the contents of the sacks left behind by the Turkish invaders beaten back at the gates of the city in 1683. The riddle was solved when they hit on the idea of roasting the green beans – and got a new elixir of life.

Intellectual Flights of Fancy

Around the end of the 19th century and in the interwar

Above: Café Griensteidl has always been a cultural hotspot

Left: Taking a break with a *Melange* at the Café Central

What to Drink in the Coffee-house:

- **Melange:** coffee with a lot of milk and perhaps a topping of whipped cream
- **Schwarzer (gross/klein):** mocha without milk or cream (double/single)
- **Brauner:** mocha with milk
- **Cappuccino:** a double *Brauner* with a topping of foamed milk
- **Einspänner:** mocha served in a glass with whipped cream

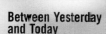

years the Viennese "public living-room" was in its heyday as the focus of intellectual life. In the Herrenhof, at Griensteidl (➤ 90) and in the Central (➤ 66), the marble tables and shabby plush benches witnessed intellectual flights of fancy. Whether literature, music, architecture, politics or psychology – all went hand in hand with a large *Brauner* and a glass of water, served on a silver tray.

The Coffee-house as Information Exchange

In the 1980s and 90s many coffee-houses became the victims of development mania, suffering the cruel fate of being transformed into banks or even car showrooms. Others were "restored" to death or upgraded into stylized theme cafés. Even so, the cafés have largely retained their essential function, serving politicians, journalists and business people as a place to see and to be seen, to meet and exchange information and to do deals. You'd think more politics happens at Sluka's (➤ 111) and Landtmann's (➤ 111) than in the Rathaus or the Parlament.

Between Yesterday and Today

All the same, many of the 500 or so coffee-houses have kept their original character. Lovers go to the romantic Sperl (➤ 134), antiques dealers and fans of the writer Thomas Bernhard congregate at the Bräunerhof (➤ 89).

At least the human element of the coffee-house from the old days has been preserved: the waiter with his black tail-coat and bow-tie, wallet on hip, and traditionally with a pair of exemplary flat feet. He knows his regular guests' tastes, greets them with "Küss' die Hand, Gnä' Frau' (May I kiss your hand, ma'am) and "Habe die Ehre, Herr Hofrat" (An honour for us, sir), and expects about 10 per cent tip.

Who Wrote Where?

Turn on the tap and you'll be amazed: out gushes the purest, freshest spring water. Truly! The quality and flavour of Vienna's water is legendary – water flows direct from sources in unpolluted mountain areas into the city. And wherever it flows out of the artistically formed figures of the city's many fountains it also refreshes the spirit.

Of Nymphs and Fauns

Vienna is indeed blessed. While other cities find it hard to keep up with the ever-increasing demand for water, in Vienna every tap is a small mountain spring. Two conduits, constructed under

A World of Fountains

This pure spring water also supplies a series of beautiful fountains. These are a world of their own. Symbolic figures crowd around the bowls and basins, vessels and jugs, beings from the realm of fantasy united in complete – or almost complete – harmony. It wouldn't be Vienna after all, if there hadn't been an element of disruption, albeit caused by something as harmless as the fountains.

Above: The main figure on the Donner-Brunnen

Far left: Pallas Athene in front of the Parlament

Left: The figure of Austria on the Freyung

Emperor Franz Joseph, bring the pure spring water to the city from the high limestone ranges of Rax, Schneeberg and Hochschwab, situated some 100km (62 miles) from the city.

The Austria Fountain

The magnificent fountain in front of the Parliament building, for example, was to have a statue of Austria as its central figure. But to spare the feelings of the other

Background: Water-jets in the Hochstrahlbrunnen

countries of the empire, Austria had to give way to Pallas Athene, the Greek goddess of wisdom. Admittedly a politically correct solution but ill-considered all the same. If you look closely you'll see that the goddess now has no specific link with the allegorical images of the four main rivers at her feet. Still, it gave the Viennese something to mock: "Wisdom stands outside Parliament, with her back to it!"

On **Freyung** square (► 58), on the other hand, it is the figure of **Austria** who is surrounded by the monarchy's four main rivers: the Danube, Po, Elbe and Vistula. Goethe's grand-daughter Alma stood as model for Austria.

The Citizens' Fountain

In 1739, the citizens of Vienna had a fountain erected on the Neuer Markt. It was the first time that a civic commission had been carried out unaccompanied by a loyal address to the emperor. Originally called Providentia-Brunnen, it is now known as the

Donner-Brunnen, after its sculptor, the 24-year-old Georg Raphael Donner. The talk of the time was the strong resemblance of the central figure in the fountain, the scantily clad Providentia, to the wife of Donner's landlord.

The Donner-Brunnen risked removal for being "a chronic traffic obstruction"

Hours and Days on a Fountain

The **Hochstrahlbrunnen** on Schwarzenbergplatz (► 130) is more astronomical than anatomical. The 365 little jets round the edge of the basin stand for the days of the year, while the island and its six fountains represent the days of the week. Twelve high jets symbolize the months, 24 smaller ones the hours and the 30 jets on the central island mark the days of the month.

The Hochstrahlbrunnen marked the opening of the first mountain spring conduit

Paradoxically, virtually none of the dishes generally associated with Vienna actually come from here. Everything that is simmered, steamed and braised in the pots and pans of the former metropolis on the Danube was inherited from other parts of the empire. Goulash comes from Hungary, dumplings from Bohemia and the ubiquitous Wiener Schnitzel from Milan. What does that prove? That Vienna has always known how to select the very best from its former empire.

To experience the flavours of the imperial era you only need to dine at a genuine

Schnitzel, Pancakes & Co

One of the corner-stones of traditional Viennese cuisine is beef. It's served as Tafelspitz (boiled) with accompaniments such as roast potatoes, spinach or dill

Viennese inn. There the empire is every-where. Emperor Franz Joseph is represented by his favourite dish, the creamy Kaiser-schmarren (sweet pancakes with raisins), the Hungarian aristocracy by the Esterházy-Rostbraten (roast beef), which gets its characteristic flavour from a rich sauce of root vegetables and sour cream, and the most famous of field-marshals by the Radetzky-Torte (cake).

Below: The Wiener Schnitzel is the undisputed number one

Above: The city's culinary visiting-card: the original Sacher Torte

Far left: Palatschinken (stuffed pancakes) are a real temptation

Left: The crowning touch on the Kaiserschmarren: a light dusting of icing sugar

sauce, as roast beef or as beef goulash. The latter is unthinkable without Kaisersemmel (crisp emperor's bread-rolls) and a cold beer.

In the "Beisl ums Eck" (pub around the corner), a typically simple and cosy inn, good, plain cooking fills the menu – often chalked up on a blackboard at the entrance. Soups are standard fare, often served with Leberknödel or Griessnockerl (liver or semolina dumplings) or Fritatten (pancakes cut into strips). And for a main course there's roast pork with dumplings, Szegedin pork and cabbage or Wiener Schnitzel with potato salad.

As well as Keiserschmarren, the exquisite desserts include Palatschinken and Buchteln (jam turnovers), strudel and poppy-seed noodles, Powidltascherl (plum-filled potato pockets) and Topfenknödel (sweet dumplings). The queen of desserts, however, is the Sacher Torte – the rich chocolate cake with a layer of apricot jam, whose original recipe has been claimed for years by both Demel (► 90) and Sacher (► 110) cafés.

Wiener Würstl (Viennese sausage)

Vienna wouldn't be the same without the Wiener Würstl. It comes as a traditional boiled sausage served hot, or as Bratwurst (fried or grilled/broiled), Leberkäs (meat loaf) and Käsekrainer (fried and filled with cheese), all served with mild or sharp mustard and pickled chillies in oil. Late at night, the sausage stand becomes the centre of Viennese gossip. Elegantly dressed visitors after a night at the opera stand eating their sausages next to cabbies and refuse collectors before their morning shift. Among the best known sausage stands are those on Hoher Markt and opposite the Staatsoper (Albertinarampe).

Did You Know ...

- ...that Vienna is the only capital city in the world with a large vineyard area? In the Middle Ages the yield was already so great that by imperial decree sour wine had to be used to mix the mortar for the Stephansdom. Today about 400 vintner families produce around 20,000hl (450,000 gallons) of wine from 690ha (1,700 acres) of vineyard.

- ...that the first woman to travel alone around the world came from Vienna. On her journeys, **Ida Pfeiffer** (1797–1858, ➤ 179) reached South America, Sumatra with its "cannibals" and Madagascar. Her diaries became bestsellers.

- ...that the famous "Kaiserschmarren" was originally called "Kaiserinschmarren". It was dedicated to Kaiserin Elisabeth in 1854, on the occasion of her marriage to Franz Joseph. As the emperor liked the dessert better than the figure-conscious empress did, it was renamed.

- ...that the Viennese have always played a large role in Hollywood? **Fred Zinnemann** (1907–97) directed *High Noon, From Here to Eternity* and *A Man for all Seasons*. The producer of *The Silence of the Lambs* and *Dancing with Wolves*, **Eric Pleskow** (born 1924), was also Viennese. **Billy Wilder** (1906–2002), the incomparable director of *Some Like it Hot* and *The Apartment*, is often thought of as Viennese; in fact, he was born in Sucha near Krakow (now Poland), but he spent his childhood and youth in Vienna.

Finding Your Feet

First Two Hours

Vienna is a city of manageable size. Whether you arrive by plane, train or car, the journey into the centre won't take long.

Wien-Schwechat Airport (VIE)

Vienna International Airport (www.viennaairport.com), situated about 15km (9 miles) southeast of the city, is Austria's most important airport. There is an information desk in the arrivals hall, and the airport's information hotline is available around the clock on (01) 70 07-222 33.

Airport Transfers

CAT, S-Bahn and bus lines operate from 6am to midnight, running once every 30 minutes.

- The **CAT** (City Airport Train) is the fastest airport transfer – you'll be in the city in just 16 minutes (U-Bahn station Landstrasse/Wien Mitte). A single ticket is €8, a return €15. The tickets are not valid on the rest of the Vienna public transport network. An interesting option for your return flight: some airlines allow you to check in your luggage in advance at the terminal Wien Mitte. You can do so the evening before and up to 75 minutes before departure.
- The least expensive option is the **Schnellbahn** or **S-Bahn** (express train): S7 takes you to Landstrasse/Wien Mitte in 24 minutes, stopping at a number of other stations. The €3 ticket entitles you to continue your journey by any other means of public transport in Vienna.
- A ticket for the **buses** operated by the **Vienna Airport Line** costs €6, but does not permit you to change to other forms of transport. The journey from the airport to Schwedenplatz takes only 20 minutes, but it may take longer during the rush hours. Another route runs from the airport to Südbahnhof and Westbahnhof stations.
- There is a **taxi** rank north of the arrivals hall. A taxi journey into the centre will take about 20 minutes and costs around €35. A cheaper option is to go to the centre by public transport, then take a taxi to your hotel.

Railway Stations

- **Westbahnhof** was built in 1950s style. Leaving the platforms you will arrive in a two-floor hall with ticket offices and shops. Like in most other stations, there is a mixed crowd milling about, so keep an eye on your luggage, though it's generally quite a safe place. The station is situated at the western end of the shopping street Mariahilfer Strasse. There is a U-Bahn station in the railway station.
- **Südbahnhof**, where trains from the south arrive, is outside the city centre, close to Schloss Belvedere. From here, S-Bahn or tram is the best way to get into the centre.

Tourist Information

Tourist-Info Wien provides free tips and information on Vienna and current events, and helps you find hotel accommodation. The Tourist-Info **Zentrum** in Wien 1, Albertinaplatz, open daily 9–7, tel: (01) 24-555, www.wien.info. The Tourist-Info **Flughafen Wien** is situated in the arrivals hall opposite the baggage hall. It is open from 8:30am to 9pm.

Getting Around

Finding your Way

Vienna is divided into 23 districts which circle around its central district Wien 1. Between Ringstrasse and Gürtel are the urban districts 2 to 9, which are home to many old buildings and the embassies. The outer districts vary significantly from each other: Wien 10, 11 and 16 are typical workers' districts, while Wien 13 and 19 are considered elegant residential areas. Districts 21 and 22, on the opposite bank of the Danube, are being developed as new suburbs with modern high-rises.

Vienna's Streets

Vienna's most important streets are:

- **Kärntner Strasse, Graben, Kohlmarkt** – elegant shopping streets in the heart of the city
- **Ringstrasse** – the road that encircles the inner city
- **Mariahilfer Strasse** – the most popular shopping street
- **Gürtel** – outer ring road, filled with traffic, popular bars and Vienna's seedy red light strip.

Public Transport

Vienna has one of the best public transport systems in Europe, with U-Bahn, tram, train (S-Bahn) and bus lines criss-crossing the city. It's run by the **Wiener Linien** (tel: 01/7909-100, www.wienerlinien.at), which has information offices scattered throughout the U-Bahn system.

U-Bahn

- The U-Bahn officially **opened in 1976**, but some routes run on tram tracks that are over 100 years old. It's the fastest way to get around the city, and the system is constantly being extended.
- The U-Bahn runs **every day from about 5am**. The last trains depart from the centre at about 12:30am. Trains run at 5-minute intervals (every 2–4 minutes during the rush hours and every 7–8 minutes after 8:30pm).
- There are **five colour-coded** U-Bahn lines (U1 – red, U2 – violet, U3 – orange, U4 – green, U6 – brown).
- On the platforms, an **electronic board** indicates the destination of the next train and the minutes until it arrives.
- Next to the station name you'll find signs in white writing indicating the **exits** (often far apart!) and **interchanges with other lines**.

Trams, S-Bahn and Buses

- **Trams** (Strassenbahn) are identified by numbers or letters (eg. 1, 10 or D), **buses** by a combination of number and letter (eg. 1A, 10A or 156B) and the **S-Bahn** (Schnellbahn) is recognizable by an S (eg. S45, S7).
- **Tram routes 1** and **2** circle the inner city in opposite directions along the Ringstrasse. They are an excellent way to get a snapshot of Vienna's best neoclassical architecture, which lines the wide boulevard.
- Not all the routes operate from 5am to midnight every day. Consult the timetables in the stations for **detailed information**. Timetables and routes can also be checked online at www.wienplan.com or www.vor.at.
- A good network of **night buses** operates nightly from about 12:45am to 5am. Normal tickets are valid on these lines; stops are marked with a blue N.

Tickets

- Within the Vienna city limits, the **same ticket** can be used on all means of transport, including changes.
- There are frequent **ticket controls**, and if you don't have a valid ticket, you may have to pay a fine of €62.
- **You can buy tickets** from the machines in U-Bahn stations and at newsagents, advance ticket sales points, or directly on the tram or bus (keep some coins ready). Tickets bought on trams and buses are more expensive than those from machines, ticket offices and newsagents.
- If you plan to visit a number of museums and exclusively use the public transport system, consider buying a **Wien-Card** (▶ 188).
- Single tickets cost €1.70 from machines, ticket offices and newsagents, €2.20 on buses and trams. A 24-hour ticket costs €5.70, a 72-hour ticket €13.60. Week Passes, available for €14, run from Monday to Sunday, while an eight-day ticket (€27.20), which is valid for eight, not necessaily consecutive days, can be used by several passengers travelling together. All tickets, except the Week Pass, must be **validated** in a blue ticket machine before beginning your journey.
- **Children** under six travel free at all times, those under 15 travel free on Sundays and public holidays, and during school holidays.

Taxis

There are plenty of taxi stands throughout the entire city. You can also hail a taxi that's available (with a lit-up yellow sign) or book one by phone (eg.: 01/601 60, 01/401 00 or 01/313 00). There is a small surcharge for night journeys and on Sundays and public holidays.

Cars

- Vienna's first district is a **short-term parking zone** operating on a **pay-and-display** basis on weekdays between 9am and 7pm; parking in districts 2–9 and 20 is chargeable from 9am to 8pm. To avoid being fined, place a valid parking ticket behind your windscreen. You can obtain free 10-minute parking tickets (which cannot be combined with other tickets), as well as tickets for 30/60/90 minutes (€0.60/€1.20/€1.80) from tobacconists/newsagents.
- The **maximum parking time** is 1.5 hours. Days of validity and maximum parking periods may vary in busy shopping streets. Check the signs.
- On the outskirts of the city you'll find **park-and-ride car parks** with U-Bahn connections, in the central districts **pay car parks**.
- Detailed information is available at **www.parkeninwien.at**

Sightseeing by Bus

The hop-on-hop-off buses stop at all major sights. Depending on your ticket, you can get on and off these buses whenever you like.
Other bus companies offering fixed sightseeing tours are www.viennasightseeingtours.com, tel: 01/712 46 83; www.cityrama.at, tel: 01/534 13-0; www.redbuscitytours.at, tel: 01/512 40 30.

Sightseeing by Horse-Drawn Carriage

Horse-drawn carriages, known as *fiaker*, are a romantic way to see the inner city. There are carriage stands at Stephansplatz, Heldenplatz and in front of the Albertina. Rides cost €40/€65/€95 for 20/40/60 minutes.

Cycling

City Bike Wien (www.citybikewien.at) offers bike rental at over 50 terminals citywide. A credit card or Austrian bank card is required to rent the bikes, but a Tourist Card (€2) available from Royal Tours (Wien 1, Herrengasse 1–3, tel: 01/710 46 06) circumvents the need for either. Bikes are free for the first hour, and around €2 for every hour after that. **Pedal Power** (Wien 2, Ausstellungsstrasse 3, tel: 01/729 72 34, www.pedalpower.at) also rents out bikes, from €5 per hour, and offers cycling tours of Vienna.

Admission Charges
The cost of admission to museums and places of interest mentioned in this guide is indicated by three categories:
inexpensive: under €3
moderate: €3–€7.50
expensive: over €7.50

Accommodation

Whatever your tastes and resources, Vienna has something for you. The city's hostels and guesthouses, while sometimes basic, are of a high standard, and its luxury establishments, with their imperial flair, are among the best on the continent. There is also a healthy array of modern hotels, which offer the most up-to-date fittings and plenty of contemporary style.

Reservations
To ensure that you find exactly what you are looking for it's worth booking in advance. The website www.info.wien.at allows you to book a room online in one of 350 hotels, guesthouses and apartments. Or book by phoning the hotline daily 9–7 on tel: (01) 245 55. If you have not booked a room before your arrival, the Tourist-Info (► 36) can help you

Hotels and Guesthouses
Vienna has some elegant **luxury hotels**, which are truly superb but not easily affordable for everyone. However, you can still enjoy the luxury of the surroundings by just having a drink or a cup of coffee in the hotel bar. **Guesthouses** are smaller and often less expensive. The reception may not be on the ground floor because many guesthouses occupy only part of the building. Room prices generally include breakfast, local and other taxes.

Apartments
For a longer stay, consider renting an apartment. Prices may vary considerably depending on location and furnishings. The **Levante Laudon** (Wien 8, Laudongasse 8, tel: 01/407 13 70, www.thelevante.com) has clean and modern apartments in a fairly central location.

Youth Hostels and Season Hotels
Vienna has a range of inexpensive hotels, but they generally fill up quickly over summer so it's best to book in advance. HI-affiliated hostels run by the **Österreicher Jugendherbergsverband** (Wien 1, Schotterring 28, tel: 01/533 53 53, www.oejhv.or.at), include **Jugendherberge Myrthengasse** (Wien 7, Myrthengasse 7, tel: 01/523 63 16), close to the centre, and **Schloss-herberge am Wilhelminenberg** (Wien 16, Savoyenstrasse 2, tel: 01/481 03 00), near the Vienna Woods with superb views over the city. Independent **Westend City Hostel** (Wien 6, Fügergasse 3, tel: 01/597 67 29, www.westendhostel.at) is another good option, handy for the Westbahnhof.

Season Hotels are student residences open to tourists during university breaks. They're often simple but value for money. **Accordia** (Wien 2, Grosse Schiffgasse 12, tel: 01/512 74 93, www.allyouneedhotels.at) is across the Danube Canal for the first district and opens from July to September.

Accommodation Prices
Prices for a double room with bathroom and breakfast:
€€€€ over €180
€€€ €120–€180
€€ €80–€120
€ under €80

Hotels

Altstadt Vienna €€€

This stylish hotel is centrally located near the Mariahilfer Strasse shopping street. It has a specially welcoming atmosphere, and the rooms are very tastefully appointed. To start the day, help yourself from the wide selection of foods on the breakfast buffet. You'll feel well looked after in this hotel as it's almost like staying with friends.

➕ 192, west of A2 ✉ Wien 7, Kirchengasse 41 ☎ (01) 522 66 66, fax 523 49 01; www.altstadt.at
🚇 Volkstheater

Art Hotel €

A young hotel in every respect, with low prices and lots of colour, although the name "Art Hotel" promises more art and design than actually can be found here. But the staff are enthusiastic, the hotel is close to the Naschmarkt and the rooms acceptable, making this hotel a perfect choice. An internet area is available to guests.

➕ 194, southwest of A1 ✉ Wien 5, Brandmayergasse 7–9 ☎ (01) 544 51 08, fax 544 51 08-10; www.thearthotelvienna.at
🚇 Pilgramgasse

Bristol €€€€

This impressive imperial building, opposite Staatsoper, has been a byword for elegant hospitality since 1892. A classic luxury hotel with beautiful rooms and elegant suites, uniformed porters, outstanding service and everything else you might expect. The in-house Korso restaurant is considered to be one of the best eateries in the city; the bar is a traditional piano bar.

➕ 193 D2 ✉ Wien 1, Kärntner Ring 1 ☎ (01) 515 16-0, fax 515 16-550; www.westin.com/bristol 🚇 Karlsplatz

Coburg €€€€

Vienna's top luxury hotel is in a 19th-century palace right in the middle of the city. All suites have stylish marble baths, some even have their own gardens. The amenities are to the highest specifications and the spa is the best place to be pampered. The Coburg restaurant has probably the most exciting food in Vienna; make sure you reserve a table.

➕ 193 E2/3 ✉ Wien 1, Coburgbastei 4 ☎ (01) 518 18-0, fax 518 18-1; www.coburg.at 🚇 Stubentor

Das Triest €€€€

This designer hotel, based in the former stables of the Vienna-Trieste post coaches, is one of the most attractive in the city. Modern design is tastefully incorporated into the old rooms. The room prices include the breakfast buffet, and use of gym and sauna. The restaurant is excellent and the Silverbar legendary. This is where Robbie Williams and David Bowie have stayed when they're in town.

🔢 194 B1 ✉ Wien 4, Wiedner
Hauptstrasse 12 ☎ (01) 589 18-0, fax
589 18-18; www.dastriest.at
🚇 Karlsplatz

Das Tyrol €€€–€€€€

Das Tyrol falls into the "design
hotel" category– everything is
bedecked in art, right down to its
hallways and reception. Rooms are
contemporary but retain a suitably
comfortable feel, and all come with
the modern fittings expected of a
top hotel. Despite being outside
the first district, its location
couldn't be better: Mariah lfer
Strasse is right outside the front
door and the Museumsquartier only
a lazy stroll away. Among the city's
best, yet still affordable.

🔢 192 A1 ✉ Wien 6, Mariahilfer
Strasse 15 ☎ (01) 587 54 15, fax 587
54-159; www.das-tyrol.at
🚇 Museumsquartier

Domizil €€€

True grandeur and genuine
Viennese charm are the plus points
in this pleasant hotel-guesthouse.
All 40 rooms have been lovingly
and individually styled. One of the
main attractions is the central
location: the Stephansdom is only
50m (55 yards) away, and the
Mozarthaus Vienna is just around
the corner. Thus the Domizil is the
ideal starting point for exploring
the Old Town. The extensive
breakfast buffet makes for a great
start to the day – enjoy it with a
glass of sparkling wine!

🔢 193 E3 ✉ Wien 1, Schulerstrasse
14 ☎ (01) 513 31 99, fax 512 34 84;
www.hoteldomizil.at 🚇 Stephansplatz

Hilton Vienna €€€€

This 1970s hotel has been
completely overhauled and renovated. Brighter, modernised and
attractive, the Hilton Vienna is now
Austria's largest conference hotel,
located right next to Stadtpark and
Ringstrasse, not far from the centre.
With almost 600 luxurious rooms
and suites, a fantastic restaurant
and the Birdland jazz club, the

Hilton is an excellent choice.
Particularly convenient is its direct
link to the airport: the City-Airport-
Train terminus is opposite the hotel.

🔢 195 E3 ✉ Wien 3, Am Stadtpark
☎ (01) 717 00-0, fax 713 06 91;
www.hilton.com 🚇 Landstrasse/
Wien Mitte

Hollman Beletage €€€

This gorgeous boutique guesthouse
in the very heart of Vienna is a
must for anyone with a penchant
for styled surroundings combined
with plenty of personal touches.
It's suitably covered in warm
browns and oranges, and offers
communal areas with CD player,
small library, piano (for those
closet virtuosos) and couches you'll
find hard to leave. Rooms are
cleverly designed – cupboards and
even bathrooms are hidden behind
sliding wall panels, creating more
space than would seem possible.
As there are only a handful of
rooms, it's advisable to reserve
ahead.

🔢 193 E4 ✉ Wien 1, Köllnerhofgasse
6 ☎ (01) 961 19 60, fax 961 19 60-33;
www.hollmann-beletage.at
🚇 Schwedenplatz

Hotel Biedermeier €€€

In the midst of the romantic
Biedermeier complex in the
Sünnhof is this well appointed and
friendly hotel, which advertises its
"rooms for wellbeing". Close to the
centre and the City-Airport-Train
terminus, a stay here is especially
festive over Advent, when there's a
Christmas market in the Sünnhof.

🔢 195 E3 ✉ Wien 3, Landstrasser
Hauptstrasse 28 ☎ (01) 716 71-0, fax
716 71-503; www.mercure.com
🚇 Landstrasse/Wien Mitte,
Rochusgasse

Hotel am Schubertring €€€

Sharing the Ringstrasse with the
city's big five-star establishments
is Schubertring, the most
affordable option on Vienna's grand
boulevard. Understandably, rooms
don't match the luxury of the

neighbours', but they are comfortable and spacious instead, and located high above the busy road (all rooms are on the top two floors of the building). As an added extra, the rooms are Biedermaier or art nouveau in style, although the predominance of flowery patterns is a little much at times.

🕂 193 E2 ✉ Wien 1, Schubertring 11
☎ (01) 717 020, fax 713 99 66;
www.schubertring.at 🚃 Tram 1, 2

Hotel am Stephansplatz €€€

Forget tramping to the U-Bahn or waiting for the bus, why not stay at Vienna's very centre? Am Stephansplatz has the luxury of looking directly onto Stephansdom, making it an easy walk from any of the first district's sights. The hotel's splendid location is matched by its impeccable eco credentials. When renovations were carried out in 2005, the family owners used only environmentally friendly building materials (right down to biological paint) and techniques, creating a hotel that feels as good to the touch as it looks to the eye. Only organic produce is used for the substantial breakfasts. If you can afford it, fork out for room 702, whose balcony hangs over Stephansplatz itself.

🕂 193 D3 ✉ Wien 1, Stephansplatz 9
☎ (01) 534 050, fax 534 05 710;
www.hotelamstephansplatz.at
🚇 Stephansplatz

Hotel-Pension Suzanne €€

Suzanne has an excellent location, just off one of the city's main streets, Kärntner Strasse, and only metres from the Staatsoper. Its rooms are more *pension* than hotel, furnished with 19th-century antiques, large, inviting beds and modern bathrooms. Staff know all about cultural events in the city, there's internet access for guests and umbrellas on rainy days, and the buffet breakfasts are a healthy selection of breads, spreads, yogurts and fruit.

🕂 193 D2 ✉ Wien 1, Walfischgasse 4

☎ (01) 513 25 07, fax 513 25 00;
www.pension-suzanne.at 🚇 Karlsplatz

Imperial €€€€

The exceptionally beautiful Ringstrassenpalais was converted into a hotel on the occasion of the World Exhibition of 1873, since when it has been one of the best hotels in the city. Guests of state enjoy the aristocratically elegant hospitality, as do actors and pop stars. A showcase hotel, right on the Ringstrasse, with a butler service unique in the German-speaking world, pressed newspapers and every imaginable kind of comfort. Instead of staying here, you can always just try the home-made *Imperial-Torte* in the pleasantly quiet hotel-café.

🕂 193 D1/2 ✉ Wien 1, Kärntner Ring 16 ☎ (01) 501 10-0, fax 501 10-410;
www.luxurycollection.com/imperial
🚇 Karlsplatz

König von Ungarn €€€€

This hotel, in the heart of the Old Town, immediately behind the Stephansdom, accurately conveys the atmosphere of traditional Viennese hospitality. Part of the hotel is based in Mozart's former residence, the Mozarthaus. The roofed inner courtyard is a particularly pleasant place to relax after sightseeing, shopping or strolling through the city.

🕂 193 D3 ✉ Wien 1, Schulerstrasse 10 ☎ (01) 515 84-0, fax 515 84-8;
www.kvu.at 🚇 Stephansplatz

Landhaus Fuhrgasslhuber €€

This rustic hotel is ideal for those wishing to combine city and country living. It's situated in the *heurigen* village Neustift am Walde, is surrounded by picturesque green vineyards. If you like a rural atmosphere, country walks and evenings with a glass of new-vintage wine, you'll enjoy your stay at this hospitable guesthouse. There's an excellent breakfast buffet and the service is very attentive – perfect relaxation is guaranteed.

🏠 194, northwest of A5 ✉ Wien 19, Rathstrasse 24 ☎ (01) 440 30 33, fax 440 27 14; www.fuhrgassl-huber.at 🚌 Bus 35A Neustift am Walde

Le Meridien €€€€

This hotel is a good example of modern hotel design, with trendy furnishings and stylish fittings. The elegant restaurant, glamorous bar and extensive spa area with gym have ensured that this establishment, opened in 2004 as part of a chain of luxury hotels, lives up to its luxury tag. Its location between the opera house, Hofburg and MuseumsQuartier is superb.

🏠 192 C2 ✉ Wien 1, Opernring 13–15 ☎ (01) 588 90-0, fax 588 90 90 90; www.lemeridien.at 🚇 Karlsplatz

Neuer Markt €€

A guesthouse on the second and third floors of a late 19th-century building, located close to Neuer Markt, and only a few minutes from Stephansdom and Kärntner Strasse. The rooms in this family-run establishment, although not modern, are clean and pleasant, staff are friendly, and the prices are low for so central a location.

🏠 193 D3 ✉ Wien 1, Seilergasse 9 ☎ (01) 512 23 16, fax 513 91 05; www.hotelpension.at 🚇 Stephansplatz

Pension Pertschy €€–€€€

Child-friendly Pertschy may be in a prime location only a stone's throw from Graben, the first district's celebrated shopping street, but it's as quiet as can be. All rooms overlook a central courtyard, typical of Vienna's older houses, and are reasonably spacious, helped along by their high ceilings. The rooms come in a range of colours – one may be soft pink, while the next warm yellow – but all are filled with Biedermaier furniture and have separate en-suites. Non-smoking rooms are also available.

🏠 192 C3 ✉ Wien 1, Habsburgerstrasse 5 ☎ (01) 534 49-0, fax 534 49-49; www.pertschy.com 🚇 Stephansplatz

Sacher €€€€

Probably the most charming of the hotels with numerous stars – rich in tradition, world-famous and still family-owned. The hotel is in a historical building, with much style – and is home to the legendary Sacher-Torte. A first-class luxury establishment with a personal touch, the Sacher is centrally located, just behind the opera house, between Kärntner Strasse and Albertinaplatz. Even if your money won't stretch to one of the superb rooms, furnished with antiques, a visit to the Sacher-Eck near Kärntner Strasse for a slice of Sacher-Torte is a must for every visitor to Vienna!

🏠 192/193 C/D2 ✉ Wien 1, Philharmonikerstrasse 4 ☎ (01) 514 56-0, fax 514 56-810; www.sacher.com 🚇 Karlsplatz

Style Hotel €€€€

The name might sound pretentious, but this is one of the city's top hotels. It occupies a former bank (the huge vault in the basement is a monumental reminder) built in the 1930s, and still retains many of the original art deco touches alongside its plethora of modern features. The rooms, decorated in warm hues, balance luxury and comfort with ease. Location is no problem either – the Albertina is only two blocks away.

🏠 192 A2 ✉ Wien 1, Herrengasse 12 ☎ (01) 22 780-0, fax 22 780-22; www.stylehotel.at 🚇 Herrengasse

Viennart €€€

A well-appointed luxury hotel, featuring functional and modern, tasteful and bright design. But what's special about the Viennart is its excellent location: in the immediate vicinity you'll find Volkstheater, Museumsquartier, Spittelberg, Ringstrasse, Mariahilfer Strasse and numerous restaurants, bars and pubs.

🏠 192 A2 ✉ Wien 7, Breite Gasse 9 ☎ (01) 523 13 45-0, fax 523 13 45-111; www.austrotel.at 🚇 Volkstheater

Food and Drink

The Viennese like to eat well, like to eat out and like to eat cheaply. This bodes well for visitors, especially at lunchtime, when restaurants offer two- or three-course meals at very reasonable prices. The choice ranges from traditional Austrian fare to world cuisine, followed by a *melange* (coffee) at one of the city's famous coffee-houses.

Traditional Food

Typically Viennese cuisine has always been "fusion" food – it's rooted in Bohemian, Austrian, Hungarian and Balkan traditions. These are still honoured today, but often they are brought up to date in combination with surprising additions from around the world.

Snacks and Small Dishes

- Traditionally, the **Viennese breakfast** consists of a bread roll or a vanilla croissant with butter and jam, plus a cup of coffee. However, other variations are also served, including some very extensive brunches.
- If hunger strikes between meals, don't forget the Viennese **Würstelstand** (sausage stall); the classic sausage snacks here are *Debreziner* (spicy!), *Käsekrainer* (sausage with cheese) and *Burenwurst* (farmers' sausage).
- A more elegant option are the traditional bread rolls at **Trzesniewski** (► 79).
- A **Beisl** (the word originates from Yiddish for "little house") is the best place to sample typical Viennese cooking. These small beer houses are usually filled with wood panelling and ageing locals, and serve hefty portions of *Wienerschnitzel* and *Tafelspitz* (boiled beef with apple and horseradish sauce); **Beim Czaak** (► 64) and **Zu den Zwei Liesln** (► 133) are classic *Beisln*, while **Immervoll** (► 65) is a modern variation.
- **Vegetarians** won't starve in Vienna. There are now many eateries focusing on meatless cuisine, and almost every restaurant offers at least a handful of vegetarian dishes. **Wrenkh** (► 64) is one of the most imaginative.

Drinks

- **Coffee** has a century-old tradition in Vienna (► 28).
- Viennese **wine** is generally drunk young (known as *Heuriger*). You can best enjoy it at a *Heuriger* wine tavern on the outskirts (for example, in Grinzing, Neustift am Walde or Stammersdorf). In the city, **Zum Haydn** (Wien 6, Haydngasse 7, tel: 01/597 21 60, May–Dec Mon–Sat 4–11, Jan–Apr Tue–Sat 4–11) also conveys a typical *Heuriger* atmosphere.
- There is also a tradition for **beer** in Vienna. One beautiful brewery tavern in a former abbey is the **Salm Bräu** (► 155).

Restaurant Tips

- To avoid disappointment, **reserve** a table at top restaurants.
- Most restaurants **stop serving** around 10 or 11pm; many close Sundays.
- Some restaurants automatically include a cover charge; if not, it's normal to add a **tip** of 5–10 per cent. In bars and cafés, round up the bill to the nearest 50 cents.

Prices
Prices are for a meal for one person, excluding drinks.
€ under €15 €€ €15–€30 €€€ over €30

Shopping

Elegant boutiques, personable shops, lively markets and functional shopping centres – Vienna makes shopping a pleasurable experience, whether you're looking for luxury goods or bargains.

Where to shop

- Vienna's main shopping street is **Mariahilfer Strasse**, between the inner city and Westbahnhof. Here you'll find all the large fashion chains and hundreds of shops with trendy gear for a young clientele. If you're after something more unusual, whether it be clothes, shoes or accessories, try **Neubaugasse**, a side street off Mariahilfer Strasse.
- In the inner city, **Kärntner Strasse**, **Graben** and **Kohlmarkt** with their designer shops, jewellers and perfumeries, are a paradise for shoppers with fat wallets.
- Trendy department stores such as **Steffl** (Wien 1, Kärntner Strasse 19) and **Gerngross** (Wien 7, Mariahilfer Strasse 38–48), as well as the **Ringstrassengalerien** (Wien 1, Kärntner Ring 5–7), have extensive shopping areas for you to explore come rain or shine.
- The edge-of-town shopping centres are typically interchangeable and soulless shopping malls. The **Gasometer** shopping centre in a former gas-container-making factory, at least has some the interesting architecture.

The Best Markets

- **Naschmarkt** (➤ 135) is Vienna's largest and most atmospheric market. On Saturdays its western end is transformed into a famous fleamarket.
- **Brunnenmarkt** (Wien 16, Brunnengasse) is a multicultural market in an area with many immigrant workers.
- **Rathausplatz** and **Spittelberg** have charming Advent markets in the pre-Christmas period, and on **Freyung** (➤ 58) farmers' markets take place, as well as Easter and Advent crafts markets.

Shopping Tips

Stylish souvenirs and traditional gifts from Vienna are known as **Wien Products**. Tourist-Info (➤ 36) has an information sheet on these products, from *Manner Schnitten* (wafers) and modern jewellery to elegant furniture fabrics, listing all the quality outlets (www.wienproducts.at).

Opening Hours

The markets set up stall as early as 6am. Supermarkets are usually open Monday to Thursday 8–7, Friday until 7:30 and Saturday until 5. Shops in Vienna's main shopping streets and shopping centres are generally open Monday to Friday 9–6:30 and Saturday 9–6; many open late on Thursdays, until 9.

Tax

Visitors from non-EU countries are entitled to reclaim VAT (20 per cent), which is included in the purchase price, on any purchases over €75. Ask the sales assistant for a Global Refund Cheque, and get this stamped at the toll booth when you leave the country. It entitles you to money back from one of 600 refund outlets. After the deduction of a handling charge, this will amount to approximately 13 per cent of the sale price.

Entertainment

From opera to disco, from jazz to DJs – there's always something going on in Vienna. Whatever your particular style of fun and entertainment, you're certain to find what you're after.

Information
The city listings magazine *Falter* is indispensable. It is published every Wednesday and lists the events of the coming week, including exhibitions, cinema screenings, guided tours, concerts, fleamarkets and special events (www.falter.at). *Falter*, like Vienna's second listings magazine, *City*, is available from newsagents; both are in German, but the listings are fairly easy to decipher. You'll also find listings online at www.hauptstadt.at.

Booking in Advance
Check out www.ticketline.cc for what's on and book tickets in advance. Telephone bookings can be made on 880 88. You can also purchase a ticket at the venue, in your hotel and from ticket offices in the centre.

Opera, Theatre, Musicals and Jazz
- **Staatsoper** (▶ 98) and **Volksoper** (Wien 9, Währingerstrasse 78, tel: 01/ 514 44 36 70, www.volksoper.at) are famous for performances and productions of world renown. The concerts at the **Musikverein** (▶ 131) and at the **Konzerthaus** (▶ 136) also promise classical pleasures.
- The **Burgtheater** (▶ 102) and its outpost, **Akademietheater**, are the most highly regarded theatres in Vienna. The **Theater in der Josefstadt** and **Kammerspiele** (www.josefstadt.org) stage traditional productions, while the **Volkstheater** (www.volkstheater.at) and the **Schauspielhaus** (www.schauspielhaus.at) tend to showcase modern drama.
- World-famous musicals can be enjoyed at the **Raimundtheater** (Wallgasse 18) and **Theater an der Wien** (▶ 136).
- Vienna's top jazz club is **Porgy & Bess** (▶ 68), closely followed by **Birdland** (▶ 158).
- The highpoints of the ball season are the Viennese **Opernball** during Carnival, which is attended each year by celebrities from around the world; the **Life Ball**, an HIV charity event in May; and the **Kaiserball** in the Hofburg, where people waltz on New Year's Eve into the New Year. It's important to book tickets well in advance for these balls!

Live Music, Bars and Clubs
- Vienna has a **good mix** of cocktail bars, live music venues, simple bars and pumping clubs. They're scattered the length and breadth of the city, although there are a few hot spots too.
- While long stretches of the Gürtel are Vienna's red-light district, a lively scene has established itself in the **Stadtbahnbögen** (S-Bahn arches). Among the most popular with an alternative crowd are **rhiz** (Lerchenfelder Gürtel Bogen 37) and nearby **Chelsea** (No 29), while a younger, more trendy set head for **Babu** (Währinger Gürtel Bogen 181) and its neighbouring bars.
- The **Bermuda Dreieck** (Bermuda Triangle, ▶ 68) has for years been known for its concentration of bars, but it's no longer the current favourite with partygoers, who now head for the **Naschmarkt** (▶ 123) and its side streets
- **Flex** (▶ 68) is the city's top club, with the **Volksgarten** (▶ 112) and **U4** (Schönbrunner Strasse 222) following close behind.

Medieval
Vienna

Getting Your Bearings

In the historic centre of Vienna every stone tells a story, and a walk through the area is like journeying back in time. But it's not all about historical significancce here: new life in the shape of shops, restaurants and bars has sprung up in these picturesque lanes.

First and foremost, though, the attraction of medieval Vienna lies in its past – there is nothing more romantic than wandering the age-old cobblestone streets and exploring inner courtyards whose walls have long been covered in ivy and roses. Any direction you take you'll find something of interest – ancient foundations of the Roman settlement of Vindobona, centuries-old churches, a soaring Gothic cathedral, the remains of Vienna's

Schottenstift
Schotten-
kirche
13 Freyung
Palais
Ferstel
Juden-
platz **11**
12
Am Hof
TUCH
Herrengasse

| 0 | 200 metres |
| 0 | 200 yards |

In the narrow lanes you'll find beautiful things at every turn

MORZIN-PLATZ

Ruprechts-kirche **9**

FRANZ-STRASSE

Donaukanal

SCHWEDEN-PLATZ Schwedenplatz

JOSEFS-KAI

JULIUS-RAAB-PLATZ

Fleisch-markt **7**

Griechen-beisl **8**

G.-COCH-PLATZ

Hoher Markt **10** Ankeruhr

ROTENTURM-STRASSE

Heiligen-kreuzerhof **6**

BAJERN-

BRANDSTÄTTE

LUG-ECK BÄCKER

SONNENFELS-STR.

Jesuiten-kirche **5**

STUBEN-RING

STEPHANS-PLATZ

Erzbischöfliches **2** Palais

ZEILE

DR.-IGNAZ-SEIPEL-PLATZ

Stephans-platz

Stephans-dom **1**

DOMGASSE

Figaro-Haus **4**

STOCK-IM-EISEN-PL.

WOLLZEILE

SINGERSTRASSE

RIEMERG.

Stubentor

Franziskaner-platz **3**

Franziskaner-kirche

★ Don't Miss

At Your Leisure

Page 47: The view from the north tower of Stephansdom

Baroque splendour: Kinsky Palace on Freyung

former Jewish quarter, beautifully renovated palaces, peaceful squares – the list seems endless. Smart shops and chic bars have found homes in the old lanes, as have upmarket restaurants. At night, too, there's plenty going on; the Viennese like to party and bars here stay open till the small hours.

In the shadow of Stephansdom, Vienna's beloved cathedral, a maze of narrow alleyways wind their way back to the Middle Ages. Enjoy the atmosphere of the thick, ancient masonry and the entrancing mysticism of the churches, before returning to modern life, with all its diversions, on the broad squares.

Medieval Vienna in a Day

9:00 am

The day begins with a visit to **❶ Stephansdom** (► 52). Walk round the cathedral, then take the lift up the north tower and marvel at the mighty "Pummerin" bell, Austria's largest and heaviest. Enjoy the wonderful views of the city before walking down Singerstrasse to **❸ Franziskanerplatz** (► 60), and a coffee at Kleines Café (► 66).

11:00 am

The **❹ Mozarthaus Wien** (► 60) where Mozart lived, is in the sleepy Domgasse. Then continue to the **❺ Jesuitenkirche** (left; ► 61) – you should pause on Dr-Ignaz-Seidel-Platz and take time to admire the beautiful early baroque facade. Stroll down the romantic alleyways Sonnenfelsgasse and Schönlaterngasse to the idyllic, peaceful **❻ Heiligenkreuzerhof** (► 61). Then continue your tour on to the **❼ Fleischmarkt** (► 62) with its numerous shops.

12:30 pm

If you lunch in the **❽ Griechenbeisl** (► 62), which is probably the oldest inn in Vienna, you certainly won't be alone, as it's a real magnet for visitors from around the world. It's well worth putting up with a bit of hubbub for the sake of the atmosphere and the delicious traditional food.

2:00 pm

Stroll along to the narrow, romantic lanes of the "Bermuda Triangle" (➤ 68). This is a very lively entertainment quarter, which – naturally – doesn't become really interesting until evening. In the centre of the area is the ivy-clad 🄉 **Ruprechtskirche** (left; ➤ 62). Walk on across the 🄂 **Hoher Markt** (➤ 63), one of Vienna's oldest and most historic squares, to 🄈 **Judenplatz** (➤ 56). On no account fail to visit the Museum Judenplatz, before moving on to 🄂 **Am Hof** (➤ 63).

4:30 pm

At 🄉 **Freyung** (right; ➤ 58) it's pretty much compulsory to go down the Palais Ferstel passage and have a coffee at Café Central (➤ 66). Then tour Freyung, taking in the magnificently renovated palaces; feel free to enter any of the pretty courtyards. The Schottenstift and the Schottenkirche are also worth a visit, but it might be better to opt for the Kunstforum (Art Gallery); if you have the time and inclination you should definitely go to the current exhibition, which is certain to be first-class. Or would you rather do a bit of shopping? There's no lack of attractive shops on Freyung – and you could always restrict yourself to window-shopping…

7:00 pm

If you feel like some jazz, then Porgy & Bess (left; ➤ 68) with its varied programme of international music will be just the thing for this evening. And you can relax afterwards with a glass of champagne in the Eden Bar (➤ 68), a Viennese institution.

❶ Stephansdom

"Steffl", as the Viennese call their beloved and revered Stephansdom, the Cathedral of St Stephen, is the undisputed central feature and the soul of the city. It is a high point of Viennese Gothic architecture, a masterpiece of the stonemason's craft. But it is more than that: the towering edifice is also the national emblem of Austria.

The technical data alone of Stephansdom are impressive. The mighty cathedral is made of 20,000cu m (26,000 cubic yards) of sandstone, stretches 108m (118 yards) in length and 39m (42 yards) in width, and the tip of the south tower rises 137m (450 feet) into the air.

The history of the church's construction goes back to the 12th century, to the time when the new rulers, the Babenbergs, needed a prestigious place of worship. They built a basilica dedicated to Saint Stephen, which was burnt down twice. Around 1260 King Ottokar II of Bohemia had a Romanesque church constructed, the remains of which now form the main entrance, great portal and west facade. Not until a generation later, under Duke Albrecht II, was any further building done. In 1359 the founder of the present cathedral, the Habsburg Duke Rudolf IV, gave the order to rebuild in the contemporary Gothic style. The choir, south tower and nave with its massive saddle roof faced with colourful glazed tiles were constructed at this time.

The Gothic pulpit, the artistic jewel of Stephansdom

Steadfast Against Many Foes

At the start of the 16th century, when the Turks posed an imminent threat to Vienna, building work on Stephansdom stopped – it was more important to fortify the city – and consequently the north tower was never finished. In 1579 the tower was capped with a helm, under which swings Vienna's favourite bell, the "**Pummerin**". Cast from the metal from

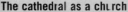

Turkish cannons and weighing a solid 21 tonnes, it is Austria's heaviest bell, and said to be the second largest in the world. Even though two Turkish cannon balls are still lodged in the facade of the south tower, "Steffl" came through the Turkish sieges relatively unscathed.

The cathedral as a church

Stephansdom is, of course, not only of cultural importance, it is also a working church. On weekdays seven services are held and on Sundays ten. On high feast days such as Easter, Whitsun and Christmas, numerous worshippers attend Mass. Special services are often broadcast live on television. On high feast days and at New Year the "Pummerin" bell is rung.

Later, the French too failed to damage it. In the last days of World War II, though, it suffered severe damage. In April 1945 a fire reduced large

parts of the nave to rubble and ash. The fire also consumed the wooden roof trusses, a brilliant example of Gothic craftmanship. Reconstruction of the cathedral was started in 1948 and, because the whole of Austria supported the work, it was so far advanced after only seven years that services were again held here. Thus "Steffl" became a symbol of solidarity after the horrors of Hitler's dictatorship.

It's worth pausing in front of the entrance to Stephansdom, with its **Riesentor** (Giants' Doorway) flanked by the two Towers of the Heathens, for a good look at the Romanesque statues. Dragons, lions and serpents symbolise demonic powers, the struggle between good and evil. As the square in front of the cathedral long served as a marketplace, the so-called Viennese measures can still be seen embedded in the masonry next to the portal: a loaf of bread and two measures of length, the (shorter) Bohemian and the (longer) Viennese ell.

The Most Spiritual Church Interior in the World

The Jugendstil architect Alfred Loos (1870–1933) called Stephansdom "the most spiritual church interior in the world". As soon as you enter you'll understand why. The soaring pillars, high ribbed vaulting and dim light give the triple aisles of the nave a feeling of rapture and timelessness. But pleasant as it is to just stand and gaze, there's plenty more to see in this mighty church.

The most famous artistic treasure of the Stephansdom is the **Gothic pulpit**. The filigree masonry, carved in 1514 from seven sandstone blocks, presents four particularly unflattering portraits of the princes of the church and, on the plinth, the image (affectionately known as *fenstergucker*, or "Peeping Tom") of

Right: On two-horsepower through the city centre

master-mason Anton Pilgram. Stone toads and lizards, symbols of evil, crawl up the staircase balustrade. These are held at bay by a dog, a symbol of good.

Other highlights include Meister Pilgram's base for the **gigantic organ** comprising 10,000 pipes. The left side-chapel contains the **Wiener Neustädter Altar** from 1447. which has 72 images of saints painted on its inner and outer wings, while the right side-chapel houses the red marble **tomb of Emperor Friedrich II**. The noble simplicity of the 650-year-old *Dienstbotenmadonna* (Serving-girl Madonna) is particularly moving. Legend has it that the innocence of a serving-girl accused of theft was proved after she appealed to this Madonna for help. The statue of Mary, which she had implored. was relocated in Stephansdom and later much-visited by servants in need

Left: Old and new – the glass facade of the Haas House and Stephans-dom's Towers of the Heathens

TAKING A BREAK

Stop off for a refreshing cup of tea at the **Teehaus Haas & Haas** (► 67), directly behind Stephansdom, before continuing your exploration of medieval Vienna.

🚼 193 D3 ⊠ Wien 1, Stephansplatz ⏰ Interior Mon–Sat 6–10, Sun 7–10;
Guided tours Mon–Sat 10:30 and 3, Sun 3 (in English Apr–Oct daily 3:45);
Lift up Nordturm Apr–Jun, Sep–Oct daily 8:30–5:30, Jul–Aug 8:30–6,
Nov–Mar 8:30–5 🚇 Stephansplatz 🚌 Bus 1A, 2A, 3A Stephansplatz
💷 Guided tours moderate; lift up Nordturm moderate
❓ www.stephanskirche.at

STEPHANSDOM: INSIDE INFO

Top tips If you're fit enough, climb the 343 steps up to the **Türmerstube im Südturm** (Watchman's Room in the South Tower, daily 9–5:30, admission: moderate). The view from the top is magnificent and it will make you forget all your troubles.
• You can only descend into the **Gruftanlagen** (crypt) with a guided tour (Mon–Sat 10–11:30/1:30–4:30, Sun 1:30–4:30, admission: moderate). The crypt contains the tombs, urns for viscera and sarcophagi of the Habsburg rulers and a number of bishops, together with skeletons from the city cemetery, which was laid out round the cathedral in the 18th century.
• In fine weather from June to September **evening tours with a roof visit** are on offer every Saturday at 7pm (English tours at 5:30). Meet at the south tower.

Hidden gem Visit the Stephansdom in the **early morning or late evening**. The quietness really enhances the atmosphere.

⓫ Judenplatz

A former Roman barracks and medieval Jewish quarter, and now a moving place of remembrance – very few squares reflect the long and varied history of the city like the Judenplatz.

For a long time the square was quite unremarkable. It wasn't until 1995 that its long history came to light when excavations undertaken for the construction of a memorial proposed by Simon Wiesenthal unveiled Judenplatz's hidden gems. This part of the city was first settled by the Romans, who in the first century AD built legionaries' barracks here for a large camp. In the 12th century the square became the centre of the Jewish quarter from which it gains its name (Jewish Square).

One of the Largest Medieval Jewish Quarters

The Jewish ghetto had 70 houses, built to form a continuous wall. In the centre stood the school- or prayer-house, first mentioned in 1205; at the time it was one of the largest synagogues in Europe. The Viennese Jewish community then formed some 5 per cent of the population of the city. Most families were not rich, but the ghetto developed into a famous centre for Jewish scholarship. In 1421, 210 Jews were burnt at the stake, the rest were expelled and the synagogue destroyed. More than five centuries later archaeologists discovered the remains of the synagogue: the foundations, parts of the tiled floor and the hexagonal *bima*, where the Torah was read.

The Holocaust Memorial

Today Judenplatz with its memorial, excavations and museum is a place of remembrance. The square is dominated by the

Rachel Whiteread's memorial on Judenplatz

memorial by British sculptress Rachel Whiteread. The reinforced concrete cube, unveiled in 2000, is a poignant reminder of the 65,000 Austrian Jews who died at the hands of the Nazis: the structure consists of 7,000 books with bindings turned

Museum Judenplatz, an annexe of the Jewish Museum

The exhibition in the lower ground floor of Museum Judenplatz

inwards, their titles forever unreadable and so lost forever. The flagstones surrounding the memorial are inscribed with all the locations where Jews were put to death.

TAKING A BREAK

For a taste of proper Viennese fast food, stop at **Würstelstand am Hoher Markt**, a tiny sausage stand on nearby Hoher Markt. Whichever type of sausage you choose from the vast array on offer, wash it down with an Austrian beer in the traditional way. As an added bonus, there's little chance of turning up and finding the stand closed – it opens from 7am to 4am.

✚ 192 C4 ⊚ Herrengasse 🚌 Bus 1A Heidenschuss/Am Hof

JUDENPLATZ: INSIDE INFO

Top tip The excavations can be viewed on the ground floor and in the cellars of the **Museum Judenplatz** (Wien 1, Judenplatz 8, Sun–Thu 10–6, Fri until 2pm, admission: moderate), and in an outreach of the Jewish Museum in the Palais Eskeles (11 Dorotheergasse, Vienna 1, tel: 01/535 04 31, Sun–Fri 10–6, Sat 10–8; U-bahn station: Stephansplatz; admission: moderate. www.jmw.at). Audio-visual equipment in three modern exhibition rooms gives information on the daily life and commercial and religious activities of the medieval community. A computer animation reconstructs the ghetto of around 1400 and lets you take a virtual tour of the alleyways and the synagogue. In addition, numerous excavated objects are displayed in showcases.

🔟 Freyung

Freyung is one of Vienna's most elegant squares. Lined with magnificent, lavishly restored palaces, it has developed into an urban centre with a special ambience, where art lovers will always find spectacular, ever-changing exhibitions. The attractive passages and courtyards of the palaces, with their pretty shops and inviting bars, also contribute to its metropolitan feel.

In the Middle Ages the triangular square had the dubious privilege of serving as the city's rubbish dump. If the mounds of rubbish were not too high, travelling entertainers and minstrels performed here, and in an emergency, gallows for traitors were swiftly erected. There is now no trace of the square's sombre past.

A temple of art

On the site of the former oratory of the Schottenkirche there now stands the **Kunstforum** of Bank Austria. Its regular exhibitions of modern art are always worth visiting. (Wien 1, Freyung 8, tel: 01/537 33; Sat–Thu 10–7, Fri 10–9; admission: expensive; www.kunstforumwien.at)

Plenty of Palaces...

The Schottenkirche on Freyung

One side of the square is formed by Lukas von Hildebrandt's **Palais Daun Kinsky**, a masterpiece of baroque architecture. Festive banquets are held in its princely rooms. Since 1994 the staterooms of the equally baroque **Palais Harrach** have been used by the Kunsthistorisches Museum (Museum of Art History) for top-flight exhibitions, lectures and concerts. The adjoining **Palais Ferstel** was built in the Italianate style in 1856–60 by Heinrich Ferstel for the Österreichisch-Ungarische Bank. Until 1877 it was the home of the Wiener Börse (Vienna Stock Exchange). Later the building deteriorated, until in 1975 it was restored, together with the Café Central (► 28, 66). Today the staterooms on the first floor are let out for conferences and banquets.

Café Central, once a meeting point for Vienna's literati

...and Plenty More

On the north side of Freyung stands the **Schottenstift** (Scottish Foundation). Founded in 1155 by the Babenberg Duke Heinrich II Jasomirgott. it actually has nothing to do with Scotland – the Duke brought monks to Vienna from Ireland, which at that time was called *Scotia maior* The monks had the right to shelter asylum-seekers, who could not be prosecuted by the courts while they were in the foundation – hence the name of the square, *freyung*, meaning "freeing". Heinrich II Jasomirgott is buried in the Schottenstift's church. On the corner of the traffic-calmed square and Renngasse stands the grand **Austria-Brunnen** (➤ 30), the Austria Fountain designed in 1846 by Ludwig Schwanthaler. Its female bronze figures symbolise the rivers Elbe, Danube, Weichsel and Po, the principal rivers of the empire. The fountain is crowned by the figure of Austria.

TAKING A BREAK

Wander down Palais Ferstel's passageway to Herrengasse and one of the city's finest coffee-houses, **Café Central** (➤ 66). Here you can sample traditional Viennese coffee and cake.

➕ 192 B/C4   Ⓤ Herrengasse, Schottentor   🚋 Tram 1, 2, D Schottentor, Bus 2A, 3A Herrengasse

---

At Your Leisure

2 Erzbischöfliches Palais

The baroque Archbishops' Palace was built between 1632 and 1641 to the design of Giovanni Coccapani. The extensive building has facades on Stephansplatz, Rotenturmstrasse and Wolfzeile. The palace was, and still is, the seat of the bishops and archbishops of Vienna. It houses the Dom- und Diözesanmuseum (Cathedral and Diocesan Museum), which has sacred art from the Gothic, Renaissance and baroque periods. At the core of the collection are objects from the cathedral treasury, including very valuable vestments from Stephansdom.

🔛 193 D3 ✉ Wien 1, Stephansplatz 6
☎ (01) 515 52-36 89 🕔 Tue–Sat 10–5
🚇 Stephansplatz 🚌 Bus 1A, 2A, 3A
Stephansplatz 💰 Moderate
❓ www.dommuseum.at

3 Franziskanerplatz

Shut off from traffic by a row of large stone balls, entering this square instantly transports you to a medieval town in Italy. This feeling is conveyed by **Franziskanerkirche**, Vienna's only ecclesiastical building in the Renaissance style, whose gable looms over a narrow facade. The high altar was created by Andrea Pozzo, the Italian master of *trompe-l'oeil* architecture, but of more

The idyllic courtyard of the Erzbischöfliches Palais

interest is the miracle-working statue *Madonna with the Axe* from the 15th century. Its name comes from a story in which the Protestants tried – and failed – to destroy it with fire and an axe: the axe is still there, sticking out of Mary's left shoulder.

🔛 193 D3 🚇 Stephansplatz
🚌 Bus 1A, 2A, 3A Stephansplatz

4 Mozarthaus Wien

A narrow, cobblestone street behind Stephansdom contains the only residence of Wolfgang Amedeus Mozart still standing in Vienna (he moved 11 times in the city). The great musician lived here from

The indestructible *Madonna with the Axe*

September 1784 until April 1797, reputedly during the happiest time of his life, and it was in this house that he composed *The Marriage of Figaro*. Originally preserved as a memorial to Mozart known as the Figaro Haus, it has now been turned into a thoroughly absorbing museum capturing the life and spirit of the city in Mozart's time.

🔢 193 D3 ⊠ Wien 1, Domgasse 5
☎ (01) 513 62 94 ⏰ Tue–Sun 9–6
🚇 Stephansplatz 🚌 Bus 1A, 2A, 3A
Stephansplatz 🎫 Moderate, Sun free

5 Jesuitenkirche

The Jesuit Church, the former university church, was built in the mid-18th century as the dining hall for the Alte Universität (Old University).

north, so Pozzo had to contend with particularly poor lighting. He therefore integrated the altarpiece, which shows the Assumption of the Virgin into Heaven, into the architecture. He set the painting into a shallow bay and created two sources of natural light by opening up narrow windows between the picture and its frame. In the chapels at the back on the right, where an adjoining high building shuts out the light, Pozzo's solution is even more interesting: he diverted the light by replacing the narrow side windows with mirrors. He included himself in the piece at the bottom left, as the Apostle Ancreas

🔢 193 E3 ⊠ Wien 1, Dr-Ignaz-Seipel-Platz 🚇 Stubentor 🚌 Tram 1, 2, D Stubentor; Bus 1A Riemergasse

Together with the Alte Universität and the Akademie der Wissenschaften (Academy of Sciences), it encloses Dr-Ignaz-Seipel-Platz. The charm of this square is particularly noticeable in the evening, when floodlights bathe the harmonious early-baroque edifice in an unearthly light. Built in 1623–31, the church was founded by Emperor Ferdinand II, when he entrusted the university to the Jesuits. Of particular interest is the *trompe-l'oeil* painting by Andrea Pozzo in the main aisle. The church faces

"Historyworld" in the Heiligenkreuzerhof

6 Heiligenkreuzerhof

Between Köllnerhofgasse and Schönlaterngasse lies a large, particularly idyllic courtyard, which belongs to the Cistercians of the Holy Cross Abbey. The residences round the

The towers of the Greek Church soar above Fleischmarkt

courtyard are let as private apartments (the famous cabaret artist Helmut Qualtinger lived here for a while). With its wrought-iron balconies,

potted plants and well-kept apartments, Heiligenkreuzerhof is a beautiful example of the city's many inner courtyards, and an excellent photo opportunity. Be sure to take a stroll down Schönlaterngasse – this narrow street, with its cellared eateries and quaint shops, is a classic example of how Vienna must have looked in medieval times.

➕ 193 E4 🚇 Stephansplatz 🚌 Bus 1A, 2A, 3A Stephansplatz

🄍 Fleischmarkt

At the start of the 18th century, with the threat of the Turks gone, Vienna grew into a key centre for trade with the East. Turkish, Levantine and Greek merchants settled in the area of Fleischmarkt (Meat Market) and developed this trade with the Orient. The Byzantine

look of the Greek Non-United Church is a reminder of this time.

➕ 193 E4 🚇 Schwedenplatz 🚋 Tram 1, 2, 21, N; Bus 2A Schwedenplatz

🄌 Griechenbeisl

In 1447 the city's records register the sale of a house named Griechenbeisl (Greek tavern), making this the oldest pub in Vienna. However, its origins long predate this – its foundations were laid in Roman times. It was here, in the mid-17th century during the plague years, that the minstrel Augustin composed and sang the famous song *Oh du lieber Augustin, alles ist hin* (➤ 20) (Dear Augustin, everything is over). The statue of Augustin, peering out of a barred-off room in the cellar, is a reminder of the minstrel. The Griechenbeisl has had many prominent customers, including Beethoven, Mozart, Einstein and Gina Lollobrigida – all of whom are immortalised on the ceiling of one of the restaurant's vaults.

➕ 193 E4 ✉ Wien 1, Fleischmarkt 11 ☎ (01) 533 19 77 🕐 Daily 11am–12:30am (hot food 11am–11:30am) 🚇 Schwedenplatz 🚋 Tram 1, 2, 21, N; Bus 2A Schwedenplatz 🌐 www.griechenbeisl.at

🄎 Ruprechtskirche

This small, ivy-clad church is Vienna's oldest. Rising above today's bar-ridden "Bermuda Triangle" (➤ 68), it stands on a mound overlooking the Danube Canal, where in the Middle Ages steps led down to a landing-stage for the salt-trading ships. The Ruprechtskirche is said to have been founded as early as 740. The plain 12th-century hall

Maître Leherb

Have a look at the house at No 6 Franziskanerplatz. Until his death in 1997, it was the home of the Viennese surrealist artist Maître Leherb. He also created the pretty dove fountain in front of the house.

church was remodelled in Gothic style in the 13th century. It still has stained-glass windows from the 1200s and a "Black Madonna", invoked in times of plague or war.

🕀 193 D4 ✉ Wien 1, Ruprechtsplatz
🚇 Schwedenplatz 🚋 Tram 1, 2, 21, N;
Bus 2A Schwedenplatz

⑩ Hoher Markt and Ankeruhr

The small square of Hoher Markt has been around for a long time – beneath its cobblestones lie Roman ruins. During the Middle Ages it was the site of the Schranne, courts of law which handed down harsh sentences, and the city's gallows and pillory. It was also home to a filthy prison used for the criminally insane and mentally disabled. For a long time the square was also a fish-market, and Vienna's first water-conduit ended here. The Vermählungsbrunnen (Wedding Fountain) in the middle was built first of wood by Joseph Emanuel Fischer von Erlach, then rebuilt in marble by his son, in 1792.

In its eastern corner is the glory of the square, the **Ankeruhr** (Anchor Clock). It was created in 1911 by the Jugendstil painter Franz von Matsch as a decoration for the Anchor Insurance Company. The clock's special feature is a parade of statues – each day, exactly on the stroke of twelve, doors open and twelve larger-than-life figures appear, illustrating the history of the city (among

The baroque splendour of the church "To the nine choirs of angels"

Roman remains

Be sure to descend the steps under the Café Salut im Garten (Hoher Markt 3) to the Roman excavations. These show the remains of the Roman camp at Vindobona and the foundations of the palace where the Roman Emperor Marcus Aurelius probably once stayed (Tue–Sun 9–1, 2–5, admission: inexpensive)

them Marcus Aurelius, Charlemagne and Rudolf I).

🕀 193 D4 🚇 Stephansplatz 🚌 Bus 1A, 2A, 3A Hoher Markt

⑫ Am Hof

In 1155, Babenberger Heinrich II Jasomirgott had a conqueror's palace built on the wide square of Am Hof. This developed into a centre of chivalric culture, where poets such as Walther von der Vogelweide appeared. Even today Am Hof has a lordly feel about it, not least thanks to the church Zu den neun Chören der Engel (To the Nine Choirs of the Angels), Collalto Palace, where the six-year-old Mozart had his concert debut, and the giant Mariensäule (Mary Column), which commemorates the menace of the Swedes in the Thirty Years War.

🕀 192 C4 🚇 Herrengasse
🚌 Bus 1A Am Hof

The "Anchor Clock" at Hoher Markt is a famous Jugendstil work

Where to...
Eat and Drink

Prices

Prices are for a meal for one person, excluding drinks.
€ under €15 €€ €15–€30 €€€ over €30

RESTAURANTS

Beim Czaak €

Tucked away in a quiet corner of the inner city is this pleasant *Beisl*, which caters for local residents, city workers and the odd tourist or two. The menu is filled with traditional Viennese cuisine – take your pick from wonderful dishes such as *Wienerschnitzel*, *Tafelspitz* (boiled beef) or hearty paprika *Huhn* (paprika chicken). In summer there's outdoor seating on the quiet square, and in winter you'll be snug indoors.

🚏 193 E4 ⊠ Wien 1, Postgasse 15
☎ (01) 513 72 15 ⓖ Mon–Sat
11am–midnight ⓜ Schwedenplatz
🚋 Tram 1, 2, 21, N

Cantinetta Antinori €€

This restaurant, close to Stephansdom, belongs to the renowned aristocratic Antinori family from Florence, who have been making wine for 26 generations. All the wines served here are from the family's own wine cellar, and the food is based on inspirational and delectable Tuscan cuisine. The interior is – like the wine, food and family – tasteful, exuding simple elegance.

🚏 193 D3 ⊠ Wien 1, Jasomirgottstrasse 3/5 ☎ (01) 533 77 22 ⓖ Daily
11:30am–midnight (hot food until 11pm)
ⓜ Stephansplatz 🚌 Bus 1A, 2A, 3A
Stephansplatz

Fabios €€€

Fabios restaurant, bar and lounge is reputed to have the finest design of any restaurant in the city. The glass doors onto the arbour are opened wide in summer, turning the whole place into a terrace. The cuisine is creative Mediterranean, light and delicate; specialities include warm braised octopus and fillets of turbot. The ambience is chic, and the place is incredibly popular with the well-to-do.

🚏 192 C4 ⊠ Wien 1, Tuchlauben 6
☎ (010) 532 22 22 ⓖ Mon–Sat 10am–
1am (hot food noon–11:30pm)
ⓜ Stephansplatz 🚌 Bus 1A, 2A, 3A
Petersplatz

Figlmüller €€

This cosy restaurant and wine bar is in the narrow alleyway between Wollzeile and Lugeck. It serves the biggest *Wienerschnitzel* in Vienna, traditionally accompanied by a mixed salad and a *g'spritzer* (spritzer). The wine is from the restaurant's own vineyards and the atmosphere is relaxed and easy.

🚏 193 D3 ⊠ Wien 1, Wollzeile 5
☎ (01) 512 61 77 ⓖ Daily 11–10:30
ⓜ Stephansplatz 🚌 Bus 1A, 2A, 3A
Stephansplatz

Gösser Bierklinik €

Even after renovation the furnishings have remained the same, traditional and very cosy, with a medieval feel. In the Gösser Bierklinik everything revolves round Gösser beer, reputed to be the best in the city. To accompany the amber nectar there's good Viennese food on the ground floor, while on the floor above the chef serves ever-changing dishes of the day. Prepare to be surprised!

🚏 192 C4 ⊠ Wien 1, Steindlgasse 4
☎ (01) 533 75 98 12 ⓖ Mon–Sat
10am–11:30pm ⓜ Stephansplatz
🚌 Bus 1A, 2A, 3A Petersplatz

Immervoll €€

This modern take on the traditional *Beisl* is a pure gem in the back streets of medieval Vienna, and so popular that it's almost impossible to secure a table at lunchtime (it's a little easier in the evening). The atmosphere is both intimate and convivial, and the interior designed by celebrated architect Hermann Czech (of Kleines Café fame,
▶ 66). Immervoll (literally "always full") shares the outdoor seating on Franziskanerplatz with Kleines Café in summer, and on a warm day it's one of the loveliest places to dine in the city.

➕ 193 D3 ⊠ Wien 1, Weihburggasse 17 ☎ (01) 513 52 88 ⏲ Daily noon–midnight Ⓡ Stephansplatz 🚌 Bus 1A, 2A, 3A Stephansplatz

Indochine 21 €€€

Far-Eastern food is all the rage in Vienna, and the culinary culture of Vietnam, Laos and Cambodia, combined with the spirit of 21st-century Europe, are the thinking behind this trendy eatery. Its charm lies not only in the Asian cuisine but also in the colonial-inspired surroundings. The wickerwork furniture and the stylish restaurant-bar-lounge, serving some of the best cocktails in town, make it special.

➕ 193 F3 ⊠ Wien 1, Stubenring 18 ☎ (01) 513 76 60 ⏲ Daily 11:30am–2am (hot food served 11:30–3, 6–midnight) Ⓡ Stubentor 🚋 Tram 1, 2; 🚌 Bus 1A, 74A Stubentor

Neu Wien €€

At Neu Wien, the possibilities are manifold. They include an *achterl* (half-litre of wine) at the bar, agreeable company, a meal at the neatly laid tables or an evening in KIK (*Kultur im Keller*, culture in the cellar). The restaurant has the pleasant atmosphere of a private living-room, and the cooking is good and not over the top trendy. With style to match, it is a sophisticated rendezvous for artists.

➕ 193 E3 ⊠ Wien 1, Bäckerstrasse 5 ☎ (010) 512 09 99 ⏲ Mon–Sat 6pm–1am Ⓡ Stubentor 🚌 Bus 1A Riemergasse

Ofenloch €€

The owner of this 300-year-old restaurant is an avid collector, who for years has been gathering whatever takes his fancy, from every possible source. The rooms are decorated with equal care – in pride of place is a substantial collection of corks. The food and wine combines the traditional and contemporary, and the menu is laid out in the form of an old newspaper, *Ofenloch's Localblatt*.

➕ 192 C4 ⊠ Wien 1, Kurrentgasse 8 ☎ (01) 533 88 44 ⏲ Mon–Sat 10am–midnight (hot food noon–10:45) Ⓡ Stephansplatz 🚌 Bus 1A, 2A, 3A Petersplatz

Oswald & Kalb €€

This mixture of fashionable bar and restaurant has been a favourite meeting place for two decades. The dimly lit rooms are rustic and comfortable, the food is traditional Styrian and delicate. Many well-known personalities and artists meet here for dinner, especially at the regulars' tables at the back of the vaulted room.

➕ 193 E3 ⊠ Wien 1, Bäckerstrasse 14 ☎ (01) 512 13 71 ⏲ Daily 6pm–2am Ⓡ Stubentor 🚌 Bus 1A Riemergasse

Wrenkh €€

Wrenkh has for years been Vienna's seminal vegetarian restaurant, though in recent times a few fish and meat dishes have crept onto the menu. No matter, its imaginative meatless dishes have kept diners coming back time and time again, and it even runs its own cooking classes (see www.kochsalon.at). The restaurant offers two faces to guests, with an informal, bar-like setting at the front and a more intimate and romantic scene to the rear.

➕ 193 D4 ⊠ Wien 1, Bauernmarkt 10 ☎ (01) 533 15 26 ⏲ Mon–Fri noon–4, 6–11, Sat 6–11 Ⓡ Stephansplatz 🚌 Bus 1A, 2A, 3A Stephansplatz

Zu den 3 Hacken €

This restaurant, once the favourite haunt of Franz Schubert and his cohorts, is still an absolutely typical inn. In the little garden in front of the house you sit at simple tables with green-and-white chequered tablecloths. The cooking is very traditional, ranging from the classical *Tafelspitz* (boiled beef) to offal dishes like braised heart, accompanied by a fine selection of wines from Austria and Italy.

✚ 193 E3 🖂 Wien 1, Singerstrasse 28 ☎ (01) 512 15 19 🚇 Mon–Sat 11:30am– midnight 🚇 Stephansplatz 🚌 Bus 1A, 2A, 3A Stephansplatz

CAFÉS

Café Central

Café Central in Palais Ferstel is legendary. For generations it has been the chosen meeting place of writers and intellectuals, including Lenin, Trotsky and the psychologist Adler. The latest round of renovations has removed its rather sleepy patina, but a lifesize figure of the writer Peter Altenberg, sitting at one of the marble tables, is a reminder of the intellectual glories of the past. You can also eat well in Café Central; the Viennese dishes and the pastries are first class.

✚ 192 C4 🖂 Wien 1, Herrengasse 14 ☎ (01) 533 37 63 61 🚇 Mon–Sat 7:30am–10pm, Sun 10–10 🚇 Herrengasse, Schottentor 🚊 Tram 1, 2, D Schottentor; Bus 2A, 3A Herrengasse

Café Prückel

Prückel has been a successful café on the Ringstrasse for over 100 years for two reasons – its excellent coffee and Viennese coffee-house flair. It acquired a retro look in the 1950s, but you'd think the waiters, with their gruff service, Viennese *schmäh* (dry wit and humour) and black jacket and bow ties, were right out of the *fin-de-siècle* years. It can get a little smoky at times, but thankfully there is a non-smoking room to the rear and pavement seating in summer.

✚ 193 D3 🖂 Wien 1, Stock-im-Eisen-Platz 2 ☎ (01) 512 79 25 🚇 Stephansplatz 7am–8pm, Sun 9–8 🚇 Stephansplatz 🚌 Bus 1A, 2A, 3A Stephansplatz

Diglas

The tasteful, roomy corner café in Wollzeile keeps up the old Viennese coffee-house traditions. It is splendidly furnished, with marble floors, wall-panelling and cut-glass doors. There is an extensive range of hot foods from breakfast to lunch, and afternoon pastries from their own shop. In the evening, discreet piano music provides a relaxing ambience for diners. The coffee-house is always crowded so it's often hard to get a table, even in the garden out front.

✚ 193 E3 🖂 Wien 1, Wollzeile 10 ☎ (01) 512 57 65 🚇 Daily 8am–10:30pm 🚇 Stephansplatz, Stubentor 🚌 Bus 1A Riemergasse

Kleines Café

Designed in the mid-1970s by the architect Hermann Czech, Kleines Café (Little Café) lives up to its name. It has just five marble tables and a few Thonet chairs and leather-covered benches. The favourite haunt of the Viennese actor Hanno Pöschl, it has a distinctive feel and is a popular meeting place for artists. In fine weather the café can take extra guests – they put a few more tables outside.

✚ 193 D3 🖂 Wien 1, Franziskaner-platz 3 ☎ No telephone 🚇 Daily 10am–2am 🚇 Stephansplatz 🚌 Bus 1A, 2A, 3A Stephansplatz

Korb

This café is not distinguished for its modern furnishings – on the contrary, everything looks pretty shabby. All the same, or perhaps even because of its agreeable patina, "the Basket" is a legendary Viennese institution. The café provides more hot dishes than many pubs and boasts of having the best *apfelstrudel* in town. The Korb is a favourite meeting place for business people and artists. In the summer, guests fill the garden. The cellar also has a particular attraction: there's an old-fashioned skittle-alley.

🏠 193 D4 ⊠ Wien 1, Brandstätte 7–9 ☎ (01) 533 72 15 ⓦ Mon–Sat 8am–midnight, Sun 11–11 ⓢ Stephansplatz 🚌 Bus 1A, 2A, 3A Stephansplatz

Teehaus Haas & Haas

In a town dominated by coffee-houses, it's refreshing to find a quality tea house in the heart of the city. And what a tea house – Haas & Haas stocks almost 50 sorts of tea from around the world, mostly in leaf form. It's also famous for its breakfasts, which include full English and continental varieties alongside the likes of more unusual Japanese and Chinese morning meals. Its courtyard setting is among the most pleasant in the inner city.

🏠 193 D3 ⊠ Wien 1, Stephansplatz 4 ☎ (01) 512 26 66 ⓦ Mon–Fri 8–8, Sat 8–6:30 ⓢ Stephansplatz 🚌 Bus 1A, 2A, 3A Stephansplatz

Where to... Shop

The narrow alleyways in the old city centre are not only suited to strolling, they are also good for shopping. There are numerous boutiques, antique dealers, bookstores and special interest shops that stock a vast array of original offerings. Many of the shops have kept their Viennese style, while others have been modernised, but the good thing is there is something for everyone here, and perhaps even for everyone's wallet.

Behind the Stephansdom

Vinothek St Stephan (Stephansplatz 6) has a vast range of international wines, rare and old vintages and single-malt whiskies, as well as olive oil and balsamic vinegar. The **Galerie Ambiente** (Lugeck 1A) specialises in traditional bentwood furniture; of special interest is the new Design Marlowe furniture, which has touches of Biedermeier, whose exhibits, however, are not for sale. The small but elegant **Schatzecke** (Treasure Trove, Wollzeile 5, Passage) has antique ornaments at all price levels, even for the smallest purse. The **Geschenks-Gewölbe** (Fleischmarkt 16) has antique and new bears and dolls, as well as pretty little antiques and gift articles. The shoe boutique **Le Petit Chou** (Kühfussgasse 2/Petersplatz 9) specialises in small sizes, with particularly cute children's shoes and accessories.

Freyung

Freyung's finely renovated palaces are filled with inviting shops. In the passage leading from the square to the Palais Ferstel arcades, two small shops merit special attention. **Katze & Kater** (Cat & Tomcat, Freyung 2) has delightful model tigers, in painted wood or porcelain and in all colours and sizes. **Xocolat** (Freyung 2) describes itself as a pleasure ground for explorers and conquerors, and with some justification, as they have every possible sort of chocolate. **Tomas Lisa Interiors** (Herrengasse 14) on the far side of Palais Ferstel, has a selection of pretty things for the home such as lamps, accessories and small lifestyle items and gifts such as note-blocks. **Klosterladen im Schottenstift** (Freyung 6), the Abbey Shop, sells religious artefacts. This specialist shop for monastic products has been in existence since the 18th century, and stocks brandies, herbal liqueurs and wine as well as groceries from its own gardens (fruit, sausages, poppy oil). As might be expected, they also do a good line in devotional books and religious objects.

Where to be...
Entertained

The oldest part of Vienna has seen many a lively evening in its time, and while things have quietened down in recent years, the party still goes on. The narrow lanes and back alleys around Stephansdom hide a number of bars, but the greatest concentration of places is in the labyrinth of streets near Ruprechtskirche, aptly nicknamed the Bermuda Triangle.

Bermuda Triangle

In the early 1970s, a vibrant entertainment area grew up around the Ruprechtskirche, in Rabensteig, Seitenstettengasse and Ruprechtsplatz. It soon gained the nickname "Bermuda Dreieck" (Bermuda Triangle), not only for its maze of lanes, but because it was so easy to disappear here for hours (or even days!). It was a place where you could eat, drink, listen to live music and then stroll next door and do it all over again. Many of the original venues are still there today, and while the area has lost its edge and popularity with many locals, it still attracts plenty of young people looking for a night out.

First Floor (Seitenstettengasse 5, tel: 01/533 25 23, Mon–Sat 7pm–4am, Sun 8pm–3am) is a classic American cocktail bar, offering over 200 mixed drinks accompanied by smooth tunes. **Ma Pitom** (Seitenstettengasse 5, tel: 01/535 43 13, Sun–Thu 5pm–3am, Fri–Sat until 4am) is an upbeat beer house with an especially fine garden by the Ruprechtskirche. **Krah Krah** (Rabensteig 8, tel: 01/533 81 93, daily 11am–2am) specialises in beer – it has varieties from all over the world. **Salzamt** (Ruprechtsplatz 1, tel: 01/533 53 32, Mon–Fri noon–2am, Sat–Sun 5pm–2am) is a popular gastropub.

Der Rote Engel (Rabensteig 5, tel: 01/535 41 05, daily 5pm–4am) is the place for live music: in recent years 700 groups have played rock, pop, funk and jazz here.

MUSIC

Already in the mid-19th century there was a theatre in the cellars of No 11 Riemergasse. Later cabaret, revue and cinema moved in. The present occupants, **Porgy & Bess** (Riemergasse 11, tel: 01/512 88 11, Mon–Sat from 7pm, Sun from 8pm) have modern, lavishly furnished rooms. Anyone interested in jazz comes here – the programme is varied and interesting.

At **Jazzland** (Franz-Josefs-Kai 29, tel: 01/533 25 75, Mon–Sat from 7pm, music from 9pm) time seems to have stood still. The place is as dimly lit and smoky as you'd expect from a true jazz club, and the mood is often excellent. The music varies from swing, blues and dixie to modern jazz.

BARS AND CLUBS

Flex (Donaukanal, tel: 01/533 75 25, daily 6pm–4am) is arguably the top club in Vienna. It doesn't look like much – strongly reminiscent of 1970s grungy punk – but the sound system is one of the best in Europe, and the world's top DJs and bands regularly grace the stage.

The legendary **Eden Bar** (Lilien-gasse 2, tel: 01/512 74 50, Mon–Sat 9pm–4am) has lost none of its charm over the years. All the Viennese celebrities come here, from industrial tycoons to leading politicians, for *reden in der Eden* (a chat at the Eden). The noticeboards outside have photos of the bar's illustrious former customers. They are a real draw in Liliengasse, as is the well-stocked bar. Every evening there's live music. Landlord Heinz Schimanko, Vienna's "king of the night", insists on strict etiquette. Gentlemen without ties are not admitted – though in emergencies the cloakroom can help out.

The Imperial City

Getting Your Bearings

More than any other, this part of Vienna bears witness to the splendour of the imperial era. The Hofburg, the Albertina and the busy surrounding streets reflect the power and elegance of the former royal city on the Danube. There are still shops here with a pleasingly dusty imperial feel, but there are also great pubs and real temples of consumerism with an international reputation.

The heart of the old imperial city beats with an almost youthful vigour. This is particularly evident in the Kohlmarkt and Graben areas, which have seen many changes in the past few years. The old has given way to the new, and everything has been updated in tasteful metropolitan style. A new, urbane flair is apparent, with numerous and elegant pubs and bars flooding the area. In the past few years the tourist attractions have also been refurbished, at great expense. From the Hofburg with its great museums through to the Hofreitschule (Riding School) and Albertina, everything has been resplendently renovated.

Above:
The Hofburg attracts crowds of people

Left: Rest your feet on Graben

Right: Swarovski's gleaming paradise

Page 69: The Kohlmarkt leads to the Michaelertor

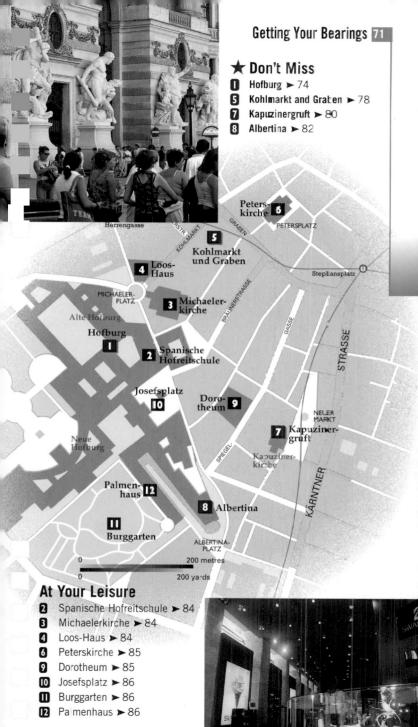

Herrengasse

Peters-
kirche **6**
PETERSPLATZ

5 Kohlmarkt
und Graben

4 Loos-
Haus

StepEansplatz

MICHAELER-
PLATZ

Alte Hofburg

3 Michaeler-
kirche

BRAÜNERSTRASSE

Hofburg

1

2 Spanische
Hofreitschule

GASSE

Josefsplatz
10

9 Doro-
theum

STRASSE

NELER
MARKT

Neue
Hofburg

7 Kapuziner-
gruft

SPIEGEL

Kapuziner-
kirche

KÄRNTNER

Palmen-
haus **12**

11
Burggarten

8 Albertina

ALBERTINA-
PLATZ

0   200 metres

0   200 yards

The Hofburg and Albertina are highlights of the imperial city, but you can experience the royal atmosphere by strolling through the streets that established Vienna as a city of elegance and splendour.

The Heart of the Imperial City in a Day

9:00 am

Start the day by exploring a royal residence with a visit to the 🚩Hofburg (left; ➤ 74). Don't just gaze at the so-called "Habsburgs' labyrinth" from the outside. The imperial apartments, the Sisi-Museum, the Silberkammer (Silver Chamber) and the Schatzkammer (Treasury) have plenty to offer through their exhibits and unique atmosphere. The celebrated 🚩Spanische Reitschule (Spanish Riding School, ➤ 84) adjoining the Hofburg, is also special.

Noon

Recharge yourself in the Hofburg café (➤ 90) and then stroll across 🚩Kohlmarkt (➤ 78). Admire the elegant contemporary jewellery at Schullin's (➤ 91) and the antique jewellery at Siedler's (➤ 91) before passing Demel's (➤ 90), which always has imaginative window-dressing, and buy some candied violets here (Sisi's favourite nibble), then stroll past the stylish displays at Chanel, Gucci and Louis Vuitton to 🚩Graben (➤ 78).

1:00 pm

Vienna's leading coffee-roaster, Meinl am Graben (right; ➤ 88) serves a choice, light lunch. Afterwards you could enjoy the window displays at the Schwäbische Jungfrau (Swabian Virgin, above right; ➤ 91), which specialises in fine linen, and then at Rasper & Söhne down nearby Habsburgerstrasse (➤ 91), a furnishing store

which has everything to make a home chic and up to date. The displays at Heldwein's and Haban's jeweller's shops (➤ 91) sparkle with life, but after this things get rather serious – steel yourself for a visit to the **7 Kapuzinergruft** (➤ 80) where you'll experience the Habsburgs' unique take on death.

3:00 pm

The bold modern architecture of the stairway and the lavishly restored rooms of the **8 Albertina** (➤ 82) art gallery will soon elevate your spirits after a visit to the Kapuzinergruft. Take in the current exhibition and then stroll around to your heart's content.

5:00 pm

The ancient, narrow side-streets off Graben are inviting to anyone who loves to rummage through beautiful old things. Here large and small antiques shops stand side by side, selling exclusive objects as well as little ornaments at more reasonable prices. Don't miss an opportunity to explore the **9 Dorotheum** (➤ 85) auction house. You'll be charmed by the mixture of art and kitsch in the beautiful palatial surroundings.

7:00 pm

Finally, take a gentle stroll through the **11 Burggarten** (➤ 86), where you'll find the **12 Palmenhaus** (Palm House, right; ➤ 86) with its butterfly house and superb brasserie: there is no better place for supper. And after that? Why not try your luck at the casino (➤ 92).

❶Hofburg

The Hofburg is often described as the "Habsburgs' labyrinth", and with some justification. This massive palace was the Habsburg dynasty's residence for six centuries, almost without interruption. During this time the rulers added one wing after another, creating a gigantic, and slightly confusing, complex.

The Sisi-Museum brings the imperial era to life

Nowadays the Hofburg feels like a city within the city. The palace is spread over an area of 240,000sq m (287,000 square yards), and comprises 18 wings and 19 courtyards with a total of 2,600 rooms. Some 5,000 people work in the Hofburg palace.

The Origins

It all began with the **Schweizerhof** (Swiss Court), named after the Swiss Guard who were stationed here during the reign of Maria Theresa. It is not known when this, the oldest wing, was built, but it is first mentioned in records in 1279. The *castro wiennensi*, a proper fortress with four corner turrets, a moat and a drawbridge, was used as a residence by the Habsburg ruler Rudolf I. The central part of this fortress is still standing, as is the **Burgkapelle** (Castle Chapel), although altered at a later date.

The **Schweizertor** (Swiss Gate), with its striking red, black and gold paintwork was constructed in 1552 by Pietro Ferabsco. The **Schatzkammer** (Treasury) is also located in this wing; here, along with many other precious secular and religious objects, you can see the insignia of the Holy Roman Empire, including the 1,000-year-old imperial crown, the orb, the sword, the cross and the fabled 15th-century Burgundian treasure.

Other Buildings

The second-oldest part of the Hofburg, the **Stallburg** (Stables), lies outside the main complex, and is separated by Reitschulgasse. This Renaissance palace was built between 1558 and 1565 by Emperor Ferdinand I for his son Maximilian, on the latter's return from

Incredible but true

In Empress Maria Theresa's time, lavish banquets were held, which the populace could watch, in order to demonstrate the power and the wealth of the rulers. Each of these meals cost as much as the construction of the Karlskirche.

Spain. Since the 18th century, this building with its three-storey arcaded courtyard has been home to the Lipizzaner horses from the **Spanische Reitschule** (Spanish Riding School, ➤ 84).

The **Amalienburg**, which dates from the 15th century, was originally a free-standing building opposite the Schweizertrakt. Later, Empress Elisabeth lived there. On 24 April 2004, to mark the 150th anniversary of the wedding of Elisabeth and Emperor Franz Joseph, the **Sisi-Museum** was opened here. It's not a museum in the usual sense but rather a celebration of the fascinating personality of the Empress. The main exhibits are Sisi's poems, portraits of the Empress and her clothes and jewellery (reproduced by the firm of Swarovski).

In 1668–80 Emperor Leopold I had the Schweizertrakt linked to the Amalienburg. Later Maria Theresa and Joseph II lived in the **Leopoldinischer Trakt** (Leopold Wing). Since 1946 the magnificent main rooms have been used as the official residence of the Austrian president, and so this part of the Hofburg cannot be visited.

The Schweizertor is one of the oldest parts of the Hofburg

The monument of Emperor Franz II stands in the Hofburg's inner courtyard

A Spectacular Baroque Makeover

Probably the most spectacular alteration to the Hofburg was made when Emperor Karl VI commissioned Johann Fischer von Erlach to design extensions. Between 1723 and 1735 the **Nationalbibliothek** (National Library) was built – its main room, the Prunksaal, is one of the finest in the world. Afterwards the **Winterreitschule** (Winter Riding School, ► 84) and **Redoutensäle** (Ballrooms) were constructed around Josefsplatz. The Winterreitschule has a suspended roof and a circular gallery supported by 46 columns.

From 1725 to 1730 Fischer von Erlach and Johann Lukas von Hildebrandt built the **Reichskanzeltrakt** (Chancellery Wing), Emperor Franz Joseph's residence from the mid-19th century. Its Kaisertor leads to the **Kaiser-appartements** (Emperor's Apartments), where the original furnishings give an authentic insight into his living and working quarters. In the neighbouring **Silberkammer** (Silver Chamber) are displays of valuable table-settings – the silver, bronze, glass and porcelain were used both for daily and state occasions.

In the early 19th century the **Zeremoniensaal** was added next to the Leopoldinischer Trakt. Many balls are still held in this Ceremonial Hall designed by Louis de Montoyer.

The Completion of the Complex

Emperor Franz Joseph carried out the last big addition to the Hofburg. He commissioned Ferdinand Kirschner to build the **Michaelertrakt**. In 1913, just one year before World War I, the building was completed; its 50m (165-foot) high copper

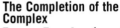
The Neue Hofburg forms one side of Heldenplatz

For kids

Children can learn about Empress Elisabeth and life in the Hofburg on a **Family Tour** through the Sisi-Museum. At the end of the tour, the greatest attraction for children is trying on clothes from the imperial era, which allows them to transform themselves into miniature royalty. (Sat–Sun and public holidays 10:30am and 2:30pm, tours last one hour, to book tel: 01/533 75 70-15, admission: moderate).

The eagle and crown on the Neue Hofburg are symbols of imperial power

roof looks especially elegant seen from Kohlmarkt. Franz Joseph was also responsible for the **Neue Hofburg** (New Hofburg).

Since the end of World War I, the Hofburg has no longer needed to house an emperor and his 1,000-strong corps of servants. The various wings now contain government and commercial offices, private apartments and conference rooms – and the Lipizzaners' stables. The Hofburg lives on.

TAKING A BREAK

From the **Café Spanische Reitschule** (Michaeler-kuppel entrance) you can watch the Lipizzaners trotting to their morning's workout.

🔲 192 C3 🔘 Herrengasse
🚋 Tram 1, 2, D, J Burgring,
Bus 2A, 3A Hofburg
❓ www.hofburg-wien.at

Kaiserappartements, Silberkammer, Sisi-Museum
☎ (01) 533 75 70 🔘 Jul–Aug
daily 9–5:30; Sep–Jun 9–5;
🏛 Expensive

Schatzkammer
☎ (01) 525 24-0 🔘 Wed–Mon
10–6 🏛 Expensive

Burgkapelle
☎ (010) 533 99 27 🔘 Sep–Jun Mon–Thu 11–3, Fri 11–1 🏛 Inexpensive

Prunksaal Nationalbibliothek
✉ Wien 1, Josefsplatz 1, 1st floor ☎ (01) 534 10-394 🔘 Tue–Sun 10–6,
Thu till 9 🏛 Moderate ❓ www.onb.ac.at

HOFBURG: INSIDE INFO

Top tip At 9:15am on Sundays between mid-September and the end of June you can hear the famous **Wiener Sängerknaben** (Vienna Boys' Choir) sing at Mass in the Burgkapelle, accompanied by members of the Staatsoper choir and orchestra. Reservations are essential (tel: 01/533 99 27); unsold tickets can also be bought on Friday at the Burgkapelle box office.

5 Kohlmarkt and Graben

Kohlmarkt and Graben are, together with Kärntner Strasse, the most elegant streets in Vienna, well worth a gentle stroll. The ever-changing face of the city is also evident here: in recent years many stylish and sophisticated stores have been replaced by multinational chains – and the exquisite outlets of famous luxury brands.

Graben

Graben (which means "ditch") is not just an expensive strip – it also has historical associations. The Romans built a broad defensive ditch here, which the Babenberger rulers filled in around 1200 during the expansion of the city. English soldiers from the entourage of imprisoned King Richard the Lionheart are said to have been brought in to help with the work – but this may just be a historic myth.

By the Middle Ages Graben was operating as a shopping street, selling bread, meat and vegetables rather than the expensive jewellery found here today. Activity on the pedestrianised street centres on **Dreifaltigkeitssäule** (Trinity Column). During the plague of 1679 some 100,000 Viennese died, and Emperor Leopold I commissioned the construction

A lively scene round the Dreifaltigkeitssäule on Graben

of a memorial column. Lodovico Burnacini created the splendid column, on which the Holy Trinity surmounts a mountain of clouds.

In the baroque era Graben became an urban centre; palaces were built and coffee-houses opened. The only survivor from that era is the **Palais Bartolotti-Partenfeld** (Graben 11), built by Johann Lukas von Hildebrandt in 1720 as an early apartment block.

The buildings which you see today on Graben mostly date from the 19th and 20th centuries. Otto Wagner's **Ankerhaus** (Graben 10) is especially worth a look. The upper floor with the glass roof extension was the home of Friedensreich Hundertwasser (1928–2000), the Austrian artist known for his bold, revolutionary architecture.

Graben seduces with its stylish shops

Kohlmarkt

The history of Kohlmarkt also dates back to the Romans, when it was part of a trade route that crossed Limesstrasse at Michaelerplatz. In the Middle Ages the Viennese could stock up on wood and charcoal here, hence the name, "coal market". The large **Michaelerhaus** (Kohlmarkt 11), where the young Joseph Haydn had a garret room, dates from the baroque era.

Today the pedestrianised Kohlmarkt is Vienna's showcase of luxury items. Here you'll find the flagship stores of famous designer brands, including Armani (Kohlmarkt 3), Gucci (Kohlmarkt 4), Chanel (Kohlmarkt 5) and Louis Vuitton (Kohlmarkt 6), the coffee-roaster and delicatessen Meinl am Graben (► 38) and the legendary patisserie Demel (► 90) with its unforgettable gâteaux and pastries.

Trzeniewski's snacks are legendary, and not just with ladies who lunch

TAKING A BREAK

Trzeniewski (Dorotheergasse 1) has the best fillings for sandwiches in town. In summer you can eat a light snack (including bacon and egg) at a table outside.

🔢 192/193 C/D3 🚇 Stephansplatz 🚌 Bus 2A, 3A Habsburgergasse

KOHLMARKT AND GRABEN: INSIDE INFO

Top tip In the narrow passage between Michaelerplatz and Habsburgergasse you'll discover an unexpected relic from medieval Vienna: a 1494 **limestone relief of the Mount of Olives** and a 1430 **Man of Sorrows**.

Hidden gem Whether you need to or not, make sure you go down into the public toilets in Graben. Wilhelm Beetz's 1904 walnut wood and Venetian glass interior is a real stunner.

7 Kapuzinergruft

The Viennese Imperial Crypt under the Kapuzinerkirche is a striking testimonial of the passing of the Habsburg dynasty. Buried here are 146 members of this aristocratic family and more than three centuries of Austrian history.

Above the steep flight of steps that leads down to the imperial vaults is written the inscription "Silentium". This request for silence is a reminder that the last resting place of the Habsburgs is consecrated ground. In 1617 Empress Anna ordered that a Capuchin monastery and a burial place for her and her husband, Emperor Matthias, be built within the city walls. In 1633 the mortal remains of the founders were buried in the Imperial Crypt. Since then a further 144 members of the royal family have found here their last resting place, conscientiously watched over by the Capuchin brothers. The dead include 12 emperors and 19 empresses and queens.

Emperor Karl VI's tomb

The Changing Cult of the Dead

The individual rooms reflect their time – as is evident from the bare "Founders' Crypt", the baroque, theatrical "Maria Theresa Crypt" and the simple "New Crypt", begun in 1960. Particularly impressive is the **Prunksarkophag von Maria Theresia und Franz Stephan** (Sumptuous Sarcophagus of Maria Theresa and Franz Stefan), adorned with bas-reliefs and designed by the imperial couple themselves. Countess Caroline Fuchs-Mollardt, the only non-Habsburg to be buried here, had a close connection to Maria Theresa – she was the Empress's tutor.

The unadorned copper coffin of Maria Theresa's son and successor, Joseph II, illustrates clearly the changing attitudes from baroque era to the Enlightenment.

The Kapuzinergruft has been frequently extended. In 1908 Emperor Franz Joseph had a suitable mausoleum built in the monastery's cellars for himself, his spouse Elisabeth and Crown Prince Rudolf. The most recent burial here was of Empress Zita, the wife of the last Austrian emperor, Karl I, in 1989.

Opposite: The elaborate tomb of Maria Theresa and Franz Stefan

Habsburg Hearts

For three centuries the Habsburgs have been laid to rest in accordance with their own particular ritual. Hearts were placed in silver goblets kept in the Herzgruft (Hearts Crypt) in Augustiner-kirche, innards stored in the Herzogsgruft (Dukes' Crypt) under Stephans-dom, and only the embalmed bodies were laid to rest in the Kapuzinergruft.

TAKING A BREAK

Just a few steps from the Kapuzinergruft is **Café Tirolerhof** (Führichgasse 8), which serves some of the best home-made *Apfelstrudel* in the city.

✚ 193 D3   ✉ Wien 1, Tegetthoffstrasse 2   ☎ (01) 512 68 53/16   ◉ Daily 10–6
◎ Stephansplatz   🚌 Bus 1A, 2A , 3A Stephansplatz   💶 Moderate   ❓ www.kaisergruft.at

KAPUZINERGRUFT: INSIDE INFO

Top tips Ask the Capuchin monk at the entrance whether any **groups or school classes** are currently visiting the crypt. The general level of noise is not conducive to the nature of the place; just return later and enjoy the memorials in peace and quiet.

Hidden gems Take your time while studying **Maria Theresa's sarcophagus**. The details and carvings are a unique symbol of the struggle between Death and the power of a determined ruling family set on continuance.

• Have a look at the **display case by the entrance**. The Capuchin monks have recently begun to exhibit here 12 objects from their treasury, such as reliquaries or a rock-crystal cross.

8 The Albertina

The Albertina was for many decades an unattractive block in the imperial heart of Vienna. But the palace, which now houses one of the largest collections of drawings in the world, was lavishly renovated and reopened in March 2003. Since then, the Albertina has become a shining light in Vienna's new museum landscape, topping all visitor records.

Seminal architect Hans Hollein was given the job of transforming the Albertina into a work of art. His grand entrance, complete with a bold, wing-shaped roof, glass and steel lift from street level and much-debated Soravia Wing, is highly striking, but it doesn't stop there. He also gave

the interior a major facelift, cladding the anteroom in marble, dressing the foyer in Travertine limestone and providing elegant space for a stylish restaurant and shop near the ticket counter.

The Albertina in renewed splendour

Eighteen Newly Resplendent Rooms

The main stairway leads up to the showcase rooms. For the first time in 100 years, these 18 Habsburg rooms have returned to their original glory. The smaller rooms of the **Herrenseite** (Gentlemen's Side), from the Goldkabinett (Golden Gallery) to the Billardzimmer (Billiard Room), are decorated in the style of Louis XVI. The **Damenseite** (Ladies' Side), on the other hand, with its Musensaal (Hall of the Muses) and Audienzsaal (Audience Chamber), is pure classicism.

The palace took its present form essentially at the end of the 18th and start of the 19th centuries, when Albert, Duke of Sachsen-Teschen, and his wife, Archduchess Marie Christine, the favourite daughter of Maria Theresa, had it remodelled to the designs of Louis de Montoyer. The classical parts

The high point of the "Ladies Side" is the Hall of the Muses

come from the next owner, Archduke Karl, who defeated Napoleon in the Battle of Aspern (1809). He gave the commission to Joseph Kornhäusel.

Other recent additions to the palace (the Albertina suffered severe damage at the end of World War II) include the **White Cube Hall** in the bastion, where modern art exhibitions are held, the **Propter-Homines-Halle** on the first floor, which is composed of 10 exhibition rooms, and, attached to the portico, the **Pfeilerhalle** (Pillar Hall), which functions as a third exhibition space.

Since its opening in 2003, the Albertina has attracted visitors by the million – 800,000 in the first nine months alone. This is not the only large number connected to the palace, however. The Albertina courts 65,000 drawings, around a million prints and 25,000 architectural plans, sketches and models in its massive collection. There's also the photographic collection, begun in 1999, which now provides Austria with its first centre of historical and contemporary photography. The beauty of such a large collection is that you can return to the Albertina time and time again and find something new to see.

TAKING A BREAK

The Albertina's very elegant **Do & Co restaurant** is ranked among the best places to eat in the city.

🚩 192 C2 ✉ Wien 1, Albertinaplatz 3 ☎ (01) 534 83 🕐 Daily 10–6, Wed until 9 Ⓤ Oper 🚋 Tram 1, 2, D, J Oper; Bus 3A Albertinaplatz 💰 Expensive ❓ www.albertina.at

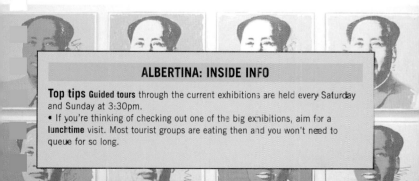

ALBERTINA: INSIDE INFO

Top tips **Guided tours** through the current exhibitions are held every Saturday and Sunday at 3:30pm.

• If you're thinking of checking out one of the big exhibitions, aim for a **lunchtime** visit. Most tourist groups are eating then and you won't need to queue for so long.

At Your Leisure

❷ Spanische Hofreitschule

If you hear the sound of hooves between the Stallburg and the Hofburg, it's bound to be the Lipizzaner horses. In 1580 the imperial stud, which bred horses for riding displays, was founded in the village of Lipica, in what is now Slovenia. Today the Lipizzaner are the oldest breed of show horses in Europe, characterised by perfect physique, intelligence and graceful strength. In the magnificent Winter Riding School visitors can watch as 64 stallions are trained every morning.

➕ 192 C3 ✉ Wien 1, Michaelerplatz 1 ☎ (01) 533 90 31 ◉ Visitor Centre (entrance Michaelerkuppel) Tue–Sat 9–4: tickets and programme for morning training with music (Tue–Sat 10–noon) and other performances 🚇 Herrengasse 🚌 Bus 2A Michaelerplatz 💰 Expensive ❓ www.srs.at

❸ Michaelerkirche

This church, where Mozart's *Requiem* was first performed shortly after his death, combines Romanesque, Gothic and baroque elements. Large parts of the triple-aisled and columned basilica date from the 13th century, as does the lower part of the slender tower. The last big alterations to the church were carried out in the 18th century. The imposing stucco relief *The Fall of the Angels*, created by Karl Georg Merville in 1782, is particularly impressive. Between 1631 and 1784, around 4,000 people were buried in the catacombs. Today, a macabre display of hundreds of painted coffins and mummified corpses can be seen there, some clad in baroque frock coats and wigs.

➕ 192 C3 ✉ Wien 1, Michaelerplatz ☎ (01) 533 80 00 ◉ Church daily 7am–10pm 🚇 Herrengasse 🚌 Bus 2A Michaelerplatz ❓ Guided tours by arrangement, tel: 0650 533 8003

❹ Loos-Haus

No other building in Vienna has provoked so much debate as the Loos-Haus on Michaelerplatz. Built by Adolf Loos in 1910–1911 for the gentlemen's tailor Goldmann & Salaatsch, the housewas ahead of its time, designed without any external ornamentation. This caused a great

The performances of the Lipizzaner horses are a great tourist attraction

Angels feature prominently inside and outside the Michaelerkirche

stir, and the Viennese nicknamed it the "house without eyebrows" due to the lack of framework around the windows. Emperor Franz Joseph loathed the place, which for him stood for a new, sober age he no longer understood, and he avoided leaving the Hofburg by the Michaelerplatz gates because of it. Nowadays the Loos-Haus is a celebrated structure, and contains the Raiffeisenbank.

➕ 192 C3 ✉ Wien
1. Michaelerplatz 3
🚇 Herrengasse
🚌 Bus 2A Michae-lerplatz

❻ Peterskirche

This fine baroque church stands on the site of an earlier, 4th-century church, which might have been the city's first. This early Christian church was constructed from parts of a barracks for the Roman camp. The present Peterskirche, designed by Gabriele Montani, was begun in 1703 on the orders of Emperor Leopold I and completed in 1733 by Johann Lukas von Hilde-brandt Seen from Graben, the church, with its great green dome and two corner towers, looks

particularly striking. The most impressive sections of the interior are Michael Rottmayr's dome ceiling frescoes and Matthias Steindl's richly decorated pulpit.

➕ 193 D3 ✉ Wien 1, Petersplatz
🕐 Daily 10–1, 4–7 🚇 Stephansplatz
🚌 Bus 1A, 2A, 3A Petersplatz
💶 Inexpensive

❾ Dorotheum

The Dorotheum, affectionately known as *pfandl* (deposit), is a Viennese institution. Founded as a *Pfandamt* (official pawnbroker) in 1707 to protect the people from usurers, it moved in 1788 to the abandoned Dorotheer convent. About 100 years ago it was given its own magnificent palace in Dorotheergasse. Today it is the largest auction house in the German-speaking world, hosting some 600 auctions each year. "Aunt Dorothy" has long been seen as a good opportunity to turn silver spoons or worn-out Persian rugs into cash. Its display rooms are filled with all manner of antiques and curiosities, and it's possible to browse them at your leisure. If something takes your fancy, it can be bought at a minor auction, held every Sunday. Not everything is priced out of this world, and some pieces can be bought direct.

➕ 192 C3 ✉ Wien 1, Dorotheer-
gasse 17 ☎ (01) 515 60
🕐 Mon–Fri 10–6, Sat 9–5
Ⓢ Stephansplatz
🚌 Bus 3A
Plankengasse
🔲 www.doro
theum.com

🔟 Josefsplatz

Because of its severe beauty and unity of style, this square is often described as one of the finest in Europe. Its qualities can be fully appreciated now that it is free of traffic. In the middle of the square stands the equestrian statue of the reforming Emperor Joseph II, created in 1795–1807 by the Tyrolese sculptor Franz Anton Zauner. On the plinth are reliefs showing the Emperor with Europa and Mercury, symbols of travel and trade. The backdrop to the square is formed by the gorgeous baroque facade of the Nationalbibliothek (National Library), adjoined right and left by side wings and ballrooms.

➕ 192 C3 Ⓢ Stephansplatz
🚌 Bus 3A Plankengasse

🔟 Burggarten

This park, originally known as the Kaisergarten, was reserved for the emperor's family and not opened to

In the Dorotheum many a collector's item goes under the hammer

the public until 1919. Laid out in front of the Neue Hofburg and the Palmenhaus, it is a good example of garden landscaping as well as a splendid green oasis in the middle of the city. You can relax by the lake with its ducks, kick back on the green grass and admire the lead, marble and bronze statues of Mozart and the emperors Franz I and Franz Joseph I.

➕ 192 C2 ✉ Wien 1, Burgring
Ⓢ Oper 🚋 Tram 1, 2, D, J; Bus 57A
Opernring

🔟 Palmenhaus

"A swan-song of Habsburg greatness" is how the Palm House in the Burggarten is often described. In fact, it is the last large orangery in Europe. The court architect Friedrich Ohmann built it in 1901, a time when it was fashionable to replace nature with "urban greenery". The bold construction of steel and glass was restored a few years ago, and now houses one of the city's most attractive restaurants (► 88), along with the Schmetterlingshaus (Butterfly House). This contains hundreds of butterflies which flit around a tropical rainforest.

➕ 192 C2 ✉ Wien 1, Burggarten
☎ (010) 533 85 70 🕐 Apr–Oct Mon–
Fri 10–4:45, Sat–Sun, public holidays
until 6:15 pm; Nov–Mar daily 10–3:45
Ⓢ Oper 🚋 Tram 1, 2, D, J; Bus 57A
Opernring 🎫 Moderate

Where to...
Eat and Drink

Prices
Prices are for a meal for one person, excluding drinks.
€ under €15 **€€** €15–€30 **€€€** over €30

RESTAURANTS

Barbaro €€
This fine Italian place with three floors on Neuer Markt has that "city feeling". The cantina is in the cellar, the bistro on the ground floor, and the spacious bar and sophisticated restaurant on the first floor. The food is Mediterranean-Italian, and one of its signature dishes is lamb with beans.

➕ 193 D3 ⊠ Wien 1, Neuer Markt 8
☎ (01) 955 25 25 🕒 Bistro daily
8am–midnight, Cantina daily
6pm–midnight, Bar-Restaurant daily
11:30am–4am 🚇 Stephansplatz
🚌 Bus 1A, 2A, 3A Stephansplatz

Do&Co Albertina €€
Two principal materials were used for this restaurant's furnishings: dark jacaranda wood hewn from a single tree and East Anatolian red Levantine marble. Their warm colours give the place an agreeable atmosphere. The marble bar is also unusual – customers sit facing each other. The food is refined Viennese cuisine and international dishes – you can watch it being prepared in the open kitchen. In summer, the large terrace looking towards the Burggarten is particularly beautiful.

➕ 192 C2 ⊠ Wien 1, Albertinaplatz 1
☎ (01) 532 96 69 🕒 Daily 10am–midnight, hot food served all day
🚇 Oper 🚋 Tram 1, 2, D, J Oper; Bus 3A
Albertinaplatz

Do&Co Stephansplatz €€€
This exclusive restaurant high up on the seventh floor in the Haas Haus is a Viennese classic. The food – traditional Viennese cuisine, alongside Asian and Middle Eastern dishes – is exceptional, although the wonderful view of Stephansdom from the terrace almost steal the show. Dinner reservations are advisable.

➕ 193 D3 ⊠ Wien 1, Stephansplatz 12
☎ (01) 535 39 69 🕒 Daily noon–3,
6–midnight 🚇 Stephansplatz 🚌 Bus
1A, 2A, 3A Stephansplatz

Esterházykeller €
This Viennese institution has been around a long time – during the Turkish siege, the city's defenders took shelter in Esterházykeller's large cellar and fortified themselves with wine. Today this traditional establishment still serves superb wine (from its own cellars in Eisenstadt) along with good old Austrian cooking, such as roasts, dumplings and hearty goulash.

➕ 192 C4 ⊠ Wien 1, Haarhof 1
☎ (01) 533 34 82 🕒 Mon–Fri 11–11,
Sat–Sun 4–11 (hot food until 10)
🚇 Herrengasse 🚌 Bus 2A, 3A
Herrengasse

Ilona Stüberl €
This small tavern is ideally situated close to Stephansplatz but in a quiet side street. Visitors can look forward to superb Hungarian specialities, including hearty stuffed cabbage, various sorts of goulash and chicken paprika. There's a small garden for summer dining.

➕ 192 C3 ⊠ Wien 1, Bräunerstrasse 2
☎ (01) 533 90 29 🕒 Apr–Sep daily
11:30–11:30, Oct–Mar Tue–Sun noon–11
🚇 Stephansplatz 🚌 Bus 1A, 2A, 3A
Stephansplatz

Levante €

The high quality of the food at this large restaurant means that it is usually packed to overflowing. Turkish specialities, including delicate hors d'oeuvres, lamb kebabs and vegetable salads, are always fresh and smell delicious. They also do a take-away service.

➕ 192 C3 ☒ Wien 1, Wallnerstrasse 2 ☎ (01) 533 23 26 ◷ Daily 11am–11:30pm Ⓤ Herrengasse 🚌 Bus 2A, 3A Herrengasse

Marktrestaurant Rosenberger €

This massive restaurant, which covers two lower ground floors. The centre is set out like a marketplace, where you can select your meal yourself. Or you can choose from a selection including "Vienna coffee-house", "summer house" or "Grandma's cooking" at your table. The menu lists Austrian favourites, Hungarian goulash, American steaks and Italian pasta dishes, and there's a separate counter with Viennese pastries and gâteaux.

➕ 193 D2 ☒ Wien 1, Maysedergasse 2 ☎ (01) 512 34 58 ◷ Daily 10:30am–11pm Ⓤ Oper 🚌 Tram 1, 2, D, J; Bus 3A Oper

Meinl am Graben €€€

This restaurant, based inside Vienna's best delicatessen, is an absolute must for gourmets. It has an enormous selection, and the standard of the food and drink is first rate. But what makes it so pleasant is the relaxed atmosphere.

➕ 192 C3 ☒ Wien 1, Graben 19 ☎ (01) 532 33 60 00 ◷ Mon–Wed 8:30am–midnight, Thu–Fri 8am–midnight, Sat 9am–midnight Ⓤ Herrengasse 🚌 Bus 3A Bognergasse

Mörwald im Ambassador €€€

Mörwald, in the Ambassador hotel, is a gourmet's delight and a favourite place for sophisticated business lunches. The cooking is imaginative and the selection of wines extensive.

➕ 193 D3 ☒ Wien 1, Neuer Markt 5 ☎ (01) 96 16 11 61 ◷ Mon–Sat noon–midnight (hot food noon–3, 6–11) Ⓤ Stephansplatz 🚌 Bus 1A, 2A, 3A Stephansplatz

Novelli €€€

This high-class Italian restaurant is opposite Café Bräunerhof in an old palace. The interior is stylish and the menu impressive, especially the fine pasta and fish specialities. The Novelli has even published a book of its most popular recipes. The large garden brings a touch of Florence to the city centre.

➕ 192 C3 ☒ Wien 1, Bräunerstrasse 11 ☎ (01) 513 42 00–0 ◷ Mon–Sat 11am–1am (hot food noon–2, 6–11) Ⓤ Stephansplatz 🚌 Bus 2A, 3A Habsburgergasse

Orpheus €€

This smart restaurant in the heart of the imperial city specializes in Greek food, in particular Cretan creations. The lamb and fish dishes are superb, and the ingredients are all organic. Orpheus's front garden is a pleasant place to while away a few hours in summer, while its cellar vaults are easily the best location for a winter night. Don't pass over a chance to sample the excellent wine and grappa.

➕ 193 D3 ☒ Wien 1, Spiegelgasse 10 ☎ (01) 512 38 88 ◷ Sun–Thu noon–midnight, Fri–Sat noon–1am Ⓤ Stephansplatz 🚌 Bus 1A, 2A, 3A Stephansplatz

Palmenhaus im Burggarten €€€

The light-flooded Jugendstil ambience of this restaurant makes it one of the most beautiful in the city, and the menus in the café, brasserie and bar are in no way inferior to the elegant setting. The choice includes fine Viennese and Mediterranean dishes and a well-selected wine list, chiefly from France and Austria, which changes each month.

➕ 192 C2 ☒ Wien 1, Burggarten, entrance behind the Albertina ☎ (01) 533 10 33 ◷ Daily 10am–2am (hot food noon–midnight; closed Mon, Tue Jan–Feb Oper Tram 1, 2, D, J Oper; Bus 3A Albertinaplatz

Sky-Restaurant €€

This stylish modern restaurant on the top floor of Steffl's department store has Viennese classics such as *Tafelspitz* (boiled beef) and international food, mainly Asian and Mediterranean. From the broad terrace there's a superb view over the rooftops towards Stephansdom.

+ 193 D3 Wien 1, Kärntnerstrasse 19 (01) 513 17 12 Mon–Sat noon–3, 7–1am (hot food until 11pm) Stephansplatz Bus 1A, 2A, 3A Stephansplatz

Trzesniewski €

If you're looking for the finest bite-size delectables in the city, head for Trzesniewski. This small but famous sandwich shop has been feeding hungry locals for 100 years. The choice of spreads is lengthy – 21 in all – but you'll have to order a few, as they're gone after a couple of quick bites. If you can't reach this branch, there are another six scattered throughout the city.

+ 194 C3 Wien 1, Dorotheergasse 1 (01) 512 32 91 8:30–7:30, Sat 9–5 Stephansplatz Bus 1A, 2A, 3A Petersplatz

Yohm €€

Yohm is a small, modern restaurant popular for business lunches and romantic evening dinners. Its speciality is top-quality Asian cuisine; there's an inviting range of sushi options but you'd also do well ordering one of the imaginative main dishes. If you reserve ahead, try to get a window table overlooking pretty Peterskirche.

+ 194 C4 Wien 1, Petersplatz 3 (01) 533 29 00 Daily noon–3, 6–midnight Stephansplatz Bus 1A, 2A, 3A Petersplatz

Yugetsu €€€

"Japan in Vienna" extends over two floors. The ground floor has the largest selection of sushi in Vienna, while the first floor is home to the gastronomic experience that is *teppanyaki* cuisine. On weekends and public holidays there's a self-service sushi bar.

+ 192 C2 Wien 1, Führichgasse 10 (01) 512 27 20 Daily noon–3, 6–midnight (hot food noon–2:30, 6–11) Oper Tram 1, 2, D, J; Bus 3A Oper

Zum Schwarzen Kameel €€

The consistent quality of its food has made this smart restaurant, which dates back to 1618, a favourite. A delicatessen fills the front room, where you can enjoy tasty filled rolls, bite-size sandwiches and excellent wine.

+ 192 C4 Wien 1, Bognergasse 5 (01) 533 81 25 Mon–Sat 8:30–midnight (hot food noon–2:30, 6–10:30) Herrengasse Bus 3A Bognergasse

CAFÉS

Aida

Aida cafés are institutions in Vienna for their divine cakes and sweets and retro design, and the most famous of them all is this branch on the corner of Kärntner Strasse and Stephansplatz. Old ladies and tourists sit side by side here, sipping a *melange* (Viennese coffee) and watching the hustle and bustle outside on the city's busiest corner.

+ 192 C2 Wien 1, Stock-im-Eisen-Platz 2 (01) 512 29 77 Mon–Sat 7am–8pm, Sun 9–8 Stephansplatz Bus 1A, 2A, 3A Stephansplatz

Bräunerhof

In this legendary café, which was the favourite of Austrian writer Thomas Bernhard (1931–89), the style and atmosphere of the old Viennese coffee-house has survived. Local antiques dealers come here for lunch, and it's a favourite spot for business meetings or a date. At weekends there's live music.

+ 192 C3 Wien 1, Stallburggasse 2 (01) 512 38 93 Mon–Fri 8am–9pm, Sat 8–7, Sun 10–7 Stephansplatz Bus 2A, 3A Habsburgergasse

Café Tirolerhof

Tirolerhof occupies a fine spot halfway between the Albertina and the Kapuzinergruft. Its interior is thoroughly Jugendstil (art nouveau) while the home made *Apfelstrudel* is among the best in the business. It's also a great place to sample a traditional Viennese coffee house, where the grumpy waiter is thrown in for free.

+ 192 C2 ⊠ Wien 1, Führichgasse 8
☎ (01) 512 78 33 ⊙ Mon–Sat
7am–10pm, Sun 9:30–8 ⦿ Oper
🚋 Tram 1, 2, D, J Oper; Bus 3A
Albertinaplatz

Demel

This former confectioner to the imperial court, founded in 1786, creates the ultimate in Viennese *Torten*. Demel sells its delicious products – chocolates, sweets and candied violets – from its streetside rooms, while its conservatory is taken over by a show bakery and its basement by a marzipan museum, which explores the confectioner's art, including elegant bonbon boxes from yesteryear. It is, however, no longer independent, having been taken over by Do&Co.

+ 192 C3 ⊠ Wien 1, Kohlmarkt 14
☎ (01) 535 17 17 ⊙ Daily 10–7
⦿ Herrengasse 🚋 Bus 2A, 3A
Herrengasse

Griensteidl

This legendary literatis' café opposite the entrance to the Hofburg is now an elegant coffee-house with Thonet chairs of black wood, upholstered in red. It has an impressive selection of foods and international newspapers.

+ 192 C3 ⊠ Wien 1, Michaelerplatz 2
☎ (01) 535 26 92 17 ⊙ Daily 8am–11:30pm (hot food until 11pm)
⦿ Herrengasse 🚋 Bus 2A, 3A
Herrengasse

Hawelka

After 60 years, this legendary café lives on. Admittedly, where once artists and writers whiled away their nights, the shabby benches are now mainly occupied by tourists, but the atmosphere remains sensational and fresh jam dumplings are still served at 10 every night.

+ 192 C3 ⊠ Wien 1, Dorotheergasse 6
☎ (01) 512 82 30 ⊙ Mon, Wed–Sat 8am–2am, Sun 10am–2am
⦿ Stephansplatz 🚋 Bus 1A, 2A, 3A
Stephansplatz

Hofburg

This pretty café with its large terrace is in the Innerer Burghof, by the entrances to the imperial apartments, the Silberkammer and the Sisi-Museum. It has taken its culinary style from the emperor's taste – the *kaiserschmarren* (raisin pancakes) are excellent. For a snack, try a "Habs-Burger", if only for the name.

+ 192 C3 ⊠ Wien 1, Innerer Burghof 1
☎ (01) 241 00-0 ⊙ Daily 10–6
⦿ Herrengasse 🚋 Tram 1, 2, D, J
Burgring; Bus 2A, 3A Hofburg

Konditorei Lehmann

Situated in the middle of Graben, this traditional Viennese café is an ideal meeting place for people with a sweet tooth. The house *torten* and pastries are first class, but smaller, more delicate snacks are also on offer. The garden is a great place to watch the busy life on Graben.

+ 192 C3 ⊠ Wien 1, Graben 12
☎ (01) 512 18 15 ⊙ Mon–Sat 8:30–7
⦿ Stephansplatz 🚋 Bus 2A, 3A
Graben-Petersplatz

Mozart

This coffee-house has a very long tradition, dating back to 1794. In the Biedermeierzeit (early 19th century) it was a favourite rendezvous for artists. One of Graham Greene's favourite haunts, it also features in *The Third Man*. Nowadays, because of its proximity to the Albertina and the Hofburg, it's an ideal place for visitors to take a break and imbibe the typical Viennese atmosphere.

+ 192 C2 ⊠ Wien 1, Albertinaplatz 2
☎ (01) 241 00–0 ⊙ Daily
9am–midnight ⦿ Oper 🚋 Tram 1, 2, D,
J Oper; Bus 3A Albertinaplatz

Where to...
Shop

Graben, Kohlmarkt and Kärntner Strasse form the heart of the inner city, and there is plenty on offer for visitors who want to take a small piece of Vienna home with them. Shoppers can choose anything they fancy from arrays of sparkling diamonds and glittering trinkets to retro-chic clothing, top chainstore brands, fashion labels, mouth-watering chocolate sensations, gorgeous art nouveau furniture...the list could go on and on.

The shopping streets around Stephansdom are ideal for buying small but elegant gift boxes, which could hold an emerald ring from the jeweller's **Haban** (Graben 12 and Kärntner Strasse 2) or **Heldwein** (Graben 13), a Viennese Jugendstil brooch from **Siedler** (Kohlmarkt 3) or a contemporary piece of jewellery from **Schullin** (Kohlmarkt 7) or **Skrein** (Spiegelgasse 5).

Somewhat larger gifts, but still typically Viennese treasures which would comfortably grace any home, can also be found here: delicate coffee cups and complete dinner services decorated with roses from the porcelain manufacturer **Augarten** (Stock-im-Eisen-Platz 3), sparkling wafer-thin glasses from **Lobmayr** (Kärntner Strasse 26), sparkling crystal glass items from **Swarovski** (Kärntner Strasse 8), exquisite household goods from **Rasper & Söhne** (Habsburgergasse 10) and the finest table linen and bedlinen from **Schwäbische Jungfrau** (Graben 26).

In recent years international luxury has also established itself on Kohlmarkt. Top designers and well-loved brands, such as **Cartier** (Kohlmarkt 1), **Armani** (Kohlmarkt 3), **Chanel** and **Gucci** (Kohlmarkt 5), **Louis Vuitton** (Kohlmarkt 16),

Ferragamo (Kohlmarkt 7) and **Chopard** (Kohlmarkt 16), have all opened outlets here.

Knize (Graben 13) is a byword for gentlemen's clothing. This elegant shop is persuasively understated. The narrow door, designed by Alfred Loos, gives no hint that, on the first floor, suites of rooms await you, with creaking parquet floors, wardrobes, display cases and courteous, obliging staff. This is not a shop to hunt for a new sports jacket, but rather a place to be fitted out with everything a man of the world needs: made-to-measure suits, hand-made shirts, cashmere pullovers and accessories. Ladies are served in their shop next door.

But the epitome of ladies' fashion in Vienna is **Adlmüller** (Kärntner Strasse 11). The firm's reputation dates back to a time when international fashion designer and couturier Fred Adlmüller would personally drape famous singers from the Staatsoper and society ladies in gorgeous flowing evening dresses.

Outside Kohlmarkt, designer brands are not so well represented, but there are nevertheless a few shops flying the youthful fashion flag. **Firis** (Bauernmarkt 9) stocks items from Belgian and Italian designers, while fans of elegant Italian handbags should head from the main Stephansdom door towards the Peterskirche: they will be in paradise with **Pitti's** trendy bags and numerous accessories (Goldschmiedgasse 5). Shoes to match are sold close by, at **d'Ambrosio** (Jasomirgottstrasse 6). **Robert Horn** (Bräunerstrasse 7) is famous for leather goods. The internationally celebrated designer creates bags and purses in the classic aesthetic tradition of Alfred Loos

The side streets off Graben have a timeless beauty and elegance. In the Dorotheergasse, Stallburggasse, Bräunerstrasse and Spiegelgasse there's one antiques shop after another, offering everything from baroque cabinets and Renaissance chests to superb carpets, pictures, lamps, porcelain and magnificent antique jewellery. Elisabeth **Reichel** and Johann **Kilianowitsch's** shop (Dorotheergasse 14) is a hidden gem, selling exquisite Jugendstil and art deco Bakelite ornaments at reasonable prices.

Doblinger (Dorotheergasse 10), the antiques section of the Musik-haus, has first editions of Strauss, Lanner and Fahrbach, along with Wiener Schule and the Wiener Klassik. They also sell sacred and choral music.

The candied violets from **Demel** (Kohlmarkt 14), made famous by the unhappy Empress Sisi, are an ideal souvenir, or stop in at **Altmann & Kühne** (Graben 30) for divine handmade sweets in elegant boxes featuring motifs from the Wiener Werkstätte. Confectionary is still traditionally crafted by hand here, according to century-old recipes.

Where to be... Entertained

During the daytime the main shopping streets of the inner city are packed with shoppers, and while things calm down come evening time, there's still enough to keep visitors entertained for hours. Bars in this area are generally smart places, serving some of the city's best cocktails.

BARS

The most famous bar in the area is the tiny **Loos Bar** (Kärntner Durchgang 10, tel: 01/512 32 83, Thu–Sat noon–5am, Sun–Wed noon–4am). Adolf Loos designed the bar in 1907, cleverly using mirrors to make the small place seem larger. It was for many years the symbol of Viennese avant-garde, but its reputation – and look –

declined in the 1980s, only to rise again in the 90s, until now it's as splendid as ever. It's also known as the American Bar because of the huge American flag above the door.

The luxurious, sleek **Onyx Bar** (Stephansplatz 12, tel: 01/535 39 69, Mon–Sat 9am–2am) in the Haas Haus is one of Vienna's hippest hang-outs for arty types and real or wannabe celebrities. It also gets points for its spectacular views of the beautifully illuminated Stephansdom. Tasty snacks and dishes from the Far East are available alongside drinks.

The **Reiss-Bar** (Marco-d'Aviano-Gasse 1, tel: 01/512 71 98, Sun–Thu 11am–2am, Fri–Sat 10am–3am), with its acclaimed architecture, is the city's "champagne spot". Here people come to "see and be seen". Whet your appetite with tasty morsels such as *tramezzini* (sandwiches), caviar and oysters.

One of the city's trendiest places at the moment is the **Sky-Bar** (Kärntner Strasse 19, tel: 01/513 17

12, Mon–Sat 1pm–3am, Sun 6pm–2am) on the top floor of Steffl's department store. The large, circular bar has live music on Tuesdays and Thursdays from 9pm. The terrace, with its views of Kärntner Strasse and the Stephansdom, is a very pleasant spot for cocktails.

Vino aficionados will love the range of wines at **Meinl's Weinbar** (Naglergasse 1, tel: 01/532 33 34-61 00, Mon–Sat 11am–midnight), available by the glass or bottle from the incredible selection in the cellar. Food is also available – fine cheeses, tasty spreads and antipasti are the house specials.

CASINO

If you want to try your luck at the tables, then the Viennese **Casino** (Kärntner Strasse 4, tel: 01/512 48 36, daily 3pm–4am) is the place for you. There's roulette and blackjack, stud poker and slot machines – you might win enough to go shopping!

The Western Ringstrasse

Getting Your Bearings

The grand boulevard of the Ringstrasse – 6km (3.75 miles) long, 60m (65 yards) wide and flanked by magnificent monuments, palaces and parks – encircles the heart of the inner city. Its western section is home to the lion's share of attractions, including the Staatsoper, Burgtheater and Kunsthistorisches and Naturhistorisches museums, not to mention the vibrant artistic MuseumsQuartier.

The Ringstrasse was built in the mid-19th century, as Vienna began its rise to the status of a major European city. A work of art in itself and unique in Europe, it includes 150 public buildings, 650 grand apartment blocks for the newly rich of the industrial and financial worlds, and a number of parks. The great thing about the Ringstrasse is that it is still virtually intact, a mirror of imperial splendour.

Nowadays, though, it's no fun for pedestrians on the Ringstrasse, affectionately called the "Ring". Day and night thousands of cars flow down the city's main traffic artery, jamming up especially behind *fiaker* (horse-drawn cabs). But provided you don't try to cross the Ringstrasse other than at designated pedestrian crossings, you can make good headway on foot along the side lanes.

Page 93: The neo-Gothic splendour of the Rathaus

A place with a history: Heldenplatz

The Burg-
theater, one
of the most
famous
German-
language
theatres

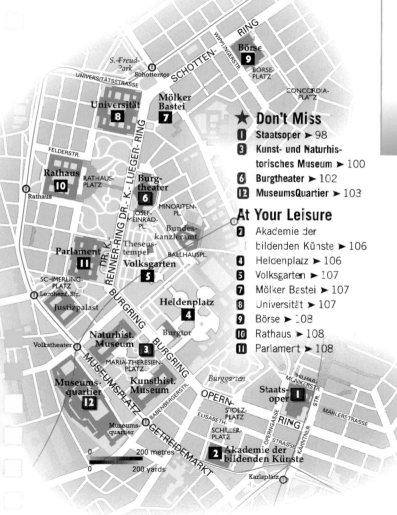

★ Don't Miss

1 Staatsoper ➤ 98

3 Kunst- und Naturhistorisches Museum ➤ 100

6 Burgtheater ➤ 102

12 MuseumsQuartier ➤ 103

At Your Leisure

2 Akademie der
bildenden Künste ➤ 106

4 Heldenplatz ➤ 106

5 Volksgarten ➤ 107

7 Mölker Bastei ➤ 107

8 Universität ➤ 107

9 Börse ➤ 108

10 Rathaus ➤ 108

11 Parlament ➤ 108

This is a busy day and you might like to return another time to appreciate all the sights. Move from one splendid building to another, then immerse yourself in the wonderful world of Vienna's museums and lively artists' district, the MuseumsQuartier, a great place to stroll, shop, eat and drink.

The Western Ringstrasse in a Day

9:00 am

Start your tour of the Ringstrasse buildings in style, with the **❶ Staatsoper** (➤ 98). Walk round the magnificent opera house and pause awhile over a coffee in the grand Sacher hotel (➤ 110). On your way to the **❷ Akademie der bildenden Künste** (Fine Art Academy, ➤ 106) you'll pass the Goethe and Schiller memorials. The Akademie, designed in a sumptuous style based on the Italian high Renaissance, is very striking. You might like to look at the building from the inside, even if you haven't the time to visit every room.

10:30 am

Cross the Ringstrasse to go to the **❸ Kunsthistorisches Museum** (Museum of Fine Arts, above; ➤ 100). Don't rush from one room to the

next, but first take in the splendour of the building itself. And when you've visited the Brueghels on the first floor, pause for a snack in the Kuppelsaal (domed hall). In the **3 Naturhistorisches Museum** (Natural History Museum, ► 101) directly opposite the Fine Arts Museum you can revel in the wonderful atmosphere of past times. The original furnishings and the numerous display cases and thousands of exhibits create a world of their own.

12:30 pm

After visiting the two museums, cross the Ringstrasse and pass through the Äusseres Burgtor to the **4 Heldenplatz** (► 106). Continue into the **5 Volksgarten** (► 107), and drop a curtsey to the marble "Sisi" memorial, then take a seat and breathe in the scent of the roses. How about lunch in the **6 Burgtheater** (above; ► 102)? The stylish surroundings of the famous theatre make eating and drinking in the Vestibül restaurant a pleasure.

2:00 pm

Stroll across Rathausplatz to the **11 Parlament** (► 108) and then across Maria-Theresien-Platz to the **12 MuseumsQuartier** (► 103). Don't let the baroque façade of the MuseumsQuartier put you off. The ancient walls conceal a very modern, state-of-the-art museum. Walk round the Museum Moderner Kunst (Museum of Modern Art), and then enjoy a restorative coffee in the newly reopened Glacis Beisl.

4:30 pm

If you still have sufficient energy, the paintings by Egon Schiele in the Leopold Museum (► 105) are well worth a visit. Otherwise, just head back to your hotel and relax before the evening's entertainments.

7:00 pm

If you haven't bought any advance tickets for a visit to the Burgtheater or Staatsoper, just ask your hotel porter. You never know, he may just "happen" to have some tickets stashed away.

❶ Staatsoper

The Vienna Staatsoper, one of the most illustrious opera houses in the world, was criticised right from the beginning; people complained it looked like a railway station. But it's the music that counts, and Vienna's reputation as a musical centre is founded on this "House on the Ring". It has since become a part of the Austrian national identity.

The new Imperial Court Opera was designed to be the first monumental building on the Ringstrasse. Begun in 1863, public opinion had "demolished" the neo-Romantic building before it had even opened in May 1869. Its loggia, side arcades and metal tunnel roof provoked such devastating

criticism that the interior designer, Eduard von der Null (1812–68), took his own life. And the engineer responsible for the construction, August von Siccardsburg (1812–68), was so distressed that he died a few weeks later of a heart attack.

In World War II, bombing raids reduced the Staatsoper to rubble, along with all its stage sets and costumes. After seven years of restoration work, its reopening on 5 November, 1955, with a performance of Beethoven's *Fidelio*, amounted to something akin to an unofficial celebration of the restoration of Vienna's 19th century splendour.

For the Opernball (Opera Ball), the Staatsoper is transformed into one vast ballroom

Art of the Highest Calibre
From the start, the Vienna Staatsoper set the very highest standards, attracting top international performers, producers

For kids

State Opera performances for young visitors are put on in the tent on the roof terrace (information tel: 01/514 44-20 19).

You can buy tickets on the street but they'll probably cost more than at the box office

and set-designers from Europe and farther afield. The list of conductors has always included important musicians, such as Gustav Mahler (1897–1907), Richard Strauss (1919–24), Herbert von Karajan (1956–64) and Claudio Abbado (1986–91). However, even the most celebrated conductor soon discovered the audience could be highly critical, and that quibbling and bemoaning go hand in hand with Viennese passion and love for music. But impress the crowd and you'll be revered and praised forever, something many world-class artists also experienced.

Impressive repertoire

The Vienna Staatsoper is one of the leading opera venues in the world. Performances are given on 300 days a year. The repertoire comprises some 50 operas and 20 ballets, including works like Verdi's *Aida*, Mozart's *Magic Flute*, Wagner's *Ring* cycle and Puccini's *La Bohème*.

Once a year, on the last Thursday of Fasching (carnival), the stage and stalls of the Staatsoper are transformed into one gigantic dance floor. The flower-bedecked hall becomes the scene of the most glittering event of the season, the Opera Ball. The "night of nights" is, what's more, a night when everyone wins: on this evening the Staatsoper actually makes a profit.

TAKING A BREAK

Have a quick espresso in the **Aida** café opposite the opera (Opernring 7). The tiny coffee tables will transport you back to the 1970s.

✚ 192 C2 ✉ Wien 1, Opernring 2 ☎ (01) 514 44-0 🚇 Karlsplatz
🚋 Tram 1, 2, D, J, 62, 65 Karlsplatz ❓ www.staatsoper.at

STAATSOPER: INSIDE INFO

Top tip You can only see the interior of the Staatsoper on a **40-minute guided tour** (admission: moderate). The starting times depend on whether rehearsals are currently being held; they are advertised on a board at the entrance. In July and August there are six tours a day (booking tel: 01/514 44-26 06, fax: 01/514 44-26 26)

❸ Kunst- and Natur- historisches Museum

From the outside the Museum of Art History (KHM) and the Natural History Museum (NHM) are identical twins. Each structure has four floors, two courtyards, a large octagonal domed tower and four smaller turrets. But inside the two buildings are worlds apart.

Both imposing museums were built by Karl von Hasenauer and Gottfried Semper in Renaissance style. They are identical, with one minor exception: whereas the Fine Arts Museum is surmounted by a statue of Pallas Athene, the Greek patron goddess of art and science, the Natural History Museum has the figure of the Greek sun god Helios.

Maria Theresa and her retinue are enthroned between the two large museums

Fine Arts

The entrance itself is worthy of the ticket price. The stairway and domed marble hall are of unsurpassed grandeur and elegance, featuring Antonio Canova's Theseus group in marble, Hans Makart's paintings in the ceiling lunettes and Ernst and Gustav Klimt's works in the spandrels. These, however, are only a taster of the treasure trove of art inside.

Most of the KHM's collection is a result of the Habsburgs' passion for collecting. The Egyptian-Oriental section has fascinating exhibits from the ancient Nile culture; the antiques collection with its miniatures and cameos is one of the most important in the world; the Münzkabinett (Cabinet of Coins) comprises some 700,000 pieces from three millennia, which provide an overview of the history and development of money; and the Kunstkammer (Art Cabinet) has a mass of larger and smaller sculptures, scientific instruments, automata and clocks.

The first floor houses the museum's *pièce de resistance*, the Gemäldegallerie (Picture Gallery), which is the fourth largest on the planet. Room X, in the East Wing, is home to the world's largest collection of Brueghels (*The Tower of Babel, The Peasant Wedding, Room X*), as well as numerous works by Dutch and Flemish painters. Rubens is also well represented here; his paintings are particularly impressive for their sensuality (*The Fur* in Room XIII shows that cellulite on the thighs wasn't always considered a blemish). The West Wing's exhibits are virtually a cross-section of the history of European painting.

The picture gallery boasts superb Rubens paintings

Natural History

While in recent years the KHM has developed into a major attraction, through events and special exhibitions, the Natural History Museum has been more of a Sleeping Beauty. And this despite possessing one of Europe's greatest scientific collections. There are countless exhibits in its 39 vast exhibition halls, including some stupendous treasures, such as the first-ever model of a sabre-tooth tiger and the *Venus of Willendorf*, the oldest known statuette of a human figure. There's also a transmission of images from live webcams, located in the USA, Australia and Spain and aimed at the sun.

Young visitors love the NHM's dinosaurs

TAKING A BREAK

Beneath the domes of both museums are **cafés** with a very special atmosphere (➤ 109).

➕ 192 B2 ✉ KHM: Wien 1, Burgring 5; NHM: Wien 1, Burgring 7 ☎ KHM: (01) 525 24-0; NHM: (01) 521 77 ⏰ KHM: Tue–Sun 10–6, Thu until 9 (Gemälde-galerie); NHM: Wed–Mon 9–6:30, Wed until 7 🚇 Volkstheater 🚊 Tram 1, 2, D, J, Bus 2A, 57A Burgring 💰 Expensive 🌐 www.khm.at; www.nhm-wien.ac.at

KUNST- AND NATURHISTORISCHES MUSEUM: INSIDE INFO

Top tips For superb views, join the guided tour **"Above the roofs of Vienna"** onto the NHM's roof terrace (tel: 01/521 77-276, Wed 5, 6:30, Sun 2, 4).
• At the NHM's **Mikrotheater**, life under the microscope is projected onto a giant screen, every weekend at 1:30, 3 and 4:15pm

❻ Burgtheater

The Burgtheater was one of the last grand structures to be built on the Ringstrasse, and the first to install electric lighting. It has always been seen as one of the finest German-language theatres, despite its at times avant-garde approach, which is not always appreciated by the audience.

The Burgtheater was built between 1874 and 1888 to the designs of Karl Hasenauer and Gottfried Semper. Just as with the Staatsoper, the reaction of the Viennese public was initially hostile. But this is long forgotten today. The auditorium proudly displays its past as the "imperial court theatre" – the boxes and circles are all clad in red velvet.

Countless renowned actors have delighted the Burgtheater's public, and appearing on its stage still represents the peak of an actor's career. Violent disputes on the nature of art are frequent. When Claus Peymann produced *Die Burg* (The Fortress) in 1986, he was accused of "deconsecrating" the house, and storms still rage over works by the current director, Klaus Bachler. For many, dramatic art stops with Schiller, and progressive or unusual productions take a lot of getting used to. And there are many such productions.

The glittering interior of the Burgtheater

TAKING A BREAK
The **Vestibül** (▶ 110) is the best place for a break.

✚ 192 B4 ✉ Wien 1, Dr-Karl-Lueger-Ring 2
☎ (01) 514 44-41 40 🕐 Box office daily 8–6 and
1 hour before performances; guided tours Sep–Jun
daily at 3 🚇 Rathaus, Herrengasse 🚋 Tram 1, 2,
D Burgtheater Moderate
❓ www.burgtheater.at

BURGTHEATER: INSIDE INFO

Top tip The bookshop **Leporello** stocks works on drama and literature (daily 5–10, except on days when there are no performances).

Hidden gem Have a look at the **frescoes** on the grand staircase. Some are by Ernst and Gustav Klimt.

⓬ MuseumsQuartier

Seen from Maria-Theresien-Platz, the MuseumsQuartier is simply a long baroque facade with two vast cubes – one black, one white – towering up behind it. But as you enter the enormous courtyard, it becomes clear that something entirely new and exciting has been created here: an urban habitat for the arts, spacious – covering an area of 60,000sq m (72,000 square yards) – and forward-looking.

For 300 years the area of the present MQ (Museum Quarter) bore the stigma of incomplete grandeur. It started when, in 1713, Emperor Karl VI commissioned the baroque architect Johann Fischer von Erlach to build imperial stables on the glacis, the open slopes outside the city walls. The plan was never completely realised, but the emperor's horses never-theless were happily housed behind Vienna's longest baroque facade.

The dark basalt hulk of the "Mumok" – Museum Moderner Kunst

In the early 20th century, times were changing. The monarchy was abolished, the invention of the automobile put the horses out of their jobs, and the gigantic stable and carriage building was no longer needed. From 1921 the former luxury quarters of the imperial horses found a new use, as a site for exhibitions and trade fairs.

Controversial New Ideas

By the end of the 20th century, the complex could no longer be described as a "palace". The facade was indeed still standing, but many of the buildings on the vast area were slowly deteriorating – until in 1980 a completely different way of using the complex was proposed. Then the arguments began.

The Leopold Museum, in gleaming white limestone

For a start, the idea of a "museum quarter" was discussed for six years, from 1980 to 1986. Several commissions put forward proposals. In 1990 the Viennese office of Ortner &

Ortner won an architectural competition. That really did it. Protests rained down, and a citizens' initiative even managed to have the planned "reading tower" taken out of the scheme.

Despite all the disputes, building started in 1998, and the biggest cultural project of the

The Leopold Café, an urban communications centre

Second Republic was underway. At the opening in 2001 the mood was quite different, now people were jubilant. It turned out that Ortner & Ortner had carried out their basic architectural concept to perfection: the mutual integration of historical and modern architecture, a spectacular blend of old and new, and art and relaxation.

Great Variety

The MuseumsQuartier has developed into an exciting cultural district and a place of great diversity. Fine arts and the performing arts, architecture, music, fashion, film, new media, culture for children and small cultural projects are just as much at home here as museums and exhibition halls.

Three large buildings give the courtyard of the complex its character: the Leopold

Museum with its cladding of white limestone, the Museum Moderner Kunst Stiftung Ludwig Wien ("Mumok", the Ludwig Foundation's Museum of Modern Art in Vienna), clad in dark basalt, its roof curving down low on the edges, and the brick-built Kunsthalle Wien (Vienna Art Gallery). The latter is hidden

For kids

The **Zoom Kindermuseum** aims to introduce children to the world of museums. In the multimedia **Zoomlab**, children from the age of seven can move between the real and the virtual world, acting as producers, sound technicians, writers and actors. The **Zoom Ocean** takes children under six on a jourey through a magic underwater world, and the **Zoom Workshop** gives budding young artists the chance to be creative.

In the evening, the MQ turns into a strolling district

behind the E+G hall, the former Winter Riding School, which now houses Vienna's dance-halls.

The **Leopold Museum** contains Rudolf Leopold's extensive, originally private collection. Works by Austrian artists are displayed on five floors, with the emphasis on 19th- and 20th-century painting. Vienna around 1900 is well represented with works by Gustav Klimt, Richard Gerstl, Koloman Moser and Oscar Kokoschka. The museum's highlight – the great Egon Schiele collection – is on the lower ground floor.

The **Mumok** is the largest Austrian museum of modern and contemporary art. The emphasis of the collection is on Classic Modernism, Pop Art, Photo-realism, Fluxus, Nouveau Réalisme and Viennese Actionism.

Visitor numbers show that the MQ is a tremendous tourist attraction from which Vienna has profited greatly: in the first year around two million came. Just over half of these came to visit exhibitions or special events, including festivals. But the other half just came to experience the unique atmosphere of the cultural district, and to enjoy its advantages as a local entertainment centre, where it is possible to meet friends, relax, sit and chat, eat

The baroque architecture has been retained at the entrance to the MQ

and drink, stroll and shop.

TAKING A BREAK

The **Kantine** has a small but tasty selection of hot meals of the day, and a comfortable lounge area.

➕ 192 A2 ✉ Wien 7, Museumsplatz 1 ☎ (01) 523 58 81, Infoline 0820 600 600 (only within Austria) 🎫 Leopold Museum daily 10–6, Thu until 9; Mumok daily 10–6, Thu until 9 🚇 MuseumsQuartier 🚋 Tram 49, Bus 48A Volkstheater; Bus 2A MuseumsQuartier 💰 MQ inexpensive, Leopold Museum expensive, Mumok expensive ❓ www.mqw.at

MUSEUMSQUARTIER: INSIDE INFO

Top tip Walk a short way up Mariahilfer Strasse to Leiner's furnishing store (Wien 7, Mariahilfer Strasse 18). It has a cafeteria where you could stop for a coffee on the **roof terrace**, with the best overview of the entire MusemsQuartier area.

At Your Leisure

2 Akademie der bildenden Künste

The frescoes and the terracotta figures in the niches between the bow windows make a striking facade for Theophil Hansen's Academy of Fine Arts. Inside, the atrium with Anselm Feuerbach's ceiling painting is even more spectacular. This world-renowned picture gallery houses works of art from five centuries, including paintings by Bosch, Cranach the Elder, Rubens and Rembrandt. Hieronymus Bosch's *Last Judgement* triptych is particularly worth seeing, with its bizarre and gruesome fantasies. The etchings room has a great range of early 19th-century pictures and old architectural plans.

➕ 192 C2 ✉ Wien 1, Schillerplatz 3
☎ (01) 588 16-0 🕐 Tue–Sun 10–6
🚇 Karlsplatz 🚋 Tram 1, 2, D, J Oper/
Babenbergerstrasse, Bus 59A Oper, 57A
Babenbergerstrasse 💰 Moderate
❓ www.akbild.ac.at

4 Heldenplatz

Heldenplatz is one of the most beautiful squares in the city. Seen from the main entrance to the Neue Burg it presents a glorious panorama:

The Italian-inspired facade of the Akademie der bildenden Künste

in the foreground the equestrian statues of Archduke Karl and Prince Eugen of Savoy, to the right the Leopold Wing of the Hofburg, then the outlines of the Burgtheater, Rathaus and Parliament, and finally the Äussere Burgtor, with the memorial to the resistance fighters killed between 1939 and 1945.

The Neue Burg contains incredible treasures: the splendid reading rooms of the Nationalbibliothek (National Library), the Ephesos Museum, the Papyrus Museum with the largest collection of papyruses in the world, and a little farther on, towards the Ringstrasse, the Völkerkundemuseum (Museum of Ethnography).

Heldenplatz became a fateful place in 1938, when, from the balcony over the main entrance to the Neue Burg, Hitler announced the *Anschluss* (Annexation) of Austria to the Third Reich. Today this large square is a starting point for a leisurely tour of the city by horse and carriage.

➕ 192 B3 🚇 Volkstheater
🚋 Tram 1, 2, D, J; Bus 2A Burgring

5 Volksgarten

The Volksgarten is a paradise for rose-lovers, with thousands of roses of every conceivable colour. The plant labels give information about whom each rose is named after. The Theseus temple, erected in 1822, is a historic gem, while the romantic memorial to Empress Elisabeth is a pilgrimage site for Sisi fans. And the cheekiest sparrows in the city flit about in the small dairy café, alighting on the edge of your plate to help themselves to some of your *Apfelstrudel*.

➕ 192 B3 🚇 Herrengasse 🚋 Tram 1, 2, D, J Dr-Karl-Renner-Ring

7 Mölker Bastei

The Mölker Bastei is one of the few remaining sections of the city's original defensive walls. In the Pasqualati House two rooms are set up as memorials to Beethoven, who composed *Fidelio* in this house (Tue–Sun 10–12, 2–6). Round the corner in Schreyvogelgasse is the "Dreimäderlhaus", famous through the operetta of the same name based on Franz Schubert's romance with the "three lasses" who lived here. The romance is invented, but the

When the roses are in bloom the Volksgarten is a scented paradise

Devastated by fire

Diagonally opposite the Vienna Stock Exchange (Börse, ➤ 108), in a plain new building, you can now see the headquarters of the Vienna police. Once the Ringtheater stood on this site. In 1881 the theatre was destroyed by a fire which killed 400 people. The fire is one of the legendary catastrophes in Vienna's history.

pretty house with the early 19th-century façade is very real

➕ 192 B4 🚇 Schottentor 🚋 Tram 1, 2, D Schottentor

8 Universität

Vienna University was founded in 1365, making it the oldest German-language institution of its kind in the world. In the 19th century many new departments were created, and in 1870 the construction of a new university building on the Ringstrasse began. The prolific Heinrich Ferstel was given the architectural job, and he gave the structure a neo-Renaissance look. In 1998, the university expanded further when the city's old hospital (dating from 1693) was turned into a university campus.

➕ 192 B4 ✉ Wien 1, Dr-Karl-Lueger-Ring 1 🚇 Schottentor 🚋 Tram 1, 2, D Schottentor

9 Börse

A brick-red facade identifies the Börse (Stock Exchange), on the right-hand side of the otherwise uninteresting Schottenring. In 1877, after numerous moves, it finally took possession of this building contructed by Theophil Hansen. Founded by Maria Theresa in 1771, the late 1980s were its heyday; for a short time it was even the fastest growing financial centre in the world. Today it is also a good place for gourmets and lovers of flowers.

➕ 192 C5
✉ Wien 1, Schottenring 16
Ⓢ Schottentor
🚋 Tram 1, 2, D; Bus 3A Börse

10 Rathaus

It was the liberals, with Kajetan Felder at their head, who in 1870 wrung from the emperor the permission to build a Rathaus (Town Hall). Today the Rathaus, constructed 1872 to 1883 by Friedrich Schmidt, is the administrative heart of the city. It has everything one would expect of a grand neo-Gothic building: open arcades, loggias, balconies, ogive

At the Börse you can buy stocks and shares – and delicious meals

windows and ornamentation aplenty. The banqueting hall is the largest in Austria. The "Rathausmann", a Viennese emblem, looks out from the top of the 98m (320-foot) high main tower. The square in front of the Rathaus has become a centre of activity. Formerly it was only used on 1 May, when socialists gathered for the May Day parade instituted by Viktor Adler in 1889. But now there's almost always something going on here.

➕ 192 A4 ✉ Wien 1, Rathausplatz ⓒ Free guided tours Mon, Wed, Fri 1 am Ⓢ Rathaus 🚋 Tram 1, 2, D Rathausplatz/Burgtheater

11 Parlament

With its harmoniously ordered facade and elegantly curving approach ramp, the Parliament counts as one of the most artistically valuable buildings of the Ringstrasse era. It was built in 1873–83 to the design of Theophil Hansen. In the last decades of the monarchy it contained both houses of the then Reichstag, the elected house and the nobility – the architect's main difficulty was to fit both into one building. He solved the problem by creating an arcaded atrium with a cube-shaped chamber on each long side. Today the Nationalrat (National Council) and the Bundesrat (Federal Council), the two houses of the Austrian parliament, sit in these chambers. The conference hall, modelled on a Greek amphitheatre, is preserved in its original form. The finest adornment outside is the monumental Pallas Athene fountain (► 30).

➕ 192 A3 ✉ Wien 1, Dr-Karl-Renner-Ring 3 ⓒ Guided tours mid-Sep to mid-Jul Mon–Thu 11, 2, 3, 4, Fri 11, 1, 2, 3, 4, Sat 11, 12, 1, 2, 3, 4; mid-Jul to mid-Sep Mon–Sat 11, 12, 1, 2, 3, 4 Ⓢ Lerchenfelder Strasse 🚋 Tram 1, 2, D, J, 46, 49 Stadiongasse/Parlament 🎫 Moderate

Where to...
Eat and Drink

Prices

Prices are for a meal for one person, excluding drinks.

€ under €15 €€ €15–€30 €€€ over €30

RESTAURANTS

Halle €

The café-restaurant of the Kunsthalle and the Wiener Festwochen (Viennese Festival Weeks) is in the former Winter Riding School. The stucco of the imperial lodge makes an interesting contrast to the modern design. The Mediterranean food is fresh and light; the breakfast menu is extensive, there's a set menu at lunchtime and sandwiches are also available. In summer you can sit outside in the courtyard.

➕ 192 A2 ✉ Wien 7, Museumsplatz 1 ☎ (01) 523 70 01 ⏰ Daily 10am–2am Ⓜ MuseumsQuartier 🚋 Tram 49; Bus 48A Volkstheater, Bus 2A Museums-Quartier

Hansen €€

With its imaginative Mediterranean dishes, inviting breakfast menu and location on the ground floor of the Börse (Stock Exchange), Hansen is one of the city's most interesting restaurants. It's also right next to the Lederleitner garden centre, and the sweet scents of flowering plants are an added bonus.

➕ 192 C5 ✉ Wien 1, Wipplinger-strasse 34 ☎ (01) 532 05 42 ⏰ Mon–Fri 9–9 (hot food until 8), Sat 9–5 (hot food until 3) Ⓜ Schottentor 🚋 Tram 1, 2, D, Bus 3A Börse

KHM/NHM €€€

The KHM's domed atrium is home to a delightful café which transforms itself into a quality restaurant every Thursday evening between 6:30 and 10. It's an expensive treat, but the food and surroundings make it an unforgettable experience. Not to be outdone, Café Nautilus in the NHM's Cupola Hall serves a variety of fine dishes and sweets and cakes from Kurkonditorei Oberlaa.

➕ 192 B2 ✉ Wien 1, Burgring 5 and 7 ☎ KHM (01) 526 13 61; NHM (01) 524 02 50 ⏰ KHM Tue–Sun 10–6, Thu 10–10; NHM Wed–Mon 9–6:30, Wed 9–9 Ⓜ Volkstheater 🚋 Tram 1, 2, D, J; Bus 2A, 57A Burgring

Korso €€€

Reinhard Gerer, often seen as the most creative of Vienna's top chefs, has for years prepared food of the highest quality in this Michelin-starred gourmet temple. Haute cuisine, fine wines and imperial elegance make every meal here an experience. The garden, squeezed between the restaurant and Hotel Bristol, offers stunning dishes, such as fried quail's eggs and pike-perch fish fingers, along with plenty of fresh air.

➕ 193 D2 ✉ Wien 1, Mahlerstrasse 5 ☎ (01) 51 51 65 46 ⏰ Sun–Fri noon–2, 6–11pm, Sat 6 pm–11pm Ⓜ Oper 🚋 Tram 1, 2, D, J; Bus 3A Kärntnerring/Oper

Mumok Café-Restaurant €

This café-restaurant in the Mumok (Museum of Modern Art) has a side entrance, so it is not dependent on the museum's opening times. It serves Italian specialities and has fresh fish every day. Snacks, ices and desserts are served in the garden. The wine bar and reading room are especially comfortable.

🏛 192 A2 ⊠ Wien 7, Museumsplatz 1 📞 (01) 525 00-14 40 🕐 Daily 10am–midnight 🚇 MuseumsQuartier 🚋 Tram 49; Bus 48A Volkstheater, Bus 2A MuseumsQuartier

Sacher €€€

Dining here is dining in pure Viennese elegance – the Anna Sacher restaurant displays a collection of Anton Faistauer paintings and contains the first electric candelabras in the city; while the Rote Bar (Red Bar) conservatory (which transforms into a terrace in summer) looks directly onto the Staatsoper. For a true Sacher experience, reserve a table for 7pm, when the piano player begins, and order the delicious *Tafelspitz* (boiled beed with vegetables) followed by a slice of world-famous Sacher Torte.

🏛 192 C2 ⊠ Wien 1, Philharmonikerstrasse 4 📞 (01) 514 56 🕐 Anna Sacher noon–3, 6–midnight (hot food until 11:30); Rote Bar daily noon–midnight (hot food until 11:30); Café Sacher daily 8am–midnight 🚇 Oper 🚋 Tram 1, 2, D, J; Bus 3A Kärntnerring/Oper

Sacher Eck' €€

If you don't want to go for the full Sacher experience, head for Sacher Eck'. The light-filled atmosphere, tall tables with bar stools and elegant bar provide really stylish surroundings for a light snack and a glass of wine. And of course the chance to sample Sacher Torte.

🏛 193 D2 ⊠ Wien 1, Philharmonikerstrasse 2 📞 (01) 514 56-699 🕐 9am–1am 🚇 Oper 🚋 Tram 1, 2, D, J; Bus 3A Kärntnerring/Oper

Shambala €€

This bar and restaurant in the new Hotel Le Meridien on Opernring is innovative and stylish. Violet and mauve felt and light beige leather are the dominant furnishings, all bathed in pink light. The cooking is international: nouvelle cuisine with influences from Asia, North Africa and other parts of Europe. The bar colours change three times a day: in the morning it is lit in green, at lunchtime in blue and in the evening in pink. Illuminated partitions of opaque glass form private alcoves into which you can retreat.

🏛 192 C2 ⊠ Wien 1, Robert-Stolz-Platz 1 📞 (01) 588 90-0 🕐 Daily 6:30–midnight (hot food until 11), bar service daily 11am–1am 🚇 Oper 🚋 Tram 1, 2, D, J; Bus 3A Kärntnerring/Oper

Soho €

Tucked away at the back of the national library is this small cafeteria that serves library staff and anyone else who might be passing by. Two daily menus are offered – one vegetarian, one meat – and the food is more imaginative than some smarter restaurants. The decor also stands out: expect to find works by local artists livening up the heavy stone walls. To find it head to the back of Burggarten and follow the signs.

🏛 192 C3 ⊠ Wien 1, Josefsplatz 1/ Neue Burg 📞 (0676) 309 51 61 🕐 Mon–Fri 9–4 🚇 Karlsplatz/Oper 🚋 Tram 1, 2, D, J; Bus 3A Kärntnerring/Oper

Una €

This restaurant in the Museums-Quartier's Architecture Centre has an interesting set-up: the French architects Anne Lacaton and Jean-Philippe Vassal clad the ceiling vaulting with Turkish tiles, creating an oriental feel. Apart from the set lunch menu it also serves Austrian, Italian and American specialities. In summer you can eat in the garden.

🏛 192 A2 ⊠ Wien 7, Museumsplatz 1 📞 (01) 523 65 66 🕐 Mon–Fri 9am–midnight, Sat 10am–midnight, Sun 10–6 🚇 MuseumsQuartier 🚋 Tram 49, Bus 48 A Volkstheater, Bus 2A MuseumsQuartier

Vestibül €€

An elegant cosmopolitan brasserie in one of the most revered places in Vienna, the Burgtheater. The rooms are marble- and stucco-clad yet modern in feel, and the atmosphere is unbeatable. The garden too is one of the finest in the city, simply for its location. The cuisine is imaginative – light Viennese, including *kalbsbeuschel* (calf's lung) and chive dumplings as well as wild duck breast and pigeon with soya beans.

➕ 192 B4 ⬛ Wien 1, Dr-Karl-Lueger-Ring 2 ☎ (01) 532 49 99 🕔 Mon–Fri 11am–midnight, Sat from 6pm (hot food 11–2:30, 6–11pm) 🚇 Rathaus, Herrengasse 🚋 Tram 1, 2, D Burgtheater

CAFÉS

Kantine

Kantine is an established café right in the heart of the trendy MuseumsQuartier. It's pleasant any time of the year, with outdoor tables on the Quartier's inner courtyard and cosy couches indoors for when the weather turns cool. Fine teas and coffees are complemented by a small selection

of home-made cakes and savoury snacks, and there's always stronger stuff for those who wish to enjoy Kantine's convivial atmosphere well into the evening.

➕ 192 A2 ⬛ Wien 7, MuseumsQuartier 1 ☎ (01) 523 82 39 🕔 Thu–Sat 10am–2am, Sun–Wed 10am–midnight 🚇 MuseumsQuartier, Volkstheater 🚋 Tram 49; Bus 2A MuseumsQuartier

Kurkonditorei Oberlaa

This café in Babenbergerstrasse is known for its delicious confectionery, magnificent *Torten* and first-rate food. As a result, it's usually very crowded. If you can't get a seat, why not try the pub in Babenbergerstrasse opposite the Fine Arts Museum instead? The food's just as good (try the Kurbadtorte). The confectionery also makes an ideal souvenir of Vienna.

➕ 192 B2 ⬛ Wien 1, Babenbergerstrasse 7 ☎ (01) 586 72 82 🕔 Mon–Sat 8–7, Sun 10–7 🚇 MuseumsQuartier 🚋 Tram 1, 2, D, J; Bus 2A, 57A Burgring

Landtmann

Since its opening in 1873, Landtmann has been acclaimed as one of the city's most elegant coffeehouses. Its status has in turn attracted some big names from Austria and abroad – Sigmund Freud, Marlene Dietrich, Romy Schneider, Burt Lancaster, Hillary Clinton and Paul McCartney have all waltzed through its grand doors. Aside from household names, actors from the Burgtheater and politicians from the nearby Rathaus, Parliament and party headquarters all flock here for the excellent Austrian cooking and wide selection of coffees and cakes. There's live piano music some evenings.

➕ 192 B4 ⬛ Wien 1, Dr-Karl-Lueger-Ring 4 ☎ (01) 24 100-0 🕔 Daily 7:30am–midnight 🚇 Rathaus, Herrengasse 🚋 Tram 1, 2, D Burgtheater

Meierei Volksgarten

The Meierei in the Volksgarten might not be a gourmets' heaven or an upscale café, but it's a loveable

piece of old-world Vienna. Its circular garden is centred around a tiny art deco pagoda, and the views of the Hofburg are truly stupendous.

➕ 192 B3 ⬛ Wien 1, Volksgarten ☎ (01) 533 21 05 🕔 Apr–Oct depending on the weather daily 8am–10pm 🚇 Herrengasse 🚋 Tram 1, 2, D, J, Bus 2A, 57A Burgring

Sluka

In the Rathaus arcades is this popular café-cum-cakeshop, which achieves the highest standards. There are some delicious fish snacks on the menu as well as special meals for people with diabetes. Officials from the nearby Rathaus tend to meet here for a sweet or savoury snack or a coffee and *torte*, and it goes without saying that many a political issue is thrashed out here.

➕ 192 A4 ⬛ Wien 1, Rathausplatz 8 ☎ (01) 405 71 72 🕔 Mon–Fri 8–7, Sat 8–5:30 🚇 Rathaus 🚋 Tram 1, 2, D Rathausplatz/Burgtheater

Where to... Shop

The western Ringstrasse is not one of the city's main shopping streets. All the same, a visit to the museum shops and one or two specialised stores could be rewarded with some pretty and original finds.

MUSEUMS SHOPS

There are some good shopping opportunities in the **Museums-Quartier**. The Architecture Centre, Kunsthalle Wien, Leopold Museum and Mumok all have their own shops, selling books, prints, T-shirts, bags and countless unusual knick-knacks. Next door to the Kunsthalle's shop, the Lomographische Gesellschaft has opened the **LomoShop**, the first in the world to stock everything to do with these cult cameras. The little **Cheap Shop** in Quartier 21 has a large selection of sound equipment and an info-centre for web-surfing. And **MQ daily**, the health food store by the main entrance, stocks high-quality organic products and snacks. There is also a stand-up café. In **KHM** and **NHM** you can spend ages rummaging through the art prints, ornaments, books and reproductions of exhibits, from dinosaur teeth to Klimt-style earrings.

OTHER SHOPS

Sädtler Classic (Opernring 13) is a stylish florists' shop selling stunning natural plants and flowers. **Demmers Teahaus** (Molker Bastei 5) has every sort of tea, including rare varieties, and all the accompaniments that turn tea-drinking into a timeless experience.

The **Sacher Confiserie** (Philharmonikerstrasse 4) sells original Sacher Torten in different sizes, packed in wooden boxes inscribed with "a sweet gift from Vienna".

Where to be... Entertained

The Staatsoper and the Burgtheater on the western Ringstrasse are famous homes of high art. Otherwise, this part of the city tends to be quiet in the evening. Apart from the MQ, pubs and bars are thin on the ground. But you can always go clubbing.

From early May to mid-September ballroom dancing is the attraction at the **Tanzcafé** in the **Volksgarten** (Heldenplatz, tel: 01/532 42 41-0, daily from 10pm), which first opened in 1824. On Friday and Saturday there's a mixed programme of boogie woogie, rock 'n' roll and all mainstream and Latin-American dances. There are dance-floors outside and, for bad weather, inside. The whole year round it's clubbing, hip-hop, house and hits from the 1970s at the equally popular **Volksgarten Clubdiscothek**, which has the motto: "we don't make parties, we live them".

Club Passage (corner of Burgring and Babenbergerstrasse, tel: 01/561 88 00) is club culture underneath the Ringstrasse: originally, the Babenberger Passage between the Hofburg and the Fine Arts Museum was intended as a pedestrian subway. But it was never used, and lay empty for years. Now the events group Sunshine Enterprises has revived it as a cool club with futuristic decor with a flexible set-up and brilliant lighting. The programme includes club, dance and house music.

The **Café Leopold** (Museumsplatz 1, tel. 01/523 67 32, Thu–Sat 10am–4am, Sun–Wed 10am–2am) is ever more popular; it has brought a quite new urban experience to Vienna. In the evening you can have drinks at the bar or a meal after midnight, and watch videos by experimental Austrian film-makers.

Schönbrunn and Wiental

Getting Your Bearings

Schönbrunn is a powerful symbol of a bygone era. Nothing represents the imperial age as well as this magnificent palace and its park. The Wiental (Wien Valley), on the other hand, is proof that the city has always had a great liking for art and sensual pleasures.

The palace, unique park and the oldest zoo in the world make Schönbrunn a marvellous advertisement for Vienna, and indeed for the whole of Austria. The entire palace and its grounds have long been a World Cultural Heritage Site. Almost no other place so well conveys the imperial family's sense of elite beauty. Here the former glory of the Habsburg monarchy has by no means faded.

Among the attractions in Wiental, farther in towards the city are the highly unconventional buildings of the Secession movement, the Karlskirche, and those great, world-famous temples of music, the Musikverein and Konzerthaus. There are also culinary delights at every corner. Along the colourful, lively Naschmarkt numerous restaurants have opened, offering the finest foods from around the world.

Page 113:
The imperial
splendour
of Schloss
Schönbrunn

Above left:
A penguin in the
Schönbrunn zoo

Right: Vitamins
galore in the
Naschmarkt

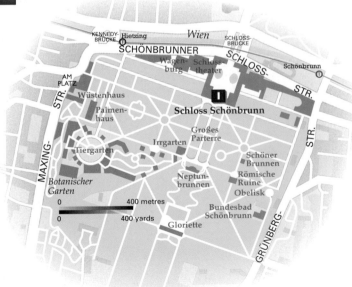

This day is entirely devoted to enjoyment. First, at Schloss and Park Schönbrunn, you will see architecture and garden design of stunning beauty, followed by a culinary journey around the world in Naschmarkt. And, finally, classical music will make a perfect end to a wonderful day.

Schönbrunn and Wiental in a Day

9:00 am

Start the day at the Habsburgs' summer residence, **❶Schönbrunn Palace** (➤ 118). As soon as you first catch sight of this palace, you'll understand at once why it is on the distinguished UNESCO World Cultural Heritage list. The effect becomes stronger as you walk through some of the splendid rooms: the Arbeitszimmer des Kaisers (Emperor's Study), the Grosse Rosa Zimmer (Large Pink Room), the adjoining Spiegelsaal (Hall of Mirrors), in which the "child prodigy" Mozart played for Maria Theresa, and the magnificent Porzellanzimmer (Porcelain Room).

11:30 am

Once outside again, take a deep breath after all that rococo splendour. It is a real pleasure to stroll through the park, all carefully trimmed and maintained according to the rules of baroque horticulture. When you arrive at the Gloriette (above), a view of the almost unreal beauty of the palace and Vienna lies before you. Pause here for a while, perhaps over a refreshing drink at the Gloriette (➤ 134).

1:30 pm

For lunch, you're spoiled for choice. At the ② Naschmarkt (right; ► 123), reached by U-Bahn line 4, you're bombarded by a wonderful variety of the most delicious aromas. Here the food ranges from Turkish to Italian, Indian, Japanese, Thai and Chinese – and each dish smells and tastes even better than the last. There's nothing for it but to stroll and sample a few.

3:00 pm

At the end of the Naschmarkt another, completely different highlight of Viennese architecture awaits you, the rectilinear ③ Secession (► 126) building, crowned with a dome of golden laurel leaves, which gave its name to an entire movement. Don't miss seeing it from the inside – if only to admire Klimt's famous *Beethoven-Frieze*.

4:00 pm

After a coffee or glass of wine in the Naschmarkt nearby, cross Karlsplatz and visit ④ Karlskirche (► 128). You'll be impressed by its bright interior, the large oval dome, which looks as though it's floating, and magnificent baroque frescoes.

5:00 pm

Walk across the remodelled Schwarzenbergplatz to the ⑥ Hochstrahlbrunnen (High-jet Fountain, below; ► 130), then take a rest. Make sure you are fit for the evening, which belongs to classical music in the Konzerthaus (► 136) or the ⑨ Musikverein (► 131). And after the inspiring notes of the Philharmonic or Symphonic Orchestras, what better way to end an evening than a nightcap in the stylish Silverbar (► 136).

❶ Schloss Schönbrunn

The Habsburgs' summer residence with its baroque land-scaped park and the oldest zoo in the world is one of Austria's most important cultural monuments. The imperial palace complex, which lies to the west of Vienna, was included in UNESCO's World Cultural Heritage list in 1997.

It all began in 1559, when Emperor Maximilian II bought the manor house in the former Katterburg, extended it to create a hunting palace and added the first zoo for rare fish and game. "Was für ein *schöner Brunnen*!" (What a lovely fountain!) said Emperor Matthias in 1612, when he was walking through this hunting ground – and that's how the place got its name.

After it was destroyed during the Turkish siege of 1683, Leopold I commissioned Johann Bernhard Fischer von Erlach in 1696 to build an imperial residence for his son Joseph I. The vast building project on Gloriette hill was to surpass the palace of Versailles in splendour and brilliance. However, this proved to be too expensive, so an economy version was built and painted in blue and pink – the characteristic "Schönbrunn yellow" was only applied in 1752. In 1728 Karl VI acquired the property and gave it to his daughter Maria Theresa. During her reign the court architect Nikolaus Pacassi extended Schönbrunn and remodelled it as a palatial rococo residence. It was the start of Schönbrunn's heyday; the palace became the centre of court and political life, and each summer the entire court, with its 2,000 servants, ladies-in-waiting, gardeners and craftsmen, transferred from the Hofburg to Schönbrunn. Empress Maria Theresa oversaw the furnishing of the palace, while her husband Franz Stephan took charge of the garden designs.

The view of the palace from the Neptune fountain is splendid

When Maria Theresa died, the palace, park and Gloriette were complete. In later years, Emperor Franz Joseph I and Empress Elisabeth regularly resided in in the palace. Franz Joseph was born and died here. In 1918 Emperor Karl I signed his abdication document in the Blauer Salon (Blue Salon). The palace suffered severe damage in World War II. After repairs, the public rooms re-opened to visitors in 1948.

A Tour of the Palace

The palace has 1,441 rooms, of which 40 are open to the public. These include Franz Joseph and Elisabeth's apartments in the west wing, the central section with the banqueting halls and function rooms, and the audience chamber of the imperial couple Maria Theresa and

Franz Stephan in the east wing. Of particular interest are the **Arbeitszimmer des Kaisers** (Emperor's Study) with portraits of Franz Joseph and Sisi, the sumptuous **Spiegelsaal** (Hall of Mirrors)

For kids

The palace has a museum and guided tours designed for children, in which they can hear all about the emperor's children, what they wore and how they were educated (weekends and public holidays).

in which the six-year-old Mozart gave his debut concert in front of Maria Theresa, and the **Chinesische Kabinette** (Chinese Rooms). When Napoleon occupied Vienna in 1805 and 1809, he made Schönbrunn his headquarters. He is said to have slept in what is now called the Napoleon Room. His son, the Duke of Reichstadt, grew up in Schönbrunn and died here at the early age of 21. The Habsburg emperors worked personally on the furnishing of the rooms – the design for the decoration of the **Porzellanzimmer** (Porcelain Room) was probably drawn up by Maria Theresa's daughter-in-law Isabella of Parma, Emperor Joseph II's first wife, and the 213 blue pen-and-ink drawings are by Emperor Franz I and some of his children. The west wing houses the **Schlosstheater** (Palace Theatre), where performances are still held today. In

Right: The young Mozart with Empress Maria Theresa, painted by Eduard Ender

the former Winterreitschule you can visit the **Wagenburg**, a collection of state and everyday carriages.

The Baroque Palace Park

South of the palace is the 185ha (457-acre) early baroque park (Schlosspark Schönbrunn), originally laid out in the French style in 1695. Maria Theresa had it remodelled in 1770. The **Neptunbrunnen** (Neptune Fountain, in operation daily 10–2) was built at the foot of Schönbrunn hill and the **Gloriette** on the hilltop. From the roof of the pavilion, which is shaped like a three-part triumphal arch, rich in ornamentation and

The Hall of Mirrors – a gorgeous example of imperial splendour

symbols, you have a tremendous view of Vienna. The mythological figures along the **Grosses Parterre** were also created under Maria Theresa, as were the **Obeliskbrunnen** (Obelisque Fountain) and the **Römische Ruine** (Roman Ruin) not far from the **Schöner Brunnen** (Beautiful Fountain), which gave the palace its name. In the western part of the park are the **Irrgarten** (Maze), the **Tiergarten Schönbrunn** (Zoo) and the **Botanischer Garten** (Botanical Gardens). The monumental **Palmenhaus** (Palm House) was erected in 1882 and is renowned for its cultivation of orchids. Nearby, the Sonnenuhrhaus (Sundial House), the last imperial project, was built in 1904; it is now the **Wüstenhaus** (Desert House), given over to the fauna and flora of the desert.

The Tiergarten

There was a game park at Schönbrunn as early as 1570, but we have Maria Theresa's husband Franz Stephan to thank for founding the first menagerie. The centre, and still the core, of this area is the **Frühstückspavillon des Kaisers** (Emperor's Breakfast Pavilion), around which 13 enclosures were arranged, some of them still extant. The first giraffe arrived in 1828, creating an enormous sensation in Vienna: hats, hairstyles, drinking vessels, pastries – everything was suddenly "à la girafe". In 1906, for the first time in any zoo, an elephant was born here. Almost 100 years later, the young elephants Abu and Mongu, also born here, are great favourites with visitors. Large enclosures and habitats appropriate for each species are the hallmark of the modern enclosures. In an enormous wooded area wolves run wild, in the rainforest house a tropical thunderstorm breaks out twice daily (2:15 and 3:15pm); and cheetahs hunt their prey, which is transported through the enclosure on a built-in ski-lift. In the Polarium penguins and seals dive, while clown fish,

Right: The café in the Gloriette has marvellous views

among other creatures, dart around in the aquarium/terrarium houses.

TAKING A BREAK

The café in the former **Frühstückspavillon des Kaisers** in the centre of the enclosures has the greatest zoo atmosphere. The **Tirolerhof**, on the mound beyond the wolves' enclosure, is more rustic. In the park you can fortify yourself at the **Gloriette** (► 134).

To the east, rather out of the way, the **Meierei** in the Kronprinzengarten exudes the charm of the 1950s – very few tourists, and the cakes are wonderful.

Tropical plants flourish under the glass and steel structure of the grand Palmenhaus

Schönbrunn Palace

🔢 198 B/C3 ✉ Wien 13, Schönbrunner Schlossstrasse
☎ (01) 81 11 32 39 🕐 Schloss Apr–Jun, Sep–Oct 8:30–5, Jul–Aug 8:30–6, Nov–Mar 8:30–4:30; Park Apr–Oct from 6am, Nov–Mar from 6:30am until dusk 🚇 Schönbrunn 🚋 Tram 10, 58, Bus 10A Schloss Schönbrunn
💶 Expensive 🌐 www.schoenbrunn.at

Schönbrunn Zoo

🔢 198 A2 ✉ Wien 13, Maxingstrasse 13b ☎ (01) 877 92 94-0
🕐 Daily from 9am; closing time Feb 5pm, Mar, Oct 5:30pm, Apr 6pm, May–Sep 6:30pm, Nov–Jan 4:30pm 🚇 Hietzing 🚋 Tram 10, 58, Bus 10A, 51A, Kennedybrücke, Hietzing 💶 Expensive 🌐 www.zoovienna.at

---

SCHÖNBRUNN PALACE: INSIDE INFO

Top tips The favourite time to visit the zoo, especially for children, is at **feeding time**. Here are the times for the most popular animals: orang-utans 10am and 2:30; koalas 4; seals 10:30 and 3:30; king penguins 11; mandrils 2; cheetahs Mon, Wed, Sun 3; tigers and jaguars Sun–Tue, Thu, Fri 2; wolves Sun–Tue, Thu, Fri 11; vultures Sun 11:30; elephants 10.

• If you have plenty of time, buy a **Schönbrunn Pass Gold** (€36). This ticket is valid for a year and entitles you to entry to all parts of the complex (once each) as well as giving certain reductions.

• Almost every day **concerts** are held in the Orangery. For information and tickets phone (01) 812 50 07 (www.lavera.at).

• The **Marionettentheater** (Puppet Theatre) in the Hofratstrakt is a real experience for children. For information and tickets phone (01) 817 32 47 (www.marionettentheater.at).

Hidden gem In front of the east facade of the palace, immediately above the former kitchens, is the gorgeous **Kronprinzengarten** (Apr–Oct from 9am). The flowerbeds in this, Schönbrunn's oldest garden, were laid out following embroidery patterns. A romantic pergola, pavilions and lemon trees make this garden fronting Crown Prince Rudolf's former apartments well worth seeing.

❷ Naschmarkt and Wienzeile

The Wien River, which gave Vienna its name, is not the idyllic stream it once was; for a long time, it's been just a thin rivulet. And the grand "Kaiserboulevard", which was to lead over the Wien to Schönbrunn, never amounted to anything. However, where the Wien has been covered over, a very interesting district has arisen.

Fate has not dealt the Wien River a kind hand. In the Middle Ages vineyards still flourished on its banks, but from then on it was all downhill. First dye-works arrived and polluted the water, to be followed by timber yards and mills and finally industry. By 1900 the Wien was as dead as a dodo.

But since in Vienna dying is always accompanied by pomp, the Wien also became a glorious corpse. Otto Wagner was commissioned to arrange this. He straightened and deepened the Wien and built embankments from where the river could be covered over. Never was a project so appropriate to the character of a city: in the last years of the monarchy a grand boulevard was to be built over a dead river – the "Kaiserboulevard" (Imperial Boulevard).

The outcome of the project was also typical. It started in great style with the arching over of the river at the Stadtpark, then came the grand buildings along Wienzeile and the miserable failure of Karlsplatz. The rest suffered the same fate as the monarchy, and the Kaiserboulevard remained a torso, a 500m (550-yard) long tunnel from Stadtpark to the end of the Naschmarkt flea market (U-Bahn: Kettenbrückengasse).

On Saturdays the Naschmarkt is joined by a flea market

Notable Buildings

From the Schönbrunn end, the **Kettenbrückengasse station** at the end of the tunnel immediately catches your eye. A few years ago Otto Wagner's Stadtbahn (urban railway) station was renovated true to his style. Around 100m (110 yards)

Theater an der Wien

Opposite the Naschmarkt is the Theater an der Wien, one of the city's theatres rich in tradition. It was originally built in 1787, but only the Papageno gate on Millöckergasse remains from the original structure. Famous works have had their premieres here, amongst them Mozart's *Magic Flute* in 1791, Beethoven's *Fidelio* in 1805, and Johann Strauss's *Fledermaus* in 1874. From 1945 to 1955 the theatre was the temporary home of the bombed-out Staatsoper, and in the 1980s it became Vienna's leading theatre for musicals, staging hits like *Cats*. It has recently returned to being an opera house.

towards the city centre, on the Linke Wienzeile, are two more admirable examples of the pioneering architect's work, the **Majolikahaus** (Majolica House, at No 40) and next door the house on the **corner of Köstlergasse** (at No 38, ➤ 24), faced with medallions by Koloman Moser.

On Saturday mornings there is always lots going on in the grounds opposite these houses. At this time the **flea market** is held here, and adjoining it a farmers' market, where country produce, from smoked meat to organic vegetables, is on sale.

The Naschmarkt

First-class fruit and vegetables are on sale at Naschmarkt

The adjoining Naschmarkt is a world in itself. It started around 1775 as a milk market, later growing into a fruit and vegetable market around the Karlsplatz area. After the Wien had been covered over, the market moved to its present location. It retains its old-world character at the end farthest from the city centre. Here the stalls are still wooden booths, fruit and vegetables remain cheap, and haggling goes on in all the languages of this multi-ethnic empire.

The farther you go towards the city centre, the grander the market becomes. In the middle, Turks, Iranians, Chinese, Japanese and Greeks have created a multi-cultural micro-climate. Here they sell fruit, vegetables, meat, cheese, olives and specialities from their own countries, and run snack-bars and restaurants, all enveloped in an aroma of kebabs.

The upper end of the Naschmarkt, towards the city, has blossomed in recent years. Here luxury delicatessens have opened, selling delectable, gourmet food (➤ 135).

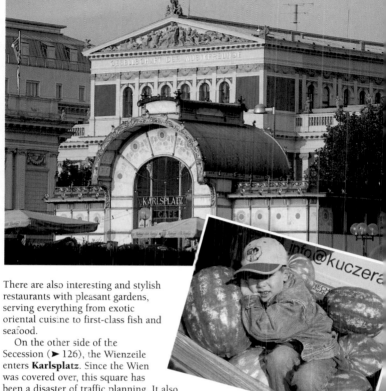

There are also interesting and stylish restaurants with pleasant gardens, serving everything from exotic oriental cuisine to first-class fish and seafood.

On the other side of the Secession (► 126), the Wienzeile enters **Karlsplatz**. Since the Wien was covered over, this square has been a disaster of traffic planning. It also has a bad reputation. After World War II this was the centre of the black market, and now the drug scene is played out at the entrances to the U-Bahn. One of the more lugubrious sights on Karlsplatz is the Wien-Museum, documenting the history of Vienna, from the first settlements on the Danube to the present day.

Top: Style fusion on Karlsplatz: Musikverein and Wagner's Stadtbahn station

TAKING A BREAK

All sorts of delicacies tempt you at every step. **Piccolo Gourmet** (► 135) serves really good Italian snacks.

📍 192 B1 ✉ Wien 6, Naschmarkt 🕐 Stalls Mon–Fri 6am–6:30pm, Sat 6–5, every 1st Sat in the month 6–6; Farmers' Market Sat 6:30–5; Flea Market Sat 6:30–6 (including public holidays) 🚇 Kettenbrückengasse, Karlsplatz 🚊 Tram 62, 65; Bus 4A, 59A Karlsplatz

Above: Tempting fruit at the Naschmarkt

NASCHMARKT AND WIENZEILE: INSIDE INFO

Top tip If you don't like crowds, **avoid the Naschmarkt** on Friday afternoon and Saturday morning when it's at its busiest.

One to miss Avoid Karlsplatz and its U-Bahn entrances **after dark**. This is where drug dealers and junkies hang out.

❸ Secession

Goldener Krauthappl, meaning "golden cabbage snack", is what the Viennese call the Secession, which is crowned by a large golden ball of laurel leaves. This affectionately disparaged building right next to the Naschmarkt is the most important example of Jugendstil architecture in the city.

The young, rebellious artists who formed their own group in 1897 and later became the leading proponents of Jugendstil in Vienna (► 24) needed their own building. And so the Secessionists, as they called themselves, asked Joseph Maria Olbrich, who had studied under Otto Wagner, to build them an exhibition hall.

The new representative building was controversial and hotly debated right from the beginning. Its plain, purist lines, the cubic block of a main building and large laurel-leaf dome met with violent opposition and distaste from the start. "Ought to be torn down!", was the vociferous demand of

The Secession, once a scandal, now a glorious advertisement for Vienna

DER·ZEIT·IHRE·KVNST·
DER·KVNST·IHRE·FREIHEIT·

The Secession style is evident in the smallest details.

many Viennese, notwithstanding the motto over the main door: "To the age its art, to art its freedom".

A Leafy Roof for Art

All the same, Olbrich succeeded, with this temple to art, in enriching Vienna with a highly attractive if unconventional building, which still looks progressive and exciting today. The "Krauthappl" with its 3,000 gilt leaves and 700 berries symbolizes the unity of art and nature – under the leafy roof art was to grow and flourish. The laurel leaf is repeated on the pilasters of the front wing and the entrance niche, as well as in the various garlands along the side elevation.

The team of lions with the Roman emperor Marcus Aurelius on one side of the Secession has much less profound origins. This was meant to be only a temporary site for the bronze group created by Arthur Strasser for the 1901 World Exhibition. It's still there – "temporary" appears to last much longer in Vienna than elsewhere.

The Secession building has remained true to its original purpose as an exhibition hall for contemporary art, and still provides the stage for numerous highly regarded changing exhibitions. It still gets people worked up today: in 1988, before it was renovated for its centenary celebrations, the artist Marcel Geiger covered it in bright red – and popular anger exploded once again.

TAKING A BREAK

Walk across the road to the **Wien & Co** bar (➤ 136) for a drink and a bite to eat.

➕ 192 C1 ✉ Wien 1, Friedrichstrasse 12 ☎ (01) 587 53 07 🕐 Tue–Sun 10–6, Thu until 8 🚇 Oper, Karlsplatz 🚋 Tram 1, 2, D, J; Bus 3A, 59A Oper, Karlsplatz 💰 Moderate ❓ www.secession.at

---

SECESSION: INSIDE INFO

Top tip Guided tours are held on Saturdays at 3pm and Sundays at 11am.

Hidden gem Take your time over Gustav Klimt's *Beethoven Frieze*. Created in 1902 for the XIVth exhibition of the Association of Fine Artists of Austria Secession, it was later detached and sold. In 1985 it returned to the Secession and is now housed in a specially constructed room on the lower ground floor. In this monumental work, 34m (111 feet) long and 2.20m (7 feet) high, Klimt interprets Beethoven's *Ninth Symphony* as a journey through illness and suffering to pure love.

4 Karlskirche

From the start this grandiose place of worship was conceived as a powerful symbol. It is an unmistakable sign of the universality of the claims of Church and Empire. The cross on the dome lantern stands for the omnipotence of God, the crowns and eagles on the two triumphal columns for the power of the emperor.

Strictly speaking, the Karlskirche is a votive church. In 1713, when the plague cost the lives of almost 10,000 Viennese, Emperor Karl VI vowed to build a church dedicated to the patron saint of plague victims, St Carlo Borromeo. In 1714, against stiff competition, Johann Bernhard Fischer von Erlach won the commission to build the church in wooded meadows beside the as yet unregulated Wien River. He, and after his death his son Joseph Emanuel, created with their budget of 300,000 guilders a unique work of art, a church which is 80m (260 feet) long and 60m (200 feet) broad and can be seen from many points in the city centre, including Herrengasse and Augustinerstrasse.

Imposing columns adorn Fischer von Erlach's baroque masterpiece

Resplendent from Outside...

In front of the central edifice, dominated by its green dome, is a porch in the form of a Greek temple, whose **Giebelrelief** (Pediment Relief) depicts scenes from the plague epidemic. St Borromeo stands on the pediment surrounded by allegories of the four virtues of contrition, mercy, piety and religion, all by Lorenzo Mattielli.

The building is flanked by two **Triumphsäulen** (Triumphal Columns) decorated with reliefs, which reach almost as high as the dome. Created by Mader and Matielli, they represent the empire's Pillars of Hercules. Beside them are two **Glockentürme** (Bell-towers) with a faint resemblance to pagodas. On each side of the **Freitreppe** (Stairway) is the mighty figure of an angel, the work of Franz Caspar.

...and from Inside

On the inside "Vienna's Hagia Sophia", as the largest baroque cathedral north of the Alps was soon called, is no less impressive. The oval **Hauptraum** (Central Hall) is crowned by the 72m (236-foot) high dome, which looks even more imposing due to Gaetano Fanti's *trompe-l'oeil* perspective paintings on its lower rim.

The **Kuppelfresko** (Dome Frescoes) were completed in 1730 by the then renowned ceiling painter Johann Michael Rottmayr. They show St Borromeo imploring the Holy Trinity for release from the plague. Rottmayr's numerous smaller paintings on the vault of the choir, in the chapels and above the organ all convey the impression of baroque opulence, as does Albert Camesina's over-lavish stucco. Johann Bernhard Fischer von Erlach's high altar, with Borromeo rising through clouds to the divine light, also makes its contribution.

TAKING A BREAK

In **Otto Wagner's Pavillon** in Karlsplatz, a Stadtbahn station converted into a café, you can enjoy a snack in fine Jugendstil surroundings.

🔢 193 D1 📧 Wien 4, Kreuzherrengasse 1 ☎ Mon–Sat 9–12:30, 1–6, Sun noon–5:45 🚇 Karlsplatz 🚊 Tram 62, 65; Bus 4A, 59A Karlsplatz 💶 Moderate 🔗 www.karlskirche.at

KARLSKIRCHE: INSIDE INFO

Top tips Be sure to take the lift up to the frescoes in the dome.
The **panorama windows** at the top have a magnificent view of Vienna.
• The **Borromeus Museum** on the first floor has interesting items from the history of the Karlskirche and the life of St Borromeo.

Hidden gem Don't miss **Henry Moore's modern sculpture** *Hill Arches* in the pond in front of the church. After all the baroque extravagance inside the church, its sober simplicity is a pleasure to look at.

At Your Leisure

5 Wien Museum

From the outside the Wien Museum (Vienna Museum, formerly Historisches Museum der Stadt Wien) in Karlsplatz, is rather off-putting with its late-1950s steel framework, but inside it has much to offer. Extensive collections document the history of the city from the Celts onwards. Of particular interest are the original stained-glass and sandstone statues from the Stephansdom, objects from the two Turkish sieges and baroque, Biedermeier and Jugendstil exhibits.

🕂 193 D1 ✉ Wien 4, Karlsplatz
☎ (01) 505 87 47 🕐 Tue–Sun 9–6
🚇 Karlsplatz 🚊 Tram 62, 65; Bus 4A, 59A Karlsplatz 🎫 Moderate

6 Hochstrahlbrunnen

The Hochstrahlbrunnen (High-jet Fountain) was meant to spring into action on 24 October 1873, in the presence of the emperor and all the civic dignitaries, to celebrate the completion of the First High Mountain Water Conduit. It caused some anxiety to its builders – it simply refused to work. After fraught minutes of waiting, however, the high column of water shot up into the sky – and since then it has carried on working (► 30). In summer the fountain is illuminated in colour. Behind it is the semicircular Befreiungsdenkmal (Liberation Monument), also known as the Red Army Memorial, which commemorates the liberation of Vienna at the end of World War II by the Red Army (► 181).

🕂 193 E1 ✉ Wien 3, Schwarzenbergplatz 🚇 Karlsplatz
🚊 Tram D Gusshausstrasse

7 Palais Schwarzenberg

Schwarzenberg Palace, which is now practically in the middle of the city, was originally built as a garden palace on ground outside the city

Caryatids in the Goldener Saal of the Musikverein

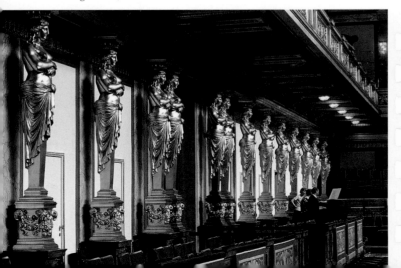

walls, with a beautiful view of the fortified inner city. In 1697 Prince Mansfeld-Fondi commissioned Johann Lukas von Hildebrandt to build it. In 1716 Prince Adam Franz von Schwarzenberg took over the site and gave the work to Johann Bernhard Fischer von Erlach. After the latter's death in 1723 it was completed by his son Joseph Emanuel. The most interesting part of the palace, which is still owned by the Schwarzenberg family, is its nicely structured facade facing the city. Today it houses one of Vienna's finest luxury hotels, which is currently undergoing a major renovation.

➕ 193 E1 ✉ Wien 3, Schwarzen-bergplatz 9 ☎ (01) 798 45 15-100 Ⓜ Karlsplatz 🚋 Tram D Gusshausstrasse

❽ Künstlerhaus

The Artists' House was built in 1868 in the style of the Italian Renaissance as an exhibition and meeting house for the "Genossenschaft der bildenden Künstler Wiens" (Association of Viennese Artists). Eight marble statues grace its facade: Dürer, Michelangelo, Raphael, Rubens, Leonardo da Vinci, Velázquez, Bramante and Titian. Recently the Künstlerhaus enjoyed a renovation and now stages spectacular and large exhibitions.

➕ 193 D1 ✉ Wien 1, Karlsplatz 5 ☎ (01) 587 96 63 Ⓜ Karlsplatz 🚋 Tram 62, 65, Bus 4A, 59A Karlsplatz

❾ Musikverein

This building was constructed to Theophil Hansen's design in 1867 for the Musikverein (Music Society), which was founded in 1814. The landlords are the Wiener Philharmoniker, but apart from the

Golden Johann Strauss in the Stadtpark

orchestra, virtually all famous international musicians have appeared in this house, and for good reason – the building has incredibly fine acoustics. In 2004 four new auditoria were added: as well as the world-famous Goldener Saal, from which the New Year's Concert is broadcast, it now has the Gläserner (Glass), Metallener (Metal, for young audiences), Hölzerner (Wooden) and Steinerner (Stone) halls.

➕ 193 D1 ✉ Wien 1, Bösendorfer-strasse 12 ☎ (01) 505 81 90, Infoline (01) 505 13 63 📦 Box office Mon–Fri 9–8, Sat 9–1 Ⓜ Karlsplatz 🚋 Tram 62, 65; Bus, 4A, 59A Karlsplatz ❓ www.musikverein.at

❿ Stadtpark

The lovingly tended Stadtpark (City Park) occupies part of what was once open ground outside the city walls. It was laid out in 1862 to the design of Josef Selleny and Rudolf Siebeck in the English landscape style. Seen from the park, the view of the Wien River is particularly interesting. After an underground passage of 2km (1.2 miles) it re-emerges through a Jugendstil gateway, flanked by walls, steps and pavilions. Many memorials commemorate notables like Schubert and Lehar. A major attraction and probably the most photographed object in Vienna is the marble and gold statue of Johann Strauss.

➕ 193 E/F2/3 Ⓜ Stadtpark

Where to...
Eat and Drink

Prices
Prices are for a meal for one person, excluding drinks.
€ under €15 €€ €15–€30 €€€ over €30

RESTAURANTS

Collio €€€

This restaurant in Das Triest Hotel specialises in northeastern Italian cooking; like the Silver Bar in the same location, it was excellently designed by Sir Terence Conran. Fresh fish is always on the menu, barbecued outside in summer. The wine list has an extensive range of Austrian, Italian and French wines.

✚ 194 B1 ⊠ Wien 4, Wiedner Hauptstrasse 12 ☎ (01) 589 18–133 ◉ Mon–Fri noon–2:30, 6:30–10,

Sat 6:30–10 ⓤ Karlsplatz
🚊 Tram 62, 65 Paulaner Kirche

Plachutta Hietzing €€

This is by far the best restaurant in the elegant residential district of Hietzing. It belongs to the Plachutti family and, like their eatery in Wollzeile 1, specialises in truly outstanding beef dishes. Everything from *Schulterscherzel* (top of shoulder) to *Tafelspitz* is served in beef broth, accompanied by a delicious selection of vegetables.

✚ 198, west of the A3 ⊠ Wien 13, Auhofstrasse 1 ☎ (01) 877 70 87

◉ Mon–Fri 11:30–3, 6–midnight, Sat–Sun 11:30am–midnight (hot food until 2:30 and 10:30) ⓤ Hietzing-Tiergarten 🚊 Tram 58, 60 Dommayergasse

ra'mien €€

This modern Asian restaurant is one of the most popular places in town with food lovers with shallow pockets. Noodles – hand-made in front of diners – are the speciality, and the noodle soups, known as *ramen*, served at lunchtime are a real delight (as are the rice dishes). In the evening there's a wide range of Thai, Japanese, Chinese and Vietnamese dishes, and the red cocktail bar is a perfect spot to wait until your table is ready. The dance lounge in the cellar is normally packed by midnight, and on some nights the price of your drink is determined by a throw of the die.

✚ 192 B1 ⊠ Wien 6, Gumpendorfer Strasse 9 ☎ (01) 585 47 98
◉ Tue–Sun 11am–midnight; Bar Tue–Wed, Sun 8pm–2am, Thu–Sat

until 4am ⓤ Museumsquartier
🚌 Bus 57A Köstlergasse

Schwarzer Adler €€

This rustic restaurant has long been known for its excellent traditional Viennese dishes. The interior features wood panelling, cast-iron fittings and a tiled stove. The impressive wine list embraces numerous excellent Austrian and international wines.

✚ 194, southwest of the A1 ⊠ Wien 5, Schönbrunner Strasse 40 ☎ (01) 544 11 09 ◉ Tue–Sat 11:30–3, 6–11 (hot food until 10:30) ⓤ Pilgramgasse
🚌 Bus 12A, 13A, 59A Margaretenplatz

Silberwirt €€

This restaurant is the epitome of a superior Viennese pub. The menu lists traditional dishes like *Schulterscherzel*, *Wienerschnitzel* and roast chicken, but also Italian pasta dishes. An inexpensive two-course set meal is available at lunchtime. The Silberwirt and neighbouring restaurants are members of the *schlossquadrat* (Castle Square), pledged to maintain high standards of food, wine and ambience.

🕂 194 A1 ⊠ Wien 5, Schlossgasse 21 ☎ (01) 544 49 07 🕘 Daily noon–midnight (hot food noon–11)
Ⓤ Pilgramgasse 🚌 Bus 12A, 13A, 59A Margaretenplatz

Zu den 3 Buchteln €

This friendly wood-panelled restaurant specialises in Viennese and Bohemian cuisine from grandmother's days. It's not a place to start counting calories, especially if you try one of the wonderful hot desserts – which you certainly should do at least once in Vienna!

🕂 194 A1 ⊠ Wien 5, Wehrgasse 90 ☎ (01) 587 83 65 🕘 Mon–Sat 6pm–midnight (hot food until 11), Closed Jul Ⓤ Pilgramgasse
🚌 Bus 12A, 13A, 59A Margaretenplatz

Zu den Zwei Lieseln €

The decor of this traditional *Beisl* hasn't changed in decades, and that suits the owners and guests just fine. Its menu probably hasn't changed either, and is filled with Viennese dishes like grandma used to make: the house special is *Schnitzel*, and this is really the thing to order here. Austrians from far and wide wait patiently at the clean tables for the breaded veal dish, which is often larger than the plate it arrives on. By tradition, it should be ordered with a side of potato salad.

🕂 194 A1 ⊠ Wien 7, Burggasse 63 ☎ (01) 523 32 82 🕘 Daily 11–11
🚌 Bus 48A Naschmarkt

Zum Alten Fassl €€

With its polished wood interior, cosy environment and massive garden at the rear, Zum Alten Fassl is one of the finest restaurants in town. Its menu is top of its list of fine points, based as it is around seasonal dishes from Vienna and the Austrian countryside beyond the city. This is the place to sample *Martinigansl* (goose) and wild meats in autumn, *Spargel* (asparagus) in spring and *Marillen-knödel* (apricot dumplings) in summer.

🕂 194 B1 ⊠ Wien 5, Ziegelofengasse 37 ☎ (01) 544 42 98 🕘 Mon–Sat 5pm–1am, Sun noon–3, 5–1 🚌 Bus 13A, 59A Ziegelofengasse

Naschmarkt

The market is in the city centre and hosts the majority of restaurants located here, but its entire stretch is slowly filling up with quality establishments. Within sight of the Secession you'll find a string of top places, including Turkish-run Umar (Stand 76, Mon–Sat 10am–midnight, hot food till 11), which is regarded as one of the best fish restaurants in the business. Close by is Indian Pavilion (Stand 74, Mon–Fri 11–6:30, Sat 11–5), a tiny Indian eatery that's filled with the delicious aromas of curry mixes and coriander – it also does take-out. Then come the Asian diners: Li's Cooking (Stand 126, Mon–Sat 10:30am–11pm) and Mr Lee (Stand 278–280, Mon–Sat 10:30–10:30) serve oriental and aromatic noodle dishes straight from the wok, and Toko Ri (Stand 261–263, Mon–Sat 11–11) tackles Japanese cuisine (sushi, maki, tempura and teriyaki, to name but a few popular options) with great gusto. All three do take-out as well. Naschmarkt Deli (Stand 421–436, Mon–Fri 8am–10pm, Sat until midnight) makes use of fresh, seasonal market produce, serving delectable little vegetable dishes and crisp salads. Its breakfast specialities are very popular, as is the coffee from a small Italian roasting house.; there's jazz on Thursdays. Directly opposite is Do-An (Stand 412, Mon–Sat 8am–midnight), a small bar-café-restaurant that has Viennese coming back time and time again for its excellent coffee and filling breakfasts, which are served till 4pm.

Café Rüdigerhof

Rüdigerhof, a popular café (particularly on Saturdays) on the edge of the Naschmarkt, is a wonderful example of Jugendstil architecture. Strong coffees and belt-busting cakes are served year round, mostly on the large terrace once summer arrives.

➕ 194 A1 ⊠ Wien 5, Hamburgerstrasse 20 ☎ (01) 586 31 38 🕐 Daily 9am–2am Ⓤ Kettenbrückengasse

Dommayer

This elegant coffee-house has a long musical history. Founded in 1787, it changed its name in 1833 to Kasino Dommayer and became the centre of Biedermeier social life. Both Johann Strauss the Elder and the Younger played here, as did Lanner. The Millefleurs Balls and *Rosenfeste* were legendary, and in the 1930s Viennese films were shot here. Today the Dommayer is as smart as the Hietzing district surrounding it. The *torten* served here are top quality, as is all the food, including classics such as goulash. On Saturday afternoons Dommayer hosts concerts from 2 till 4, and from May until September plays are performed on the garden stage (from 5:30pm).

➕ 198, west of the A3 ⊠ Wien 13, Auhofstrasse 2 ☎ (01) 877 54 65 🕐 Daily 7am–10pm Ⓤ Hietzing-Tiergarten 🚊 Tram 58, 60 Dommayergasse

Drechsler

For years, Drechsler has served the Naschmarkt stallholders and workers breakfast and strong coffee to kick-start their day, and as a by-product fed night owls on their way home from a night out. The café's recent makeover – turning it into a stylish establishment with cream sofas and dark wood furniture – may have changed its image and attracted a more upmarket clientele, but on weekends it's still filled with the hard-working regulars and partygoers of yore.

➕ 194 B2 ⊠ Wien 6, Linke Wienzeile 22 ☎ (01) 581 20 44 🕐 Tue–Sat 3am–2am, Sun 3am–midnight, Mon 8am–2am Ⓤ Kettenbrückengasse 🚌 Bus 57A Köstlergasse

Gloriette

The view from this café above Schönbrunn Palace is spectacular – the park and the palace are right before you, and beyond them the whole western part of the city. From 9am at weekends you can breakfast royally at the buffet to the sound of classical music.

➕ 198 B2 ⊠ Wien 13, Schlosspark Schönbrunn, Gloriette ☎ (01) 879 13 11 🕐 Daily 9am until an hour before the park closes Ⓤ Schönbrunn 🚊 Tram 10, 58; Bus 10A Schloss Schönbrunn

Museum Café

Designed by Alfred Loos, this café museum opened in 1899. All was set out in his strict purist style. The decor was simple and free of ornamentation, and the café soon became known as the "Nihilism Café". In 2003 it was thoroughly renovated and now, stripped of even its coffee-house patina, it looks more nihilist than ever, but it's a popular, central meeting-place.

➕ 192 C2 ⊠ Wien 1, Opperngasse 7 ☎ (01) 586 52 02 🕐 Mon–Sat 8am–midnight, Sun 10am–midnight Ⓤ Karlsplatz 🚊 Tram 62, 65; Bus 4A, 59A Karlsplatz

Sperl

This famous coffee house has retained its fine old character, thanks to careful renovation. Around 1900 the spacious café was the haunt of artists and high-ranking officers, and today it's a popular hangout for artists, intellectuals and romantics.

➕ 194 B2 ⊠ Wien 6, Gumpendorfer Strasse 11 ☎ (01) 586 41 58 🕐 Mon–Sat 7am–11pm, Sun 11am–8pm; Jul–Aug closed Sun Ⓤ MuseumsQuartier 🚌 Bus 57A Köstlergasse

Where to...
Shop

The Wiental between Secession and Kettenbrückengasse is the best place to shop. The flea market and the Naschmarkt offer all sorts of opportunities to acquire something interesting.

The **Flohmarkt** (flea market) is very busy every Saturday (6:30am–6pm). Traders, some of whom are professional dealers, arrive in the early hours to unpack their treasures; and you can then rummage through them all day to your heart's content. The choice of goods ranges from old glasses to china, books, records, furniture and – if you're lucky – genuine (or almost genuine) Jugendstil lamps and antique linen. With luck there's always the chance of picking up something special.

The **Naschmarkt** is a paradise for shopaholics. At one end you can buy seasonal fruit and vegetables. The choice of exotic fruit from across the globe is extraordinary – this is where Vienna's many foreign residents, who work in international organisations such as the United Nations, buy their food.

For many years **Strmiska** (Stand 248) has been known for the best sauerkraut and delicious pickled gherkins in the city. **Urbanek** has also long been a focal point; the tiny delicatessen (Stand 46), which sells marvellous ham, cheese and wine, is often overflowing with the Viennese "in-crowd".

The top end of Naschmarkt specialises in luxury foods. **Pohl** (Stand 168) has excellent breads, salami, olive oil and pasta, as well as one of the best hams in Vienna. **Käseland** (meaning cheese-land, Stand 172) has a large selection of cheeses from around the world including unusual ones such as Vorarlberg mountain cheese and

"Wilder Kaiser". Next door is **Kurkonditorei Oberlaa** (Stand 175), a small, elegant shop with great *torten* and confectionery; buy a picnic here and enjoy it in one of Vienna's beautiful open areas.

Gegenbauer (Stand 111–114), on the other hand, is the place for perfect vinegar: it has rarities such as blackcurrant vinegar, balsamic quince vinegar, matured in oak for five years, and "Edelsaurer", a drinkable vinegar.

Linke Wienzeile opposite Naschmarkt is also of great culinary interest. **Piccini** (Linke Wienzeile 4) has specialised for many years in Italian delicacies: mortadella, prosciutto, pasta and *antipasti*. If you want a tasty Italian snack to eat on the spot, drop in at **Piccolo Gourmet** next door (Linke Wienzeile 4, Mon–Fri 11–7:30, Sat 10:30–3:30). This shop–bar with a Jugenstil courtyard also prides itself on its *antipasti* – it has an astonishing selection of 60 in the window.

Where to be...
Entertained

The Naschmarkt and its side streets in particular are excellent for a night out– here you'll find an ever-increasing number of fine bars, attracting a very mixed crowd. But it's not all about drinking: this part of the city also hosts some of Vienna's greatest music halls.

Aux Gazelles (Rahlgasse 5, tel: 01/585 66 45) is one of the most beautiful bars in the city. Its 2,000sq m (2,400square-yard) space offers all sorts of delights with a North African twist. The café/delicatessen (Mon–Sat 11am–2am) provides a variety of breakfasts, a set lunch menu, Mediterranean specialities and oriental salads (also take-out), while the elegant Caviar & Oyster Bar does just as it says (Mon–Sat 8am–2am).

The Brasserie (Mon–Sat 6pm–midnight) is separated from the kitchen by a courtyard; it serves French and North African specialities. The Club Bar (Mon–Thu 9pm–2am, Fri–Sat 9pm–4am) with its oriental feel is strikingly beautiful, and varied a programme of music is put on here. The absolute hit at Aux Gazelles is its large *hammam* (Mon–Sat noon–10), an oriental steam bath with three temperature zones and a wonderful tea-room next door, where you can relax in style afterwards.

The chic and elegant **Theater-café** (Linke Wienzeile 6, tel: 01/585 62 62, Mon–Sat 9:30am–2am, Sun 3pm–1am) next to the Theater an der Wien quickly became the place to be seen for famous painters and musicians, as well as for would-be celebrities. At lunch, superior Viennese cooking is served, and in the evenings the Viennese "in crowd" meets in the long cool bar. And if evening stretches until early morning, there's nothing lost – the Drechsler café (▶ 134) is only a few steps away.

The **Wein & Co** bar (Getreidemarkt 1, tel: 01/585 72 57, Mon–Fri 10am–midnight, Sat 9am–midnight, Sun 11am–midnight) is a must for wine-lovers. An enormous selection of Austrian and international wines is sold at the bar, and because of the restaurant, the attached shop stays open while others close. You can eat small snacks or Mediterranean specialities from the cold buffet with your wine. Sundays from 11am to 4pm is "Happy Sunday", when house wines are half price.

The **Silverbar** in Das Triest hotel (Wiedner Hauptstrasse 12, tel: 01/589 18-133, Mon 6pm–2am, Tue–Sat 7pm–3am, Sun 4pm–midnight) is worth a visit simply for its elegant and unusual design, for which no less a person than Sir Terence Conran was responsible. The award-winning bar has an interesting selection of cocktails, and for entertainment there's jazz, Latino and soul. It's a good place just to chill out.

The modern **Schikaneder** bar in the former lobby of the old repertory cinema of the same name (Margaretenstrasse 22–24, tel: 01/585 28 67, daily 6pm–4am, or 30 minutes before the film starts) is quite special. The unusually long bar, and equally long seating opposite, make for an atmosphere with flair. The clientele is invariably clad in black, and on weekends the place is full to overflowing.

Also worth a mention are **Orange One** (Margaretenstrasse 26, tel: 01/586 22 20, daily from 4pm) and the **Kunsthallencafé** (Treitlstrasse 2/Karlsplatz, tel: 01/587 00 73, daily 10am–2am); the former is a laid-back local attracting a 30-something crowd and the latter a glass box of a café with a convivial vibe and superb desserts. Many of the Naschmarkt cafés and eateries are also fine places for an evening out.

MUSIC

This part of the city has the two institutions, which, together with the Staatsoper, form the basis for Vienna's reputation as world capital of music and in which the famous "Viennese style" was created. The **Konzerthaus** (Lothringerstrasse 20, tel: 01/242 00, information on 01/24 20 01 00, box office Mon–Fri 9–7:45, Sat 9–1) is home to the Wiener Symphoniker orchestra, while the **Musikverein** (▶ 131) has the Philharmoniker orchestra.

The gorgeous **Theater an der Wien** (▶ 124, Linke Wienzeile 6, tel: 01/588 85, box office daily 10–7) opposite the Naschmarkt hosts a vast array of highbrow cultural events, including opera, classical concerts, ballet and children's performances. Check www.theater-wien.at for the lastest schedule.

Belvedere, Prater and Danube

Getting Your Bearings

This area of the city, with both the Belvedere Palace and stunning buildings of Friedensreich Hundertwasser, has exciting architecture of very different styles. Juxtaposing these are the Prater and the banks of the Danube, Vienna's great relaxation and recreation grounds.

The Belvedere, Prince Eugene's palace, is a grandiose baroque edifice set in a magnificent park. And the architect Friedensreich Hundertwasser, with his colourful, adventurous buildings, created structures well beyond the ordinary. With its vast stretches of wood and meadow, the Prater simply invites you to take a walk, relax in the sun or play sport. One part of "Vienna's green lung", the Wurstelprater, is however reserved for another branch of fun: for many years the funfair with its dodgem cars, ghost ride and hall of mirrors has provided the Viennese with entertainment and a jolly good time.

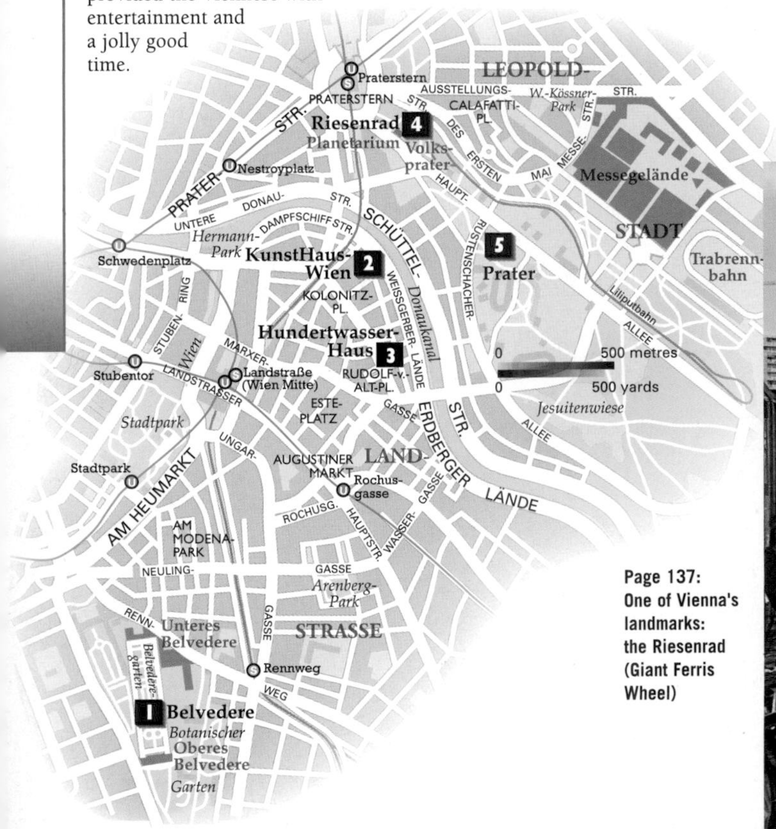

**Page 137:
One of Vienna's landmarks:
the Riesenrad
(Giant Ferris
Wheel)**

Thanks to the Danube, Vienna has a beach. The Gänsehäufel (a bathing beach), Old Danube and Danube Island are the places where the Viennese can play sport and enjoy a bathe – otherwise it would have to be the city baths. And on Copa Cagrana it's holiday-time all summer long, with wonderful aromas of multiethnic food and resounding music from distant lands filling the air.

On Donauinsel (Danube Island) you'll know you're on holiday

★ Don't Miss

1 Belvedere ➤ 142
2 KunstHausWien ➤ 144
4 Riesenrad ➤ 146
5 Prater ➤ 148

At Your Leisure

3 Hundertwasser-Haus ➤ 152
6 Gänsehäufel ➤ 152
7 Alte Donau ➤ 153
8 Donauinsel ➤ 153

First you'll immerse yourself in baroque architecture and works of art, then in the eccentrically colourful world of Friedensreich Hundertwasser. The rest of the day is devoted to pure pleasure: in the Prater and along the Danube, fun entertainment and relaxation are the order of the day.

Belvedere, Prater and Danube in a Day

9:00 am

The day starts with the **❶ Belvedere** (➤ 142). In the Upper Belvedere you'll find the splendid baroque architecture of the palace and the magnificent paintings of Klimt, Kokoschka and Schiele. Before you walk through the park to the Lower Belvedere (below), stop to take in the view of the city spread out before you. Then you'll understand the name of the palace: Belvedere – beautiful view.

11:00 am

Friedensreich Hundertwasser's **❷ KunstHausWien** (➤ 144)) is as demanding on your feet as it is on your eyes. The undulating floor forces you to tread carefully, and you also have to cope with the abundance of colours and forms that crowd in on you. But as you make

your way through the exhibition halls, you'll find that the surroundings take less getting used to than you first thought – and that in the end you don't really want to leave. But you don't have to, because there's a café with a beautiful garden where you can continue, absorbing the unique atmosphere.

12:30 pm

After a visit to the multicoloured world of Hundertwasser the reality outside looks rather grey. But this impression soon vanishes in the **5 Prater** (above; ➤ 148). Here everything is colourful and noisy. Ride the **4 Riesenrad** (➤ 146), and then plunge into the throng. Want a snot of adrenalin? Try the wild Volare (big dipper). before hopping on the Liliput railway for a miniature sightseeing tour. Then lunch at Schweizerhaus (➤ 155) – the house special is *Stelze* (pigs' trotters) washed down with a fine Czech beer.

3:30 pm

Drink your coffee in the peace and calm of the Lusthaus (left; ➤ 155). After all the turmoil a little time out is called for – you still have the Danube to explore.

5:00 pm

A bit of jogging or a refreshing bathe in the river? You can do either on the **8 Donauinsel** (Danube Island ➤ 153), but be careful to reserve enough energy if you plan to pub-crawl at Copa Cagrana (➤ 158). If not, simply enjoy the sunset.

7:30 pm

You could carouse into the small hours at Copa Cagrana, dancing to the sounds of sirtaki or salsa, and quite likely you will want to, but there are many alternatives. One would be to spend the evening in the Tribüne Krieau open-air cinema (➤ 18).

❶ Belvedere

The Belvedere complex, with its magnificent gardens, represents the apex of perfection in baroque architecture. This world-famous palace, which lies on a low hill outside Vienna, houses great works of art. It also offers an incomparable view of the city.

Prince Eugene of Savoy (1663–1736) was anything but handsome. Small and not very sociable, he wasn't the image of a dazzling hero. And yet the prince, who was born in Paris, became the most important military commander of his day. It was thanks to his strategic skill that Austria defeated the Turks and won significant victories in the War of the Spanish Succession (1701–14).

These victories paved the way for the Habsburgs' rise to power, and for that they didn't mind spending a bit. The size of Prince Eugene's reward can be guessed by looking at the Belvedere: the prince spared no expense, when in 1714 he commissioned Johann Lukas von Hildebrandt to build his summer palace, which is really two palaces in one.

Oberes Belvedere

The Upper Belvedere is the more sumptuous of the two. From the beginning it was only intended for grand events, and was furnished accordingly. The facade alone conveys the feeling of baroque luxuriance. This impression is reinforced inside by Santino Bussi's white stucco in the **Sala terrena** and Carlo Carlone's frescoes in the **Gartensaal** (Garden Room) and **Marmorsaal** (Marble Room). Prince Eugene never lived in his grand palace, but later it housed some famous personalities. In 1896 the composer Anton Bruckner spent the last year of his life here. Afterwards, it was the residence of the heir to the throne, Franz Ferdinand. After his assassination in 1914 in Sarajevo the palace stood empty for years. In 1955 it saw a historic

The Upper Belvedere, a showcase palace

The Marmorsaal is the centrepiece of the Lower Belvedere

event: in the Marmorsaal the Allies' foreign ministers signed the Austrian Treaty, and Chancellor Leopold Figl spoke the legendary words: "Austria is free!" from the balcony.

The Upper Belvedere now houses the Austrian 19th- and 20th-Century Gallery, an important collection of Austrian art. The highlights include paintings by Klimt (*The Kiss* hangs on the first floor in Room 4), Schiele, Kokoschka and Waldmüller.

Unteres Belvedere

The way to the Lower Belvedere leads through an extensive park with a view over Vienna. From the outside the palace looks almost modest, but the rooms are really something. Here, too, the centrepiece is a frescoed **Marmorsaal**, but the **Goldkabinett** and the **Marmorgalerie** (Marble Gallery) are no less sumptuous. The Baroque Museum is here, and the Museum of Medieval Art is in the Orangery.

TAKING A BREAK

Have a piece of Belvedere *Torte* in the café-restaurant **Schloss Belvedere** (➤ 157).

➕ 195 D1 ✉ Oberes Belvedere: Wien 3, Prinz-Eugen-Strasse 27; Unteres Belvedere: Wien 3, Rennweg 6 ☎ (01) 795 57-0 🕑 Tue–Sun 10–6; Oberes Belvedere also until 9 on Wed 🚊 Oberes Belvedere: Tram D Schloss Belvedere, Tram 0. 18, Bus 13A Südbahnhof; Unteres Belvedere: Tram 71 Unteres Belvedere 💰 Expensive ❓ www.belvedere.at

---

BELVEDERE: INSIDE INFO

Top tip "Einblicke" (Insights) is the name of the 30-minute guided tour which takes you round the **gallery's highlights** (Fri–Sun and during school holidays Tue–Sun 11 am).

Hidden gem If you're thinking of getting married in Vienna, the palace chapel in the Upper Belvedere provides a suitably grand setting for your vows.

2 KunstHausWien

This building, designed by Friedensreich Hundertwasser, is a museum that obeys none of the accepted norms. Colourful, curving and cheerful, it's a modern architectural adventure, striving to unite the creativity of nature and the creativity of man, an extraordinary experience for eyes and feet.

When at the end of the 1980s an appropriate home was being sought for the Austrian painter Friedensreich Hundertwasser's (1928–2000) extensive work, Vienna's third district offered the former furniture factory (1892) of the Thonet Brothers, near the Danube Canal. It took two years (1989–91) to adapt the site, making two houses into one. When it was opened in April 1991 it was a sensation.

A Bastion Against the False Dominance of the Straight Line

The master-architect oversaw the design of the museum himself. "The architecture of KunstHausWien is the first bastion against the dictatorship of the straight line, the ruler and T-square, a bridgehead against the grid system and the chaos of the absurd," he announced, leaving not a stone standing. He added a porch on the street side and a staircase on the courtyard side. Within the house his treatment of every room on the four floors was highly unusual. Colourful pillars, curving lines, coloured window-frames and bright tiles make it into a fantastic Villa Motley.

The most important stylistic device is that in many areas the floors undulate in great irregular waves. You can't just wander through without watching where you put your feet. This is a quite new experience, for which Hundertwasser

Feast your eyes on Hundert-wasser's colour-soaked paintings

Don't get confused!

Despite appearances, the Hundertwasser-Haus and the KunstHausWien are not one and the same. The former was built by Hundertwasser as a private residence for the city of Vienna (left; ► 152), and the latter, also built by Hundertwasser, is the museum described here.

evolved his very own theory: "An uneven and animated floor restores the human dignity, which has been violated in our levelling, unnatural and hostile urban grid system." The asphalted floors beloved by his contemporaries, he felt, were alienating man from his relationship with nature.

Hundertwasser and Other Artists

KunstHausWien is privately financed, with no public subsidies or taxpayers' money. It has a total exhibition space of around 4,000sq m (4,780 square yards). The ground floor houses the ticket-counters, cloakrooms, museum shop and a café-restaurant. The first and second floors house a permanent exhibition with a wide cross-section of Hundertwasser's work: paintings, drawings, tapestries and architectural models. The third and fourth floors are reserved for changing international exhibitions, including for example, the photographic work of Cecil Beaton and Lord Snowdon. The exhibitions' high standard generally attracts a large public.

TAKING A BREAK

If after touring the museum you can't yet tear yourself away from the bright colours and curving lines, spend a while in the **KunstHausCafé** (► 157). Enjoy and marvel at the extraordinary atmosphere – you won't easily find its like anywhere else in the world.

Not of this world: the garden of the KunstHaus-Wien café

➕ 195 F4 ✉ Wien 3, Untere Weissgerberstrasse 13 ☎ (01) 712 04 91
🕐 Daily 10am–7pm 🚇 Schwedenplatz 🚋 Tram N, O Radetzkyplatz
💶 Expensive ❓ www.kunsthauswien.com

④ Riesenrad

After Stephansdom, the second big emblem of Vienna is the Giant Ferris Wheel, visible from far and wide. The fact that it was rebuilt after World War II, at almost the same time as Stephansdom and "Steffl", shows how important it is to the Viennese, at the very least as a powerful symbol of the city's will to survive.

Emperor Franz Joseph's Golden Jubilee was what prompted Vienna, following the contemporary trend, to get itself a giant panoramic wheel. The commission went to the British engineer Walter Basset, who built it between 1896 and 1897. Admittedly, his designs were not unique to Vienna: he also constructed similar panoramic wheels for London, Blackpool, Chicago and Paris.

Instant Success

The giant wheel was a hit with the public from the outset. The Viennese enjoyed looking down from one of the 30 red cars on their town and "Venedig in Wien" (Venice in Vienna; ► 149). The technical data is also impressive (► opposite), and from the 1920s onwards the wheel was frequently used as a film location – scenes from *The Third Man* (1949) by Carol Reed were shot here. In 1944 the mighty mechanism came to a halt when it was damaged by a fire. But it was soon repaired and in 1947 the big wheel began turning again. For safety reasons, the wheel has operated with only 15 cars since then. Visitor numbers show how popular the leisurely

The giant wheel was an instant attraction

journey into the airy heights is: since the 1950s, some 30 million people have travelled on it. There are two luxury wagons – one in the style of 1892, the other in Jugendstil.

The Riesenrad today, as popular as ever

In the Course of Time

The Riesenrad doesn't just turn in a circle – it has recently experienced radical new additions. In 2002, eight cars that had been lost reappeared. They are now set up at the wheel's base, with lavish technical installations and a giant screen inviting visitors to take a virtual tour through 2,000 years of Vienna's history. And at night, thanks to installations by the British light-artist Patrick Woodroffe, it is bathed in different colours: the wheel shines a soft gold, while the pylons are cool silver.

Technical data
- highest point: 64.75m (212.43 feet) above ground level
- wheel diameter: 60.96m (200 feet)
- axis of the wheel: 10.78m (35.37 feet) long, 0.5m (1.64 feet) thick, 16.3t (16.04 tons) in weight
- weight – entire structure: 244.35t (240.98 tons); all iron structures: 430.05t (423.26)
- speed: 0.75m/sec (2.46 ft/sec = 2.7km/h (1.68mph)

TAKING A BREAK

With its large terrace, the new, stylish **Café** by the entrance to the ticket-hall is a good place for some refreshments before or after your "trip aloft".

➕ 196 A5 ✉ Wien 2, Prater 20 ☎ (01) 729 54 30 🕐 May–Sep daily 9am–11:45pm; Mar–Apr, Oct 10–9:45; Jan–Feb, Nov–Dec 10–7 45
🚇 Praterstern 🚊 Tram 0, 5, 21 Praterstern 💰 Expensive
❓ www.wienerriesenrad.com

RIESENRAD: INSIDE INFO

Top tips Make sure you see the Riesenrad by **night**, because after dark it becomes a clock-tower, sending out light signals instead of acoustic ones. Two minutes before each hour it starts to flash out the number of hours. If it flashes twice, you know it's two in the morning. And if it flashes three times, then the Viennese know it's time to hit the sack – t's 3am.

• The Riesenrad's cars can also be **hired** – for small parties, press conferences, a romantic dîner à deux ... whatever. It costs €98 for half an hour and €196 for one hour in ordinary cars. For the privilege of riding in one of the two luxury cars it's €260 for the first hour, €188 for the second and €116 for the third. Could there be a more romantic place to pop the question?

5 Prater

A quiet place to relax from the bustle of the city and a vibrant, noisy pleasure-ground – the Prater is both, which makes it Vienna's leisure wonderland.

Once a real hit with the Viennese: the "Russian swings"

The history of the Prater is as varied as its attractions: once it was a swampy meadowland, then an imperial forest and hunting grounds, and finally it became one of the world's first pleasure-gardens. Today the 6sq km (2.3square-mile) area contains old horse-racing tracks and the modern exhibition centre, idyllic avenues and thrilling fairground attractions.

From Water Meadow to Day-Trip Destination

For a long time the Prater was owned by various monasteries and aristocratic families, until in 1564 Maximilian II declared it a Habsburg hunting preserve. The populace was excluded from the attractive stretch of countryside until Emperor Joseph II opened the Prater to all. Soon after, pub

The Lusthaus was always a destination for romantic outings

Above left: The indestructible nostalgic chute "Tobogan"

landlords, coffee-brewers and gingerbread sellers set up their stalls at the western end, followed by swings, merry-go-rounds and skittle-alleys – the Wurstelprater (funfair) was born. In 1814 the Congress of Vienna was celebrated here in 40 inns, 50 skittle-alleys and several coffee-houses. The "Volksprater" (People's Prater) became a European tourist site whose fame reached its climax with the World Exhibition of 1873. That was when the fairground "Venedig in Wien" (Venice in

Above right: "Volare" is not for those with weak stomachs

Vienna) was unlike the **Riesenrad** (► 146) set up; however, it didn't last. Since 1928 the **Liliputbahn**, a miniature steam loco, puffs its way from the Volksprater along the main avenue to the stadium and back. You'll find the railway station behind the giant wheel (www.liliputbahn.com; admission: moderate).

Above: You can drive off in style at the Freudenau golf club

The Green Prater

The greater part of the Prater area is taken up by the "green Prater", broad stretches of natural country with meadows, woods and ponds. Here you'll also find the modern exhibition centre, a golf course, the Ernst Happel stadium and the stadium swimming baths. The splendid chestnut avenue, almost 5km (3 miles) long, which leads from the Lusthaus to the Praterstern (star), was planted in 1537 by Emperor Ferdinand I. Here wealthy Viennese used to stroll, Napoleon's troops paraded here, and at the Congress of Vienna they danced in the coffee-houses

The Pratermuseum

In the planetarium near the Riesenrad, the Pratermuseum traces the spectacular history of the Viennese Prater (tel: 01/726 76 83 Tue–Fri 9–12:15, 1–4:30, Sat–Sun and public holidays 2–6:30. Admission: inexpensive, Fri am and Sun: free).

The view from the Blumenrad is tremendous

in the avenue. Today it's crowded with runners, cyclists and skateboarders, as since 1963 cars have been banned from the **Prater Hauptallee** (the Prater's main avenue). The **Jesuitenwiese** (Jesuits' Meadow) has the largest playing fields in Vienna, and here and in the numerous other playing fields and campsites there's ample space to play football or just hang out. Next to the **Lusthaus** (▶ 155) is the **Freudenau**, where the horse racing and the listed imperial lodge are well worth seeing.

Wiener Wurstelprater

This popular entertainment area takes its name from the Hanswurst (clown) who used to amuse the children in the puppet theatres. In the early years visitors were enticed into the Prater by sensational events such as waxworks, the Prater variety show, the vivarium or strange freak-shows. It always had the most modern attractions: the first steam carousel in 1844, the first cinema in 1896, the Riesenrad in 1897. After it was destroyed in World War II, the Wurstelprater was rebuilt, but on a smaller scale. Every year it produces more amazing, faster, wilder and more breathtaking attractions. One of the newest challenges to daredevils eager for thrills is "Volare", a big dipper where you speed along lying flat, at a height of 24m

Who was Calafatti?

You'll come across his name again and again in the Wurstelprater. At one time, Basilius Calafatti, born in 1800 in Trieste, was the uncrowned king of the Prater. With his wife and nine children the small-time salami and cheese merchant built up a mini-empire, performed as a magician in front of the emperor and had the first steam carousel constructed. In the middle of this merry-go-round stood a 10m (33-foot) tall figure with exotic features, the "Great Chinaman", which became the emblem of the Prater and was erected again after the war. From its position on Calafatti-platz it reminds us still of the Prater pioneer.

For kids

In the vast area of **Kids Welt** (Kids' World) your children can, for a single entry fee, let off steam in many attractions while you relax at your table (Strasse des Ersten Mai 118, tel: 01/729 51 02; daily Mar–Oct 10–7, admission: expensive

(79 feet), through a 420m (460-yard) long jungle of rails (at Calafattiplatz). But some traditional activities have also stood the test of time, for example the 1887 Ponykarussell (opposite the Schweizerhaus), the wooden **Zwergerl-Hochschaubahn** (Miniature Railway, by the bike-hire) and the nostalgic chute "**Tobogan**" from the 1950s. Antique

attractions beside high-tech slot-machines, the chance of a win in the amusement arcades, rapid dodgem cars, plenty of music and still more fun – this is how the Wurstelprater presents itself today.

Top choice on the Schweizerhaus menu: *Stelzen* (pig's trotters)

TAKING A BREAK

The **Meierei** (Dairy) can be found in the main avenue (May–Sep). In 1873 "American drinks" were served in the pavilion of the World Exhibition. later it was mineral water, from 1924 sweet and soured milk, and now there's the usual café-restaurant menu, with traditional Viennese and light, modern fare.

🔢 196 A–C 1–5 🕐 **Attractions**: Easter–Oct 10am–1am 🚇 Praterstern 🚋 **Tram** 0, 5, 21 Praterstern ❓ www.prater.at

PRATER: INSIDE INFO

Top tips Take a trip on the 35m (115-foot) high **Blumenrad** (Flower Wheel; inexpensive), a smaller version of the Riesenrad. In the early evening the view from the revolving cars is spectacular.
• **Cycling** is a great way to explore the "green Prater". You can hire bikes by the Schweizerhaus, or the main avenue side (tel: 01/729 58 88, www.radverleih-hochschaubahn.com).

Hidden gem Behind the box office of Europe's biggest and longest **Geisterbahn** (Ghost Train, Zufahrtstrasse 143) sits a Prater character: the producer and actor Hermann Molzer. He had theatrical pictures mounted along the track and is always ready with some nice stories about the Prater.

One to miss Beautiful though it is in daytime, the green Prater can be dark and distinctly **unpleasant at night**. It is therefore best avoided at this time – stay on the illuminated roads.

At Your Leisure

3 Hundertwasser-Haus

The Hundertwasser House on the corner of Löwengasse and Kegelgasse is a colourful oasis in a grey urban desert. In a district where the buildings are mainly modest, so-called "period" houses or social housing, you suddenly come across a building with riotous shapes and brilliant colours. It consists of a jumble of windows of various sizes and with different frames, small balconies, bow-windows, strips of mosaic, onion towers and pillars, hanging gardens, and trees and shrubs sprouting from terraces and roof. Friedensreich Hundertwasser designed this building with 50 apartments in 1983–85. The crazy "eco-architecture" is continued inside the house. Out of respect for the privacy of the tenants, many of whom knew the artist, the building can only be seen from the outside, but it's well worth it.

➕ 195 F3 ✉ Wien 3, corner Löwengasse/ Kegelgasse 🚃 Tram N Hetzgasse

Friedrich Stowasser

Friedensreich Hundertwasser was born Friedrich Stowasser in 1928 in Vienna. The *enfant terrible* of the artistic world, he developed a unique, very colourful pictorial language and carried out numerous architectural projects in Austria, Germany, Switzerland, California and Japan. New Zealand became his second home. He died of a heart attack in 2000, on the *Queen Elizabeth II* in the Pacific Ocean.

6 Gänsehäufel

The Gänsehäufel is something of a Viennese institution. Its history is closely linked to the rise of the workers' movement and the development of an independent culture of physical activity. In 1907 the city of Vienna took over the island in the Old Danube and constructed there the first civic bathing beach with changing rooms for 4,000 people. In 1926–27 the island was linked by a bridge to the "Viennese mainland". During bombing raids in World War II the complex suffered 130 hits and was severely damaged. Rebuilding was a high priority for the city. This was quickly done,

One of the oldest bathing beaches: the Gänsehäufel

On the other side of the Danube, high-rise residential and office blocks are creating a modern district

and thousands of Viennese could once again occupy their cabins and enjoy the summer on the Danube beach. With a total area of 33ha (82 acres) and a length of 1,000m (1,100 yards), the Gänsehäufel is now the biggest inland bathing beach in Europe.

➕ 197 F2/3 ✉ Wien 22, Moissigasse 21 ☎ (01) 269 90 16 🕐 In summer Mon–Fri 9–8, Sat–Sun 8am–8pm 🚇 Kaisermühlen 🚌 Bäderbus (baths bus) from U-Bahn station Kaisermühlen ✋ Moderate

7 Alte Donau

The 1870–75 regulation of the Danube created in the north-east of the city the Old Danube, a lake no longer joined to the river.
By 1900 it had already become a bathers' paradise, which it still is today. In summer the Viennese flock here to swim, sail and row. Between the New and the Old Danube lies the Danube Park. Formerly the site of the 1964 Viennese International Horticultural Show, it is now a leisure park with footpaths and cycle lanes. The 252m

(827-foot) high Donauturm (Danube Tower) which rises above the park has a revolving restaurant offering splendid views. The mosque and minaret of the Islamic Centre on the nearby Hubertusdamm are also sure to catch your eye.

➕ 197 D5–F4 🚇 Alte Donau 🚌 Bus 20B Alte Donau

8 Donauinsel

When, in order to control flooding, a second river bed was excavated in the 1970s, an island (Donauinsel) was created. 21km (13 miles) long and 200m (220 yards) wide. It became a leisure paradise for the Viennese. Cyclists, joggers, roller-bladers and walkers are undisturbed by traffic here. The Schotterstrände (pebble beaches), some 40km (25 miles) long, are great for sunbathing and swimming, with a view of an exciting skyline. Surrounding UNO-City, which is shaped like a huge Y, an ultramodern district has arisen, with the Austria Centre, the Andromeda Tower, the residential park Donau-City and a series of glass-and-steel office tower blocks. As a counterpoise, the Millennium Tower soars into the sky on the other side of the Danube.

➕ 197 D2/3–F1 🚇 Donauinsel

Where to...
Eat and Drink

Prices

Prices are for a meal for one person, excluding drinks.
€ under €15 €€ €15–€30 €€€ over €30

RESTAURANTS

Altes Jägerhaus €€

This inn with its four old-fashioned dining rooms and beautiful, large garden is immediately opposite the Lusthaus. The menu offers a wide range of interesting Viennese dishes, including the ever-popular Wiener Schnitzel, as well as many seasonal and fish specialities. The delicious pastries are made in-house, and the long wine list includes both Austrian and international wines.

✚ 196, east of C1 ⊠ Wien 2, Freudenau 255 ☎ (01) 728 95 77 ⏰ Apr–Sep daily 9am–11pm (hot food 11:30–10); Oct–Dec, Mar Wed–Sun 9am–11pm (hot food 11:30–10); Jan–Feb Wed–Sun 9–6 (hot food 11:30–5) 🚌 Bus 77A Lusthaus

Amon €€

Refurbished from the bottom up, Amon specialises in traditional Viennese dishes like Wurzelfleisch (meat with root vegetables) and Zwiebelrostbraten (onion roast). It still puts on its popular specialities weeks, offering dishes from a particular region or country, but in the front of house, a wine and beer bar has been added, the conservatory and the gardens have been redesigned, and there's an indoor play area for children. In the "vinotheque" regular customers can settle in with wine boxes. House specialities are also available to take away.

✚ 196 B1 ⊠ Wien 3, Schlachthausgasse 13 ☎ (01) 798 81 66 ⏰ Mon–Sat 10am–midnight, Sun 10–4 Ⓤ Schlachthausgasse 🚋 Tram 18A 🚌 Erdbergstrasse: Bus 74A, 77A, 79A, 80A, 80B, 83A, 84A Schlachthausgasse

Contor €€

Contor is a tiny slice of Spain in a very Viennese neighbourhood. There are delicious tapas aplenty but even so their number is outweighed by the choice of wines on offer. The atmosphere is calm and cosy, and impromptu Spanish guitar concerts are occasionally held here, making it a perfect place for a romantic evening.

✚ 195 D5 ⊠ Wien 2, Leopoldsgasse 51 ☎ (01) 219 63 16 ⏰ Mon–Thu 5pm–1am, Fri 5pm–2am, Sat 10am–2am 🚋 Tram 21, N Karmeliterplatz, Bus 5A Karmeliterplatz

Gesundes €

Gesundes specialises in healthy food, hence the name (literally "healthy"). All dishes are vegetarian, some are vegan, and everything is prepared in accordance with the Chinese five elements. The menu changes daily and uses ingredients in season. The experienced chefs also offer cooking courses.

✚ 193 E5 ⊠ Wien 2, Lilienbrunngasse 3 ☎ (01) 219 53 22 ⏰ Mon–Sat 9–3 Ⓤ Schwedenplatz 🚋 Tram 21, N Lilienbrunngasse

Hansy €

On one of the busiest traffic spots in the city, the corner of Praterstern and Praterstrasse, Hansy is all that a good traditional Viennese inn should be. The bar is tiled, the furnishings simple and the garden spacious. Good plain cooking and seasonal specialities are available all day – and they brew their own beer, "Hausy-Bräu", also available as a wheat or a strong beer.

┼ 195 E5 **⊠** Wien 2, Praterstrasse 67 **◷** Daily 9am–11pm **ⓠ** Praterstern **█** Tram 5, 21, 0; Bus 80A Praterstern

Kiang €€

Once you've made your way through the blue entrance cube, you'll find yourself in what seems like a germ-free lab. But the coolly minimalist styling of Kiang is complemented by one of Vienna's most interesting Asian menus. As well as sushi there are frequently changing chef's recommendations

┼ 195 F2 **⊠** Wien 3, Landstrasser Hauptstrasse 50 **☎** (01) 715 34 70 **◷** Daily 11:30–3, 6–11:30 **ⓠ** Rochusgasse **█** Bus 4A, 74A Rochusgasse

Lusthaus €€

This delightful pavilion at the end of the main Prater avenue has a long history. From 1560 a small

hunting lodge stood on this spot, called the "Grünes Lusthaus". Emperor Joseph II commissioned architect Isidore Canavale to remodel it, and in 1781 he converted the single-storey building into its present octagonal form, with eight columns and a balcony running around its edge. As you drink your coffee on the little terrace or dine on fine Viennese cuisine in the restaurant, you can still feel the atmosphere of the imperial era: the menu includes truffles and stag, Barbary duck and pike perch. The Lusthaus is popular for family celebrations and company functions. Booking is advisable for evenings.

┼ 196, east of C1 **⊠** Wien 2, Freudenau 254 **☎** (01) 728 95 65 **◷** May–Sep Mon–Tue, Thu–Fri noon– 11, Sat–Sun noon–6; Oct–Apr Thu–Tue noon–6 **█** Bus 77A Lusthaus

Salm Bräu €

This traditional brewery tavern is in the cellars of the baroque Salesian

monastery. The beers, brewed from historical recipes, are first-class. The food is simple, hearty and good, and during the week there's an inexpensive set menu.

┼ 195 E1 **⊠** Wien 3, Rennweg 8 **☎** (01) 799 59 92 **◷** Daily 11am– midnight (hot food until 11) **█** Tram 71 Unteres Belvedere

Schöne Perle €

This pearl of a restaurant has an ever-changing menu filled with modern takes on classic Viennese dishes. Only organic ingredients are used, and generally only what's in season. The decor is suitably modern and minimalist, and there's a brilliant table. Going against the general trend of Viennese restaurants, children are very welcome here, but dogs are not.

┼ 195 D5 **⊠** Wien 2, Grosse Pfarrgasse 7 **☎** (0664) 243 35 93 **◷** Mon–Fri noon–midnight, Sat–Sun 11am–midnight (hot food till 11) **█** Tram 21, N Karmeliterplatz; Bus 5A Karmelitermarkt

Schweizerhaus €

Karl Kolarik's Schweizerhaus in the Prater is famous for serving the crispest Stelzen (pigs' trotters) and the best-kept draught Czech Budvar beer in Vienna. But it has much more: it's also known for authentic Bohemian specialities such as Spiegelkarpfen (mirror carp) and Szegedin goulash. The atmosphere in the enormous beer garden, with room for 1,300 people, is always great.

┼ 196 A5 **⊠** Wien 2, Strasse des Ersten Mai 116 **☎** (01) 728 01 52–13 **◷** 15 Mar–Oct Mon–Fri 11–11, Sat–Sun 10am–11pm **ⓠ** Praterstern **█** Tram 5, 21, 0; Bus 80A Praterstern

Seidl €

Seidl is a typical Old Viennese inn with cosy alcoves. The cooking is also Viennese, delicate but genuine and far removed from fashionable affectations. The roast chicken is said to be among the best in town, and the roast liver and goulash are also a dream. The wine list is substantial, with a choice of 400 different wines. Once a month there's a set menu with wine.

195 E2 ⊠ Wien 3, Ungargasse 63 ☎ (01) 713 17 81 ⚑ Mon–Fri 10am–11pm (hot food 11–10) ⛙ Tram 0 Neulinggasse

Stadtwirt €

This establishment has three parts: a bar with stand-up tables to the right of the entrance, an inn for light dishes and drinks to the left, and a smart restaurant in the rear. The food is modern Viennese and first-class Burgenland/Upper Austrian at affordable prices. The place is always crammed full, so booking is essential.

195 E3 ⊠ Wien 3, Untere Viaduktgasse 45 ☎ (01) 713 38 28 ⚑ Mon–Fri 10am–midnight, Sat 4pm–1am (hot food until 11), Sun 11–4 ⛙ Landstrasse/Wien Mitte ⛙ Tram 0, Bus 74A Landstrasse/Wien Mitte

Steirereck €€€

The Reitbauer family's legendary Michelin-starred Steirereck is one of the best restaurants in Austria. In 2004 it moved from Rasumofsky-gasse to the Stadtpark. In its new, romantic setting the standard of its "new Viennese cuisine" remains first-class, and the selection of breads, cheeses, wines and whiskies is outstanding.

195 D3 ⊠ Wien 3, Meierei im Stadtpark ☎ (01) 713 31 68 ⚑ Mon–Fri 11:30–3, 6:30–midnight ⛙ Landstrasse/Wien-Mitte ⛙ Tram 0; Bus 74A Landstrasse/Wien-Mitte

Wild €€

This typically cosy Viennese tavern on Radetzkyplatz specializes in regional cooking. The most popular dishes are classics, including offal, though prepared with imaginative additions – try the roast liver, for example. For weekday lunch there are two menus, one vegetarian, one meat. Neither are at all expensive.

195 F4 ⊠ Wien 3, Radetzkyplatz 1 ☎ (01) 920 94 77 ⚑ Daily 10am–1am (hot food Mon–Sat 11am–11:30pm, Sun 11–10) ⛙ Landstrasse/Wien Mitte ⛙ Tram N, 0 Radetzkyplatz

Taverna Lefteris €€

The Greek owner comes from Crete, and his taverna is one of the best Greek restaurants in the city. The atmosphere is Mediterranean and welcoming. The bread is home-baked, and the choice of mezes is impressive. The owner strives to prove that he can serve more than the well-known classics, but nowhere else does a moussaka taste so tempting.

195 F3 ⊠ Wien 3, Hörnesgasse 17 ☎ (01) 713 74 51 ⚑ Mon–Sat 6pm–midnight ⛙ Rochusgasse ⛙ Bus 4A, 74A Rochusgasse

Zur Steirischen Botschaft €

This traditional restaurant, whose name means literally "To the Styrian Embassy," has a garden planted with beautiful old walnut trees. The menu, as is to be expected, majors in Styrian (central Austrian) food, but there are also some inter-national dishes. Salads are made with Kernöl, the nutty pumpkin-seed oil which, because of its dark-green colour, is often mockingly called "Styrian axle-grease". And the numerous wines include the Styrian Schilcher. On weekdays there's a choice of three inexpensive lunch menus.

195 D2 ⊠ Wien 3, Strohgasse 11 ☎ (01) 712 33 67 ⚑ Mon–Fri 11:30 am–11pm, Sun 11am–3pm (hot food until 2:30, 6pm–10pm) ⛙ Landstrasse/Wien Mitte ⛙ Tram 0 Ungargasse; Bus 4A Neulinggasse

CAFÉS

Galerie Zum Hundertwasser-Haus

Besides coffee and cakes or snacks, such as mozzarella and tomato salad, this café offers great views of the stunningly colourful facade of the Hundertwasser-Haus opposite. In summer you can sit in the garden in front of the Hundertwasser-Haus and admire the grand view.

195 F3 ⊠ Wien 3, Kegelgasse 37–39

(01) 961 77 71 · Daily 9am–11pm · Tram N Hetzgasse

KunstHausCafé

This café is just as cheerful, colourful and eccentric as the rest of the KunstHausWien. A hundred different, brightly painted Thonet chairs are placed around tables, assembled from a variety of wooden boards. In summer the garden is sensational for its many wonderful exotic flowers. The food is less eccentric: traditional Viennese, with *Schnitzel* and *Tafelspitz*.

195 F4 · Wien 3, Untere Weissger-berstrasse 13 · (01) 712 04 97 · Daily 10–9 · Schwedenplatz · Tram N, 0 Radetzkyplatz

Schloss Belvedere

The café in the Upper Belvedere, with its beautiful, large garden, is ideal for a short break after a visit to the palace. It serves home-made *torten* (Belvedere-Torte), pastries, snacks and its own ice cream, as well as traditional Viennese dishes, such as *Schinkenfleckerl* (a baked ham and pasta dish), along with Italian pasta. So there's always something for the exhausted tourist.

195 D1 · Wien 3, Prinz-Eugen-Strasse 27 · (01) 798 88 88 · Summer Tue–Sun 10–6; winter Tue–Sun 9–5 · Tram D Schloss Belvedere, Tram 0, 18; Bus 13A Südbahnhof

Zartl

Zartl is one of the finest traditional Viennese coffee-houses with alcoves and a billiard table. The menu has mainly Viennese dishes, and breakfast is served until late. An unusual feature is the side-room where Viennese magicians hold their weekly meetings – though behind closed doors. On Sunday afternoons in winter there's live piano music (3:30–6:30).

195 F3 · Wien 3, Rasumofskygasse 7 · (01) 712 55 60 · Daily 8am–midnight · Rochusgasse · Tram N; Bus 4A Rasumofskygasse

Where to... Shop

Vienna's third district is well supplied with shops for both tourists and locals. Visitors to the city will strike it lucky above all in the museum shops.

Landstrasser Hauptstrasse has been renewed in stages over the past few years. With its numerous businesses, it is the shopping street with the greatest turnover in District 3, home to one interesting shop after another. There are boutiques, shoe shops, perfumeries and, of course, supermarkets. And dotted amongst them are cafés to satisfy the thirsty and hungry. At the start of the street, the market in the Wien-Mitte Centre provides an abundance of fresh groceries, meat and vegetables. For visitors, the greengrocers and delicatessens in the **Rochusmarkt** are particularly inviting. **Arrigo's** wine-merchants (Rochusmarkt, Stand 33) stocks a superb selection of fine Italian, Spanish and Austrian wines and delicatessen items.

For imaginative presents for the children back home try **Norbert Navara** (Ausstellungsstrasse 63), which stocks a wide range of wooden toys, hand puppets, old-fashioned toys and kaleidoscopes to please any child.

Museum shops are the place for unusual and intriguing gifts. The shop in **KunstHausWien** is a treasure trove of diaries, mugs, wrapping paper, roller-pens, key-rings, silk scarves and posters with Hundertwasser motifs. The shops in the Upper and Lower **Belvedere** have a similar selection of objects for all occasions, this time featuring motifs relating to the palaces, as well as Gustav Klimt's designs. There are shawls and umbrellas, beautiful art books, diaries, jewellery and posters.

Where to be... Entertained

In this part of Vienna every evening can be party night. The name Copa Cagrana, which comes from the neighbouring district of Kagran, has become a synonym for fun, celebrations and long nights (and early mornings) by the Danube. On this part of Danube Island new pubs are always springing up, but there's plenty of other nightlife to discover.

Copa Cagrana

In the balmy summer months, from March to October, night owls, thrill-seekers and gourmets flock to the open-air bars and pubs in this fun-filled district (take U-Bahn 1 to Donauinsel for Copa Cagrana).

Rembetiko (left bank, tel: 01/263 66 33, daily 10am–2am) is a Greek taverna, popular for its fish and lamb dishes.

The **Ios** (left bank, tel: 01/263 35 04, daily 11am–2am) next doorputs its customers in holiday mood with barbecued kebabs, retsina and ouzo, plus obligatory sirtaki music.

All' Isola (the last bar on Copa Cagrana, tel: 06645/57 10 83, daily 10am–2am) has the finest Italian cuisine here, with delicious *antipasti* (snacks), fresh fish and sophisticated pasta dishes.

MUSIC

Since May 2004, top performers of jazz, pop and world music have appeared at **Birdland** (Landstrasser Hauptstrasse 2, Hilton Vienna, tel: 01/21 96 39 3, daily 6pm–2am), the former bar of Austrian jazz legend and keyboard artist Joe Zawinul, who died in September 2007. The sophisticated jazz club is named after the legendary Birdland in New York, for which this club is meant to become a worthy counterpart.

International cooking provides culinary pleasures to accompany the musical ones. Joe Zawinul's favourite dish, *Paprikahendl* (chicken paprika), is always on the menu.

BARS

In **A bar shabu** (corner of Rotensterngasse and Glockengasse, tel: 0650/544 59 39, daily 5pm–4am) not everything revolves around a high-alcohol green drink, but a lot does. A glance at its name will tell you that – this small bar in District 2 proudly bears the sub-title "Absinth Bar". It also frequently puts on exciting art projects.

If for nothing else, the small **Biedermeier-Bar** in the Mercure Hotel (Landstrasser Hauptstrasse 28, tel: 01/71 67 15 28, daily 5:30pm–1am) is worth seeing for its beautiful early 19th-century surroundings in Sünnhof, which won the 1984 Europa Nostra Prize. It's fitted out in Biedermeier style, with cherry-wood furniture.

Excellent classic cocktails are served to pleasant live piano music. **Fluc** (Praterstern 5, tel: 01/218 28 24), daily 6pm–4am) is one of the city's edgiest bars. The clientele is a mix of students, artists, drunks and the occasional TV celebrity, and the music – live or DJ-supplied – is always contemporary and loud. If you're looking for the bar and arrive at a prefab schoolroom, you've come to the right place.

More absinth drinks, plus vodka, gin and whisky mixes, awaits visitors to the **Hamburg Bar** (Neulinggasse 21, tel: 01/718 98 18, Tue–Sat 6pm–midnight), but there are also hangover drinks and non-alcoholic choices. The American Bar plays jazzy background music, and sometimes there's live music.

The cocktail bar **Magic** in Vienna's third district (Marxergasse 14, tel: 0676/917 16 13, Mon–Sat 9pm–4am) has a small dance floor. There are snacks on offer, and for entertainment table football or a selection of party games.

Excursions

Vienna is a wonderful city to explore, but it can be just as rewarding discovering the city's surrounds. No matter which direction you point yourself, you'll find something worthy of your time, whether it be an age-old monastery, lush woodlands, scenic wine valley – or another country's capital.

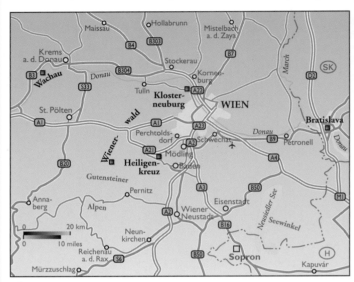

Klosterneuburg

The Augustinian abbey of Klosterneuburg is often likened to Spain's Escorial palace, not least because of its great size. It has become a world-famous site thanks to its art treasures and superb wines.

The abbey of Klosterneuburg was founded in the early 1100s by Babenberg Leopold III. By 1485 the abbey had become the national sanctuary, and, soon after, the treasury for the national crown. Karl VI began to extend the Klosterneuburg in 1730, and abbey and imperial palace were merged into one giant baroque complex. When Karl died 10 years later only a quarter of his ambitious plans were realized, but his efforts can still be seen today.

A climb up the **Kaiserstiege**

Page 159: The entrance to the imperial palace at Klosterneuburg

The Marian Column, an expression of profound piety

The medieval towers of the abbey church belong to the oldest part of the complex

(Imperial Stairway) to the **Kaiserzimmer** (Imperial Room), which Karl VI only used for a single night in 1739, reveals the extent of the complex's splendour and wealth. It becomes even more apparent one floor higher up, when you see the valuable collections of the **Stiftsmuseum** (Abbey Museum). Its highlights include an 8m (26-foot) long illustrated Babenberg family tree, panels by Rueland Frueauf the Younger and exquisite ivory carvings.

The fact that the baroque structure remained unfinished is not a l bad for it meant that large parts of the medieval complex were preserved for posterity. The best Romanesque and Gothic vestiges can be seen on the external walls of the **Stifts-kirche** (Abbey Church).

The baroque interior of the abbey and the most valuable treasures can only be seen by guided tour. The tour takes you through the cloisters to the Leopold Chapel where the **Verduner Altar** (Verdun Altar) is kept. Created in 1181 as a pulpit face by goldsmith Nikolaus von Verdun, it has 45 enamel plaques depicting scenes from the Bible. In 1330, it was remodelled as a winged altar. A second Gothic winged altar, the **Albrechts-Altar**, is in the Sebastiani Chapel.

Every year on 15 November (St Leopold's Day) the *fasslrutschen* takes place here: both young and old get the chance to slide over a 300-year-old barrel nicknamed the "1,000 bucket barrel".

Fine wines
A guided tour through the four-storey baroque cellars of Austria's oldest and largest wine-growing estate, including wine-tasting, is an experience not to be missed (Tours daily at 4pm; admission: moderate).

✉ Klosterneuburg, Stiftsplatz 1 ☎ (02243) 411-212 ◉ Stiftsmuseum
Daily 9–6; guided tours daily 10–5 English tours daily at 4pm 💷 Moderate
❓ www.stift-klosterneuburg.at

Directions: 12km (7.5 miles) north of Vienna; train S40, bus 239 to Weidling or Kierling

Wienerwald

The Vienna Woods are often described as a "symphony in green". This green belt bordering the city's western fringes is typical of Austrian countryside, and this excursion, which dips into the southern reaches of the wood, allows visits to charming wine towns and a former imperial spa.

The Vienna Woods passed into Austrian hands in 1002, when the German emperor Heinrich II signed a deed which gifted the lands between Triesting and Liesing to the Babenbergs, the Austrian royals at the time. For nearly 800 years the heart of this large wooded area remained a primeval forest. But at the beginning of the 19th century the Wienerwald was discovered as a romantic recreation ground by Vienna's populace, and it became a popular destination for country outings and summer holidays.

Perchtoldsdorf
Vineyards have long been a dominant feature south of Vienna. Here, one of the most picturesque wine villages is Perchtoldsdorf, whose streets are lined with wine taverns, each of which has romantic vine arbours, flowering oleander and a rustic ambience. Before you settle in the first one, though, take a stroll through the village and visit the restored 14th-century **Herzogsburg** (Ducal Fortress), the Gothic **Hallenkirche** (Hall Church), the **Rathaus** (Town Hall) and the **Wehrturm** (Fortified Tower). The town's ancient walls withstood the Turkish siege in 1683.

Mödling
The neighbouring town of Mödling is today a pulsating commercial hub and an important centre for education. However, its Old Town is still graced with late Gothic and Renaissance manor houses, and a walk through the centre is like stepping back in time. Some of Austria's greatest artists and musicians, such as Schubert, Grillparzer and Waldmüller, once walked these streets, and Beethoven himself spent the summers of 1818 to 1820 here,moving – as he was apt to do – no less than four times. The **Beethoven-Gedenkstätte Hafnerhaus** (Beethoven Memorial) commemorates his years in Mödling.

   Hinterbrühl and the fortress of **Burg Liechtenstein**, Austria's largest secular Romanesque structure, are a favourite destination for excursions from

The charming village of Mödling, with its quaint Old Town

There are fabulous views in the Vienna Woods

Mödling. The **Höldrichsmühle**, a mill, is said to have inspired Schubert's *The Linden Tree*, and the **Seegrotte** has Europe's largest underground lake.

Gumpolds-kirchen and its Vineyards

Gumpoldskirchen has something very special to offer: its idyllic **Weinwander-weg** (Wine Walking Path), which leads up into the vineyards. The strong aroma of vines and soil accompanies this half-hour walk, which winds its way into the hills and offers a series of fine views over the ancient village, its Renaissance estates and the Gothic parish church of St Michael managed by the Deutscher Orden. Along the walk, illustrated boards provide information on the area's viticulture and Rotgipfler and Zierfandler, typical grape varieties around Gumpolds-kirchen. Note the 19th-century cross stations along the way, a testament to the piety of the vinters.

Baden – Chic Spa Town with an Imperial Touch

The lovingly tended small town of Baden possesses a unique ensemble of Bieder-meier-style houses – all thanks to a catastrophe. In 1812

The Vienna Woods are ideal for extensive rambles

a conflagration destroyed the entire town and it was rebuilt in pure neoclassical style. One of the most prolific architects at the time was Josef Kornhäusel, who designed the **Rathaus** (Town Hall), the **Florastöckl** in Frauengasse, **Metternichhof** and the **Theresienschlössl**.

In its heyday during the late Habsburg era, Baden was an elegant spa for those suffering from rheumatism, with its elegant parks, hotels and villas. The spirit of the imperial age can still be felt today, at a concert in the **Kurpark** (Spa Park), in the **Doblhoffpark** with its magnificent roses and at the

Trabrennen (Trotting Race). Numerous splendid villas are also reminders of the higher officials and famous spa guests who used to come here, including Mozart, Schubert, Nestroy and Grillparzer.

While Baden may seem like a picture-book town today, it has a very dynamic economy, having established itself as both a commercial and educational centre. A great attraction for visitors is the **Casino** in the Kurpark, along with the **Römertherme** (Roman Baths), which are lavishly designed and topped by a giant glass roof.

The Baden Casino is more than a gambling house, it's also a venue for glamourous events

Baden is also proud of over 250 years of theatrical traditions. Both director Max Reinhardt and actress Katharina Schratt were born here, and every year the town hosts a popular operetta festival in its Summer Arena.

Hafnerhaus
✉ Mödling, Hauptstrasse 79
☎ (02236) 241 59 🕐 Mon–Wed 9–1
✋ Inexpensive

Hotel-Restaurant Höldrichsmühle
✉ Hinterbrühl, Gaadnerstrasse 34
☎ (02236) 26 27 40 🕐 Daily
11–10 🚌 From Mödling station Bus
364 and 365 to Höldrichsmühle

The Undine fountain in the Kurpark

Seegrotte
✉ Hinterbrühl, Grutschgasse 2a
☎ (02236) 263 64 🕐 Apr–Oct daily 9–5; Nov–Mar daily 9–noon, 1–3,
Sat–Sun until 3:30 🚌 From Mödling station Bus 364 and 365 Seegrotte
✋ Moderate

Casino
✉ Baden, Kaiser-Franz-Ring 1 ☎ (02252) 444 96 🕐 Daily from 3pm

Römertherme
✉ Baden, Brusattiplatz 4 ☎ (02252) 450 30 🕐 Daily 10–10 ✋ Expensive

Directions: Mödling is 15km (9 miles), Gumpoldskirchen 20km (12.5 miles) and Baden 28km (17 miles) south of Vienna. S-Bahns S1 and S2 depart from Südbahnhof in the direction of Wiener Neustadt, stopping at Gumpoldskirchen, Mödling and Baden. Buses 364 and 365 leave from Mödling station to Hinterbrühl. From 2:20pm to 3:15am, the Casino Bus shuttles half-hourly between Wiener Oper and Casino Baden. Badener Bahn shuttles between Wiener Oper and Baden-Josefsplatz every 15 minutes (day), every 30 minutes after 8:12pm.

Heiligenkreuz

Heiligenkreuz Abbey lies in the hollow of a valley amid the rolling hills of the Vienna Woods, surrounded by meadows and fields. Not only has it been a cultural centre for 850 years, but it was also the site of a royal tragedy.

Founded in 1133 by the Babenberg ruler Leopold III, the future patron of Lower Austria, the Cistercian abbey is still a place of harmony and beauty. Its name, meaning "Holy Cross", refers to a fragment of the Holy Cross. which Duke Leopold V brought back from his pilgrimage to Jerusalem and donated to the abbey in 1188. Today, the **Kreuzreliquie** (Relic of the Crucifix) can be see in the modern parish church.

Large parts of the abbey complex, the final resting place of the Babenberg rulers, date from the Middle Ages. The long nave of the Romanesque buttressed church, Gothic hall choir, cloisters and fountain house were built as early as the 12th and 13th centuries, and have been preserved in their original form. The outbuildings, towers, choir stalls (note the wooden sculptures on these) and magnificent trinity column created by Venetian sculptor Giovanni Giuliani, the Joseph fountain, library and sacristy all date back to the 17th

Gastronomic peak

Between Heiligenkreuz and Mayerling, you'll come across the beautifully styled Hanner hotel and restaurant (Mayerling 1, tel: 02258/23 78, daily noon–2, 6–10). The cuisine has been highly rated by the Gault-Millau team.

The abbey church is adorned with beautifully carved choir stalls

Pure romance

From Heiligenkreuz Abbey, pass through the Wiener Tor to the baroque **Cloisters**, created by Master Giuliani. An avenue of winter-flowering lime trees takes you past the stations of the cross and statues of the saints on its way to the Chapel. Cross the road and you'll get to the wooded cemetery, where you'll find the **grave** of Mary Vetsera. Its inscription reads: "Like a flower a human being blossoms and is broken."

century. All are splendid examples of the baroque style.

The **Klostergasthof** (Abbey Inn) is almost as old as the abbey itself. The best of traditional Austrian fare is dished up in its vaults or in the shaded garden in summer, accompanied by wines from the abbey's own cellars.

Mystery and Tragedy

The small village of Mayerling, 5km (3 miles) from Heiligenkreuz, was the scene of a tragedy that shook the empire. On 30 January, 1889, Crown Prince Rudolf committed suicide in the Jagdschloss (Hunting Lodge), together with his mistress, Mary Vetsera, who was only 18 years old at the time. It has never been possible to establish for certain the reasons for the double suicide. Austria lost its heir to its throne and with him any hope for renewal and reform. The room where the lovers died is now a memorial church. Three further rooms in the Hunting Lodge have been transformed into a museum.

Heiligenkreuz

☎ (02258) 87 03-0 ⏰ Daily 8am–8pm, guided tours Mon–Sat 10, 11, 2, 3 and 4, Sun from 11am 💶 Moderate ❓ www.stift-heiligenkreuz.at

Jagdschloss Mayerling

✉ Mayerling 3, Karmeliterkloster ☎ (02258) 275 ⏰ Mon–Sat 9–12:30, 1:30–6, Sun from 10am, in winter until 5pm 💶 Inexpensive

Directions: 30km (18.5 miles) southwest of Vienna; Postbus 1140 from Baden station; Bahnbus 364 from Mödling station (➤ 164); stop at Heiligenkreuz, Badner Tor for Heiligenkreuz Abbey and Mayerling for the Jagdschloss (Hunting Lodge)

A River Cruise through the Wachau

For a very special Sunday adventure, take a river cruise on one of the most romantic stretches of the Danube, the picturesque Wachau. This beautiful landscape is steeped in history, legend and culture.

The large cruise ship leaves Vienna, gliding past the **Donau-turm** (Danube Tower) and the modern skyline of Vienna on the right bank, and Kahlenberg and Leopoldsberg on the left. Shortly beyond the city limits, at **Korneuburg**, the green hills of Tullner Feld begin. At twice 470 horsepower, the MS *Admiral Tegetthoff*, flagship of the Danube River Cruise Company, chugs upriver to the flower-bedecked town of **Tulln**, past Zwentendorf, transporting its passengers to **Traismauer**, a village with Roman and Nibelungen pedigree.

Above: Captain of the Danube up-river cruise

Romantic Wachau

The next stop is the twin town of **Krems-Stein**. Its superb Old Town proudly exhibits snippets of its millenary history, which has brought it and the entire Wachau valley World Heritage status.

It is at Krems that the **Wachau** proper begins. This section of the Danube valley guarantees an unforgettable experience in summer, which begins with apricot blossoms in April and ends with the grape harvest in September. At 449m (1,473 feet) above sea level, **Stift Göttweig** (Abbey Göttweig), a splendid Benedictine abbey often described as the Austrian Montecassino, commands the left bank of the Danube. The boat continues upriver past wildly romantic countryside; steep stone terraces where Romans once cultivated vines and apricot trees contrast with densely wooded hills and picturesque villages with beautiful, old churches.

Krems Old Town is a historical gem

Where Richard the Lionheart Languished

The **Dürnstein Ruin**, towering high above the Danube, is one of Wachau's

Vines have been grown in the Wachau since Roman times

DDSG Blue Danube Schiffahrt GmbH

The DDSG river cruises operate from April to October every Sunday on the Vienna–Dürnstein–Vienna stretch (day return: €25). Departure Reichsbrücke: 8:35am, arrival Dürnstein: 2:30pm
Departure Dürnstein: 4:40pm, arrival Reichsbrücke: 9pm
✉ Wien 2, Handelskai 265/Reichsbrücke
☎ (01) 588 80 (seats need to be reserved)
🕒 Mon–Fri 9–6 🚇 Vorgartenstrasse 🚌 Bus 11A Vorgartenstrasse ❓ www.ddsg-blue-danube.at

emblems. It was here that Richard the Lionheart, king of England, was imprisoned in 1192 while returning from the crusades. Legend has it that his loyal servant Blondel discovered his master's whereabouts by singing the king's favourite ditty – Richard answered with the second verse from the castle's dungeon. He was freed in 1193 for a huge ransom, which was used to extend the fortress and found the town of Wiener Neustadt.

From the boat, the church tower of Dürnstein is especially noticeable. Restored to its original blue and white, it is one of the most beautiful baroque towers in Austria. It is part of the **Augustinerchorherrenstift** (Augustinian Abbey), of which the impressive portal and the courtyard are well worth seeing.

Almost too beautiful to be true: Dürnstein and the Augustinian abbey tower

The boat stops here for two hours, time enough for a pleasant stroll through Dürnstein. Apart from the former **Klarissinnenkirche** (Church of the Order of St Clare) and the **Stadttor** (Town Gate), you will discover romantic Renaissance courtyards, splendid manor houses and historical vintners' houses in the winding alleyways. In between you can fortify yourself with a Wachau speciality – Wachau ham and a glass of white wine – on the famous terrace of the hotel Schloss Dürnstein (tel: 02711/212, hot food served daily Apr–Oct 12–2, 6:30–9). Just make sure that you don't get distracted as you take in the local sights and delicacies and forget the 4:40 departure of the MS *Admiral Tegetthoff* back to Vienna…

Stift Dürnstein
✉ Dürnstein 1 ☎ (02711) 375 🕒 Apr–Oct 9–6 💶 Inexpensive

Bratislava

Only a few generations ago, when great-grandmother wanted to nip across from Vienna to Pressburg, as the town was called at the time, she only had to hop on a tram. Today's Bratislava is not quite as easy to get to from Vienna, but this beautiful city is still within easy reach.

The two towns on the Danube, once so close thanks to excellent transport connections, were very far apart during the Cold War; for a long time it was impossible to travel to Bratislava. But now that the Iron Curtain has gone, the country's two capitals are once more within easy striking distance of each other.

Pulsating life in the street cafés of the Old Town

When Bratislava became the capital of the Slovak Republic in 1993, this city of 450,000 inhabitants quickly developed into a political, economic and cultural centre. No longer a sad and grimy town, Bratislava gives the impression of having been freshly spruced up.

The proud fortress of Bratislava, towering above the Danube

View from the Top

Before hitting the town, climb up the palace stairs to the **Burg** (Fortress). This former Roman outpost has been constantly remodelled since the 9th century, most recently in 1953–62. From its battlements you can see **Petrzalka** on the right bank of the Danube, a socialist city within a city, where one prefabricated tower block stands next to another, dating back to socialist days. Of

Feasting as in grandmother's days

Delicious roasts and dumplings, accompanied by a beer, can be enjoyed at **Prašna Bašta** (Zamocnicka 11; tel: 02/5443 4957) or **Arkadia** (Zámocké schody/ Schlossstiege), which has views across the Danube.

all the central European cities, Bratislava is the most densely populated.

Old Town and Magnificent Palace

Returning from the fortress hill, you enter the **Old Town** via the Corvinus Gate. The Old Town is grouped around three squares: Hauptplatz (Central Square), Franziskanerplatz and Primatialplatz. Much has been restored here in recent years, with the thick ancient walls being brought to life again, and a charming hint of the former Austrian empire pervading the place again. Start at **Martinsdom** (Cathedral of St Martin). The Gothic church harbours evidence of the once close

Opera, operetta and ballet

The Slovak National Theatre is well worth a visit. You can buy tickets at the box office (Komenského námestie, tel: 0042 02/5778 2110; Pribinova 17, Mon–Fri 8–6, Sat 9–1).

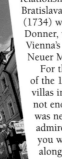

relationship between Vienna and Bratislava: the statue of St Martin (1734) was created by Raphael Donner, who also designed Vienna's Donner Fountain in Neuer Markt (► 30).

For the Hungarian aristocracy of the 17th and 18th centuries, villas in Vienna and Prague were not enough: one in Bratislava was needed as well. You can admire some of these palaces as you walk from Martinsdom along Ventúrska and Michalská streets to **Michaelstor** (St Michael's Gate). On the way to the Old Town Hall you'll see the Archbishop's Palace, the largest of them all. At the **Primatialpalais** (Primaciálny

Beautiful historical buildings can be found near the Michaelstor

námestie, behind the Old Town Hall), the Treaty of Bratislava was signed in 1805 after Napoleon's victory at Austerlitz. There's a municipal museum inside the grand **Altes Rathaus** (Old Town Hall, Hlavné námestie, Tue–Fri 10–5, Sat–Sun 11–6).

The Old Town is ideal for strolling. In between the lavishly restored historical buildings are lively pedestrianized areas and shopping boulevards lined with expensive boutiques, street cafés and bars. The most famous "Viennese" coffee-house is **Mayer** (Hlavné námestie near the Old Town Hall).

Directions: 60km (37 miles) east of Vienna; express trains depart daily from Südbahnhof, buses from Südtirolerplatz (seat reservation tel: 01/93 00 03 43 05); from May to 18 October the DDSG (► 168) also operates hydrofoil boats to Bratislava

Walks & Tours

1 THROUGH THE DANUBE MEADOWS

Cycle Tour

The wildly romantic countryside of the Lobau is tailor-made for cyclists: well-marked cycle paths take you along even ground through the Viennese stretch of the Danube meadows. Cycle in the footsteps of Napoleon's army, and relax in the green spaces of Auwald.

DISTANCE: 16km (10 miles) **TIME:** 3 hours
START/END POINT: Bicycle hire Ostbahnbrücke 📞 (0664) 397 21 02
🚇 Kaisermühlen, then 🚌 Bus 91A Lobau

1,000 million kilowatt-hours of electricity a year. When you reach the Lobgrundtor, turn left into the Donauauen National Park.

2–3
At Lobgrundstrasse you'll soon see red–white–red signs for the first of six **Napoleonsteine.** These memorial stones were erected in 1859 to commemorate the Battle of Aspern (1809). In this battle, Arch Duke Karl (➤ 106) defeated Napoleon for the first time, thus arresting his triumphal progress. The first stone, called **Am Brückenkopf** (At the Bridgehead), dates back to the time when the Danube was still unregulated and the French could only cross it on pontoon bridges. Cycle along Lobgrundstrasse through **Ölhafen Lobau** (Oil Port Lobau) on your right. You'll pass impressive oil tanks and pipelines, which transport gas on suspension bridges across the river to the refinery at Schwechat. At Königsgraben, turn left onto the cycle path along the Danube-Oder-Canal.

3–4
As early as the 14th century, the **Danube-Oder-Canal** was intended to link Vienna with the Oder River, some 3,000km (1,864 miles) away. In 1939–43 a short stretch of the artificial waterway was built in Lobau and

1–2
From the **bicycle rental outlet** your route takes you down-river on Danube Island, crossing the Steinspornbrücke to the Lobau; the path runs beside the New Danube, past **Kraftwerk Freudenau,** a power station producing over

FASANGARTEN
BIBERHAUFEN
ROTER HIASL
NAPOLEONSTRASSE
ESSLING

Hire a bicycle next to Ostbahnbrücke

Page 171: Romantic Grinzing with its lovely church

Marchfeld. At the end of the Lobau section, in the middle of the woods, you'll find a refreshing **bathing spot.** Continue straight on to the next Napoleon stone, called **Übergang der Franzosen** (Crossing of the French). Here, the French

army crossed the Danube, 42 days after the Battle of Astern, before defeating the Austrians at Deutsch-Wagram.

large circle around the Lobau, and you'll understand why its name means "water woods".

4–5

In the middle of the meadows, a short way from the cycle

path, there are two more Napoleon stones: **Napoleons Pulvermagazin** (Napoleon's Magazine) and **Franzosenfriedhof** (French Cemetery) The cemetery is said to contain a mass grave of 3,000 French soldiers. Now continue cycling in a

Guided tours and bicycle rental

The staff at the National Park offer free guided tours for groups of six or more people, (reservation: 02212 34 50). Bicycles can be rented from the Radverleih Ostbahnbrücke (at reduced rates for those taking part in the guided tour). 🛈 www.donauauen.at

When to go?

Sunny weekends are the busiest times at Lobau and you should definitely book any visits you plan to make in advance; you'll find more peace during the week. Note that the bike rental outlet only opens at 11am Monday to Friday, but at 9am on Saturday and Sunday. It's closed from November to February.

Map labels

- Napoleonstein
- Biber-gehege
- Napoleons Pulvermagazin
- Franzosen-friedhof
- Übergang der Franzosen
- Deml-kreuz
- VORWERKSTR.
- FÖRSTER STEIG
- Wildbade-stelle
- Lobau-museum
- Wurzel-station
- Donau-Oder-Kanal
- VORWERKSTR.
- Napoleons Hauptquartier 1809
- Am Brückenkopf
- Königs-graben
- Ölhafen Lobau
- GRUND...STA...
- Ölhafen
- NAPOLEONSTR.
- Panozza-lacke
- Kraftwerk Freudenau
- LOBGRUND TOR
- RAFFINERIESTR.
- Neue Donau
- Donauinsel
- Donau
- STEINSPORN-BRÜCKE
- RAFFINERIESTR.
- Lobau
- Radverleih
- OSTBAHN-BRÜCKE
- ESSLINGER FURT

1 km

1 mile

ESSLINGER FURT

grounds became a national park. Continue along Vorwerkstrasse to the next **Napoleon stone**. This memorial stone marks the end of the road along which 96,000 soldiers and countless horses once made their way to the Aspern battlefields.

6–7

Return via Napoleonstrasse to Lobgrundstrasse, then along Stadtwanderweg 11 (Municipal Footpath 11) past the last Napoleon stone, **Napoleons Hauptquartier 1809** (Napoleon's 1809 Headquarters) to the idyllic **Panozzalacke**, a natural bathing spot and a vast meadow for games and sunbathing.

7–8

The footpath will take you back to the National Park entrance, and upriver from here is the cycle rental place.

A memorial commemorating Napoleon's main camp

Taking a break

Hungry cyclists like to stop at **Uferhaus Staudigl** (Lobaustrasse, tel: 02249/27 33, closed Tue), a cosy, rustic tavern with a shaded restaurant garden. You'll find it, just before the "Übergang der Franzosen", by crossing the Grossenzersdorfer Danube Arm on the wooden bridge on the right. At the end of your tour, a refreshing drink awaits you at the **Imbiss an der Panozzalacke**.

observed in the evening twilight. Or take a detour past the **Demlkreuz**, a cross commemorating Franz Deml, a policeman who was shot here in 1920. At the **Wurzelstation** (Root Station) you can admire the impressive roots of one of the water meadow trees; the teaching pond lets you explore the unique habitat of the water meadows; and the "Hohle Pappel" (hollow polar) is a giant tree which you can walk inside. Return on Vorwerkstrasse, and after Förstersteig you'll come across the **Lobaumuseum** on the right (open at weekends and by arrangement). This local museum has aquariums and educational slides that explain all about the wildlife in the water meadows. It also tells the story of how the imperial hunting

With a bit of luck you may spot a heron fishing in one of the ponds, or other rare birds among the willow and polar trees. The old tributaries, cut off from the main river for more than 130 years, seem unspoiled, just like the uncultivated fields. Continue along this unique nature reserve up to Esslinger Furt.

5–6

Turn left now and cycle up to Vorwerkstrasse.
Here, in the heart of the Lobau, you'll come across a number of interesting sights: there's a **beaver enclosure** at the Förstersteig, for example, with two beavers, which are best

Top:
The fascinating Lobaumuseum
Above: idyllic Panozzalacke

2 GRINZING
Walk

Grinzing is Vienna's oldest and most famous wine tavern district. Situated in picturesque vineyards, it has preserved its charming village character. Here, mighty gateways open out into quiet drives and tiny gardens, and welcoming vintners' houses largely date back to the 16th and 17th centuries.

DISTANCE: 2km (1.2 miles) **TIME:** 1.5 hours (or longer, depending on time at the wine tavern)
START POINT: Himmelstrasse Grinzing 🚋 Tram No 38
END POINT: Fernsprechamt Heiligenstadt 🚌 Bus No 38A

1–2
Tram No 38 is locally known as the "Heurigen-express", because it is the fastest way for the Viennese to get to the much-loved *Heurigen*, or new-vintage wine taverns. From the terminus walk up Himmelstrasse on the left, past the 14th-century **Pöllinger Freihof** (Pölling Palace), used for a short period in 1730 by Empress Maria Theresa, to the late-Gothic Grinzing Church. Twelve vintner families built the **Kirche zum Heiligen Kreuz** (Church of the Holy Cross) from 1417 to 1426, financing it with their own money.

2–3
If you like, make a detour from the church along Managettagasse and Managettasteig to **Grinzing Cemetery**. It's the last resting place of Gustav Mahler, whose modernist tombstone was commissioned by his widow Alma Mahler-Werfel, who is also buried here. The graves of one-armed pianist Paul Wittgenstein, brother of the philosopher Ludwig Wittgenstein, and of the writers Heimito von Doderer and Thomas Bernhard, can also be found here.

3–4
Back at the church walk uphill on Himmel-strasse and turn right into Feilergasse, which

Destination: heurigen wine taverns

Tip
Force yourself to climb up to the vineyard **Am Reisenberg** (Oberer Reisenbergweg 15, tel: 01/320 93 93, early May–end Sep Mon–Fri 4pm–midnight, Sat–Sun 10am–midnight). Your efforts will be rewarded with excellent wine and great views of Vienna.

leads to the **Altes Presshaus** (Old Presshouse, Cobenzlgasse 15, tel: 01/320 02 03, daily 3pm–midnight, closed Jan–Feb); dating from 1527, it is the oldest wine tavern in Austria. Apart from a 250-year-old wine press and giant vats, the impressive cellars also have an entrance to an underground path which, many centuries ago, was dug by the vintners as an escape route to Grinzing Church.

4–5

Turn down Cobenzlgasse, and past Grinzing's oldest house, the **Trummelhof**

(Cobenzlgasse 30, tel: 01/328 90 61, Mon–Sat from 7pm). It was built by the Babenberg rulers in 1150 on the site of a Roman settlement; today it is a bar. A few steps farther along it's worth stopping at the **Heuriger Reinprecht** (Cobenzlgasse 22, tel: 01/320/14 71 0, daily 3:30pm–midnight, closed mid-Dec to Feb). In the nearly 400-year-old vaults of this former monastery, some 150,000 litres (33,000 gallons) of wine are served every year. You can also admire the world's oldest and largest collection of corkscrews here, comprising well over 3,000 items.

5–6

Continue along Cobenzlgasse, which, at the village end, leads into Sandgasse. Sandgasse eventually becomes Grinzinger Strasse. On the walls of **House No 64** a plaque commemorates Franz Grillparzer and Ludwig van Beethoven, who both spent several months here in 1808.

Taking a break

The countless *Heurigen* restaurants offer a wide variety of foods, both cold and hot buffets in a typical atmosphere, and often accompanied by live music. **Feuerwehr-Wagner** (Grinzinger Strasse 53, tel: 01/320 24 42, daily 4pm–midnight) is famed for its *backhendl* (roast chicken); **Martin Sepp** (Cobenzlgasse 34, tel: 01/320 32 33-0, daily 11:30am–midnight) specialises in seasonal foods; the elegant snack bar **Liebstöckl & Co** (Sandgasse 12, tel: 01/328 83 10, daily 11am–midnight, hot food 11–11) serves traditional Viennese with a twist; and the **Neuland** tavern (Cobenzlgasse 7, tel: 01/320 00 63, daily 11am–1am) boasts a stylish ambience.

6–7

Turn left into Armbrustergasse. Opposite the former residence of **Bruno Kreisky**, the Austrian Federal Chancellor (Armbrustergasse 15), is Probusgasse, a tiny alley that leads to another **Wohnhaus Beethovens** (Beethoven Residence, Probusgasse 6, Tue–Sun 10–1, 2–6). It was here that Beethoven wrote the *Heiligenstädter Testament* in 1802, a letter which recorded his despair over his advancing deafness. Beethoven had hoped that his

Wine, women and song

summer residence at Grinzing would bring relief from his hearing problems. When there was no noticeable improvement, he wrote a passionate and angry letter to his brothers, which he never posted.

7–8

Beethoven moved home more than 80 times in Vienna, and so it's no surprise that at the end of Probusgasse, on Pfarrplatz, there is yet another Beethoven residence. It was in this mid-17th-century building that the composer worked on his Ninth Symphony in 1817. Today

celebrities and wine lovers meet here at the Heuriger **Mayer am Pfarrplatz** (Pfarrplatz 2, tel: 01/370 33 61, Mon–Sat 4pm–midnight, Sun 11am–midnight). The facade of the romantic house is decorated with a statue of St Florian who is believed to have saved the house during a fire. Continue past **Heiligenstädter Jakobskirche** (Heiligenstadt Church of St Jacob), one of Vienna's oldest churches with structural remains dating back to the 2nd century AD on Nestelbachgasse, which leads back to Grinzinger Strasse. From here the 38A bus will transport you to the U-Bahn station Heiligenstadt.

When to go?
The best time for this walk is the afternoon. It allows you to finish off the day with a pleasant glass of wine in one of the many Heuriger taverns.

In Sandgasse, where time seems to have stood still

3 ST MARX CEMETERY
Walk

Whether it's spring, when the lilac blossoms, or autumn, as mist hangs between the rows of graves – the early 19th-century Friedhof St Marx is a romantic place to visit. In fact, it's no longer a cemetery but a park. Established in 1784, the cemetery was only in use until 1874, when Vienna's Central Cemetery was opened and the mortal remains of the famous were moved to memorial tombs. Only the tombstones remain in St Marx.

DISTANCE: 1.5km (1 mile) **TIME:** 1 hour
START/END POINT: 🚈 St Marx or 🚋 Tram 18, 71

1–2
From **S-Bahn station St Marx** walk along Leberstrasse, away from the city centre. Soon you will see the A23 concrete bridge. The **cemetery entrance** is just before the bridge on your right, a few steps back from the road. As soon as you've passed through the red-brick entrance gate, the cemetery's peaceful and tranquil atmosphere will envelop you. A broad central avenue lined with chestnut trees leads straight ahead. Note the Angels of Death either side of the avenue.

2–3
Walk up the avenue and step into one of the rows on the left. You'll spot many fascinating inscriptions on the tombstones. One says, for example:

The tombstone of one Josef März, with an unusual inscription

The entrance of St Marx Cemetery

"In memory of Herr Josef März, representative of the civilian salaried coachman and proprietor in Leopold-stadt No 138." Also on the left is the grave of **Ida Pfeiffer** (1797–1858, ▶ 34). As soon as her children had left home, this intrepid woman set out to travel around the world solo. In the Biedermeier period that was most unusual.

3–4

Where the rows of graves end, the former **grave shafts** begin. Here the dead were buried without much ado, as was typical for the time, in unmarked grave shafts holding up to six corpses. Wolfgang Amadeus Mozart was buried in such a pauper's grave. The **"Mozartgrab"** (Mozart's Tomb) was not built until 1859 and only roughly marks the spot where the composer was actually buried. The grave, featuring a broken column (a symbol of the freemasons) and the Angel of Grief is always adorned with fresh flowers. Continue along the central avenue, and admire the romantic tombstones and angels.

4–5

On your return, take a look at the graves to the right of the avenue. In the rear of the cemetery is the grave of **Moritz Michael Daffinger** (1790–1849), the most famous portrait and flower painter of his day. Near the common graves, but this time on your right, you'll see the grave of **Josef Madersperger** (1768–1850), the inventor of the sewing machine, and beyond it, quite close to the cemetery exit, the grave of **Michael Thonet** (1796–1871), a pioneering furniture-maker who invented the world-famous bentwood furniture.

The "Mozartgrab", a lasting memorial

Map labels

Schachtgräber

Josef Madersperger

Schachtgräber

»Mozartgrab«

A 23

S 23

Moritz Michael Daffinger

③

④

Taking a break

The cemetery and its surrounds have no refreshment stops. It is therefore a good idea to take something to snack on for the walk.

🚇 Wien 3, Leberstraße 6–8
🕐 Nov–Mar daily 7–dusk; Apr–Oct /–3; May–Sep /–6; Jun–Aug /–/
💰 Free

4 IN THE FOOTSTEPS OF *THE THIRD MAN*

Walk

The city walk in the footsteps of Carol Reed's famous film *The Third Man* (1949) takes you into the subterranean sewage system and through the streets of post-war Vienna, when the occupying Allies and the black market dominated a wrecked city.

DISTANCE: 3km (2 miles) **TIME:** 2.5 hours
START POINT: Stadtpark ⊞ 193 E2 Ⓜ Stadtpark
END POINT: Teinfaltstrasse ⊞ 192 B4 Ⓜ Herrengasse, Schottentor

The story

Vienna 1948: The American writer Holly Martins (Joseph Cotten) wants to visit his friend Harry Lime (Orson Welles) in Vienna, but arrives too late – Lime has allegedly been killed in a traffic accident. Martins soon becomes embroiled in the shady world of penicillin smuggling; a witness claims to have seen a third man at the site of the accident. A spectacular chase through the Vienna sewage system ensues, leading to a dramatic final showdown...

You'd like to watch the film (again)?

Catch the film – in the orginal English – at the Burg Kino (Wien 1, Opernring 19, tel: 01/587 84 06) at 6:45pm every Monday, Tuesday and Wednesday.

Invitation for an organised Third-Man guided tour

Konzerthaus, but for the film, the pillar was rebuilt on Am Hof (more about this later). Now let's go down into the underworld!

2–3

You will enter the **Vienna Sewage System,** via a narrow spiral staircase – but you can only do this with a guided tour. The sewers measure 2,300km (1,430 miles) in length. After a cholera epidemic in 1830, all the waterways within the city limits were covered over and two large intercepting sewers running parallel to

1–2

From **Stadtpark** walk down Lothringer Strasse to the **Lifassäule** (advertising pillar) where Harry Lime disappeared into a subterranean world. It's located between Beethovenplatz and the opposite

Molly Darcy's Irish Pub

Am Hof

TUCHLAUBEN

FREYUNG

HERREN-

⑦

Mölker-steig

TEINFALTSTRASSE

⑧

⑨

the Wien River were built. After a set of narrow

Into the pillar and down to the sewers

stairs you'll get to listed tunnel vaults, designed by Otto Wagner and completed around 1900. This monumental structure covered the Wien River between Stadtpark and Naschmarkt, cutting it off from daylight. More than 100 years later, the intercepting sewers canals have become too small for the city of millions: a new canal is being constructed. For several years, because of

construction works, the subterranean part of the guided tour will be restricted to this tunnel, where the exciting chase sequences with Harry Lime were filmed. Back on the

surface, walk along Lothringer Strasse up to Schwarzenbergplatz.

3–4

Near the High-Jet Fountain, you'll see the **Heldendenkmal der Roten Armee** (Red Army Memorial). The nearly 12m (40-foot) high figure representing a Russian soldier was unveiled on 19 August, 1945, at a parade of Soviet, American, English and French troops. From 1945 until 1955, Vienna was divided into four zones, with the inner city admini-strated by all four Allies together. Continue to Ringstrasse, where on your left you'll see the **Hotel Imperial**.

You'll need strong nerves, and possibly nose plugs, for a visit down to the Viennese sewage system

4–5

During Vienna's post-war occupation, the elegant hotel was the headquarters of the Russian secret service. From here continue along Ringstrasse, and then turn right towards the **Staatsoper** (➤ 98). Behind the opera house is another secret film location, **Hotel Sacher**. The hotel, built in 1860, was used to station the English forces, among them Graham Greene, author of the novel the film is based on. In the hotel's files he found all the inspiration he needed to write his black-market thriller.

5–6

Café Mozart (➤ 90), immediately behind the hotel, was a favourite drinking hole of Greene, who used its garden and interior as the locations for a number of scenes. The café overlooks Albertinaplatz, once dominated by a large residential block, known as Philipphof, with an air raid shelter in the cellars; the block was bombed in 1945, burying some 300 people alive. Today a **memorial** against war and fascism by sculptor Alfred Hrdlička marks the spot. Continue down Augustinerstrasse to Josefsplatz. Opposite Emperor Joseph II's equestrian statue you'll see the **Palais Pallavicini**, Harry Lime's home in *The Third Man*.

6–7

Via Reitschulgasse you'll reach **Michaelerplatz**, where Café Marc Aurel was reconstructed for the film. Take Kohlmarkt and Bognergasse to the next famous film location – **Am Hof** (➤ 63), where you'll find the famous advertising pillar through which Harry Lime enters the sewers. It was rebuilt in wood and shot in wideangle.

7–8

Walk along Freyung and Teinfaltstrasse to **Mölkersteig**. The archway of No 8 Schreyvogelgasse is another

Hotel Sacher was the base for the English Allied forces

Taking a break

One of the best places to have a coffee before the start of your tour are the terraces of Steiereck im Stadtpark (Wien 3, Am Heumarkt 2, tel: 01/713 31 68, Mon–Fri 9am–10pm, Sat–Sun 9–7).

key location in the film: it is the spot where Holly Martins – and the viewers – first catch sight of Harry Lime's face.

8–9

If you've joined an organized tour, you will arrive at **Molly Darcy's Irish Pub** (Wien 1, Teinfaltstrasse 6) where the *Harry Lime Theme* will be played for you on the zither. You'll also hear anecdotes about the composer, Anton Karas, and the production of the film.

Guided tours

The Timmermann family organise guided tours all year round on Mondays and Fridays at 4pm; no need to book. Meeting point is the U-Bahn station Stadtpark, exit Johannesgasse (tel: 01/774 89 01, www.viennawalks.com, expensive).

Practicalities

GETTING ADVANCE INFORMATION

Websites
- www.austria.info
- www.info.wien.at
- www.jugendinfowien.at
- www.wien.gv.at

In Austria
Albertinaplatz/
Maysedergasse
1010 Wien
☎ 01 24-555
email: urlaub@austria.info

In the UK
Austrian National Tourist
Office
☎ 0845 101 18 18
email: holiday@austria.info

BEFORE YOU GO

WHAT YOU NEED

● Required
○ Suggested
▲ Not required

	UK	Ireland	USA	Canada	Australia	France	Netherlands	Spain
Passport/National Identity Card	●	●	●	●	●	●	●	●
Visa	▲	▲	▲	▲	▲	▲	▲	▲
Onward or Return Ticket	▲	▲	▲	▲	▲	▲	▲	▲
Health Inoculations (tetanus or polio)	▲	▲	▲	▲	▲	▲	▲	▲
Health Documentation (➤ 188)	●	●	●	●	●	●	●	●
Travel Insurance (➤ 188)	○	○	○	○	○	○	○	○
Driving Licence (national)	●	●	●	●	●	●	●	●
Third-Party Car Insurance Certificate	●	●	n/a	n/a	n/a	●	●	●
Car Registration Document	●	●	n/a	n/a	n/a	●	●	●

WHEN TO GO

Vienna

High season   Low season

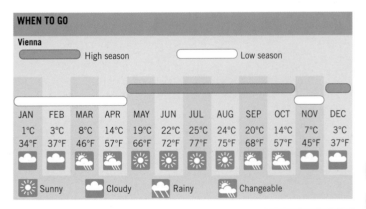

JAN	FEB	MAR	APR	MAY	JUN	JUL	AUG	SEP	OCT	NOV	DEC
1°C	3°C	8°C	14°C	19°C	22°C	25°C	24°C	20°C	14°C	7°C	3°C
34°F	37°F	46°F	57°F	66°F	72°F	77°F	75°F	68°F	57°F	45°F	37°F

☀ Sunny   ☁ Cloudy   🌧 Rainy   ⛅ Changeable

The temperatures indicated are the **average daytime temperature** in the respective months. Vienna has a continental climate, with cold winters, hot summers and rainy periods in spring and autumn. The Danube ensures a good supply of fresh air. Although Vienna is always in season, the most beautiful period to visit the city is from May, when the lilacs bloom, to October, when the leaves in the vineyards around Vienna start to change colour. Throughout the year there is an impressive programme of cultural events: theatre, music and numerous museums make it possible for you to enjoy yourself even when the sun isn't shining. Christmas and New Year is an attractive time to visit; Vienna hosts a plethora of traditional Christmas markets, and Silvester (New Year's Eve) is celebrated throughout the city with fireworks and plenty of revelry.

GETTING THERE

By Plane Vienna International Airport Wien-Schwechat is about 15km (9 miles) southeast of the city centre. It is served by 80 airlines, which connect Vienna to destinations around the world, although most flights arrive from the European continent. Schwechat is also served by charter flights

Ticket Prices Ticket prices vary considerably. If you're lucky you may get a bargain because there is so much competition. The so-called "Red Ticket" of Austria's national airline AUA is generally good value; they also have tickets at permanently low prices and regular specials. Check www.aua.com or with your travel agents for current offers. No-frills airlines Air Berlin (www.airberlin.com) and Sky Europe (www.skyeurope.com) offer cheap flights between Vienna and a number of European cities.

By Train Vienna can be reached by IC, ICE, Eurocity and regional trains. Trains from the west (Germany and Switzerland) arrive at **Westbahnhof**, while trains from the south (Italy and Slovenia) arrive at **Südbahnhof**. Regional trains to northern Austria depart from **Franz-Josefs-Bahnhof**. Information on trains is available at www.oebb.at.

By Car The A1 Westautobahn (western motorway) links Vienna with Salzburg and Linz, the A2 Südautobahn (southern motorway) with Klagenfurt and Graz.

TIME

  Vienna is in the Central European time zone (MEZ), ie one hour ahead of Greenwich Mean Time (GMT). From the end of March until the end of October clocks are adjusted one hour forwards for summer time (GMT +1).

CURRENCY AND FOREIGN EXCHANGE

Currency Austria's currency is the euro (€). Euro notes are available in the following denominations: €5, €10, €20, €50, €100, €200 and €500; coins to the value of 1, 2 and 5 cents (bronze-coloured), 10, 20 and 50 cents (gold-coloured), and the two-coloured €1 euro and €2 coins are available.
An **exchange rate calculator** is available on the internet: www.oanda.com.

Exchange Exchange bureaux can be found in the railway stations and at the airport. **Travellers' cheques** can be cashed at most banks, which are plentiful throughout the city. Outside of bank opening hours, **ATMs** (*Bankomaten*) are available in many locations.

Credit cards are accepted in an increasing number of hotels, restaurants and shops. VISA and MasterCard cards with four-digit PINs can be used at most ATMs.

GMT	Vienna	Paris	New York	Los Angeles	Sydney
12 noon	1 pm	1 pm	7 am	4 am	10 pm

WHEN YOU ARE THERE

CLOTHING SIZES

UK	Austria	USA	
36	46	36	**Suits**
38	48	38	
40	50	40	
42	52	42	
44	54	44	
46	56	46	
7	41	8	**Shoes**
7.5	42	8.5	
8.5	43	9.5	
9.5	44	10.5	
10.5	45	11.5	
11	46	12	
14.5	37	14.5	**Shirts**
15	38	15	
15.5	39/40	15.5	
16	41	16	
16.5	42	16.5	
17	43	17	
8	36	6	**Clothes**
10	38	8	
12	40	10	
14	42	12	
16	44	14	
18	46	16	
4.5	36	6	**Shoes**
5	37	6.5	
5.5	38	7	
6	39	7.5	
6.5	40	8	
7	41	8.5	

HOLIDAYS

1 Jan	New Year's Day
6 Jan	Epiphany
Mar/Apr	Good Friday, Easter Sunday and Monday
1 May	Labour Day
May/June	Ascension Day, Whit Sunday and Monday, Corpus Christi
15 Aug	Assumption
26 Oct	National Holiday
1 Nov	All Saints' Day
8 Dec	Immaculate Conception
25 Dec	Christmas Day
26 Dec	St Stephen's Day

OPENING HOURS

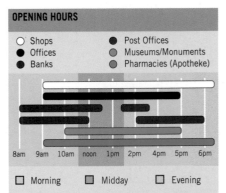

○ Shops   ● Post Offices
● Offices   ● Museums/Monuments
● Banks   ● Pharmacies (Apotheke)

8am   9am   10am   noon   1pm   2pm   4pm   5pm   6pm

☐ Morning   ☐ Midday   ☐ Evening

Shops The liberalisation of shop opening hours is currently much debated. Generally, most shops in the centre are open Monday to Friday from 9am until 6:30pm and on Saturdays from 9am until 6pm. Many supermarkets and shops in main shopping areas stay open later on Thursday and Friday evenings.

Banks Bank opening hours are Monday to Friday 8am until 12:30pm and 1:30pm until 3pm, Thursdays until 5:30pm.

Museums Opening hours vary considerably from one museum to the next.

EMERGENCIES:

POLICE 133

FIRE 122

RESCUE SERVICES (and AMBULANCE) 144

PERSONAL SAFETY

Vienna has always been considered a relatively safe city. Recently, however, there has been a sharp rise in property crime. Car break-ins and handbag theft are particular problems for visitors. Make sure you keep your handbag closed. Do not make life easy for thieves – firmly hold on to your bags and keep an eye on your valuables at all times.

- The U-Bahn is a favourite hunting ground for pickpockets. Always be aware of what is happening around you.
- Especially at night you are advised to avoid Karlsplatz and nearby U-Bahn exits as many drug dealers and users tend to congregate in this area.

Police assistance:
☎ 133 from any phone

TELEPHONES

The ubiquitous mobile phone has made public phones almost unnecessary, but some still exist. Public phones take coins and phonecards, which can be bought at post offices or newsagents. To phone another country, leave out the initial 0 after the country code.

International Dialling Codes:
UK:	00 44
Ireland	00 353
USA/Canada	00 1
Australia	00 61

POST

There are post offices in all districts. Smaller offices open Mon–Fri 8–noon and 2–5, larger offices do not close at lunchtime. The central post office (Wien 1, Fleischmarkt 19) is open 6am–10pm, the branch at Westbahnhof Mon–Fri 7am–10pm, weekends 9am–8pm, while the branches at Südbahnhof and Franz-Josefs-Bahnhof open Mon–Fri 7am–8pm, weekends 9–2.

ELECTRICITY

The power supply in Austria is 220 volts. Sockets take two round-pin plugs. Travellers from outside continental Europe should use an adaptor.

TIPS/GRATUITIES

Generally, restaurant, drinks and taxi bills are rounded up – 5 per cent is a good rule of thumb.

Hotel porters	€1–2
Chambermaids	€1–2
Tour guides	on own discretion
Lavatory attendants	30 cents

EMBASSIES AND CONSULATES

UK	**USA**	**Australia**	**Canada**	**Ireland**
☎ (01) 71613-0	☎ (01) 31339-0	☎ (01) 506 740	☎ (01) 531 38-33 25	☎ (01) 715-4246
www.britishembassy.at	www.usembassy.at	www.australian-embassy.at	wwww.kanada.at	

HEALTH

Insurance: Special travel health insurance is recommended, particularly for visitors from non-EU countries. Nationals of EU countries can receive health care in Austria by presenting a European Health Insurance Card (EHIC), though in general this will not cover you for non-emergencies. Doctors are listed in the yellow pages of the phone book. The medical emergency service (Ärztlicher Bereitschaftsdienst) can be reached on tel: (01) 531 16-0.

Dental Services: Dental treatment for non-Austrian visitors can be expensive. The dental emergency service (Zahnärztlicher Notdienst) can be reached on tel: (01)512 20 78 or 141. Addresses and telephone numbers for dentists are listed in the phone book's yellow pages.

Weather: Vienna can be unbearably hot at the height of summer. Protect yourself against sunburn and drink plenty of fluids.

Drugs: There are many pharmacies (*Apotheken*) selling prescription and non-prescription medicines. Find out from the paper or the Apotheken-Bereitschaftsdienst (pharmacy emergency service) tel: 15 50 (recorded message) which pharmacy is open outside normal opening hours.

Safe Water: Tap water is suitable for drinking, but water from public wells has been treated with chemicals – watch out with dogs, too!

CONCESSIONS

Reduced admission tickets to sights are usually available for senior citizens, the disabled and soldiers, on presentation of the appropriate ID. Concessionary tickets are also usually available for children, young people and school groups.

The **Wien-Card** is good value for money. At €18.50 it allows 72 hours unlimited travel on U-Bahn, trams and buses. In addition you will pay lower ticket prices at many museums and sights. You can buy the card at the Tourist-Infos (► 36) and public transport offices.

TRAVELLING WITH A DISABILITY

Vienna's old trams and buses, which are notoriously difficult to board for persons with reduced mobility, are slowly being replaced with new models that have lower floors. **U-Bahn stations** are better equipped for disabled visitors. A plan of **U-Bahn stations for sight-impaired visitors** is available from the Wiener Linien (tel: 01/7909-100). Detailed information on access for disabled visitors at restaurants, museums and sights is available on the internet at www.info.wien.at. Click first on your language, then "Specials" and finally on "Accessible Vienna".

CHILDREN

Children are welcome almost anywhere. Children's theatre and special kids' programmes in museums are the norm. For detailed information see www.kinderinfowien.at.

LAVATORIES

Public lavatories can be found in stations and near all major sights.

LOST PROPERTY

Zentralfundamt Wasagasse 22, Wien 9, tel: 01/ 313 46. For public transport tel: 01/4 35 00; railway tel: 01/93000-22222.

VIENNA PLACE NAMES

For ease of use this guide uses "ss" instead of ß in all cases. You may however find the correct German spelling on street signs, for example in "Straße".

The following German terms have been used throughout:

U-Bahn underground railway (subway)

S-Bahn overground (often overhead) local and regional railway

SURVIVAL PHRASES

Yes/no **Ja/nein**
Good day **Grüss Gott or Servus**
Good evening **Guten Abend**
Goodbye **Auf Wiedersehen, Auf Wiederschauen, Tschüs** (informal)
How are you? **Wie geht es Ihnen?**
You're welcome **Bitte schön**
Please **Bitte schön or Bitte sehr**
Thank you **Danke**
Excuse me **Entschuldigung**
I'm sorry **Es tut mir Leid**
Do you have …? **Haben Sie…?**
I'd like … **Ich möchte …**
How much is that? **Was kostet das?**
I don't understand **Ich verstehe nicht**
Do you speak English? **Sprechen Sie Englisch?**
Open **Geöffnet** Closed **Geschlossen**
Push/pull **Drücken/Ziehen**
Women's lavatory **Damen**
Men's lavatory **Herren**

DAYS OF THE WEEK

Monday **Montag**
Tuesday **Dienstag**
Wednesday **Mittwoch**
Thursday **Donnerstag**
Friday **Freitag**
Saturday **Samstag**
Sunday **Sonntag**

OTHER USEFUL WORDS & PHRASES

Yesterday **Gestern**
Today **Heute**
Tomorrow **Morgen**
Could you call a doctor please?
Könnten Sie bitte einen Arzt rufen?
Do you have a vacant room?
Haben Sie ein Zimmer frei?
 – with bath/shower
mit Bad/Dusche
Single room **Das Einzelzimmer**
Double room **Das Doppelzimmer**
One/two nights **Eins/zwei Nächte**
How much per night? **Was kostet es pro Nacht?**

DIRECTIONS & GETTING AROUND

Where is…? **Wo ist…?**
 – the train/bus station
der Bahnhof/Busbahnhof
 – the bank **die Bank**
 – the nearest toilets
die nächsten Toiletten
Turn left/right **Biegen Sie links ab/rechts ab**
Go straight on **Gehen Sie geradeaus**
Here/there **Hier/da**
North **Nord**
East **Ost**
South **Süd**
West **West**

NUMBERS

1 **eins**	13 **dreizehn**	31 **einunddreissig**	300 **dreihundert**
2 **zwei**	14 **vierzehn**	32 **zweiunddreissig**	400 **vierhundert**
3 **drei**	15 **fünfzehn**	40 **vierzig**	500 **fünfhundert**
4 **vier**	16 **sechzehn**	50 **fünfzig**	600 **sechshundert**
5 **fünf**	17 **siebzehn**	60 **sechzig**	700 **siebenhundert**
6 **sechs**	18 **achtzehn**	70 **siebzig**	800 **achthundert**
7 **sieben**	19 **neunzehn**	80 **achtzig**	900 **neunhundert**
8 **acht**	20 **zwanzig**	90 **neunzig**	1,000 **tausend**
9 **neun**	21 **einundzwanzig**	100 **hundert**	
10 **zehn**	22 **zweiund-**	101 **einhunderteins**	
11 **elf**	**zwanzig**	102 **einhundertzwei**	
12 **zwölf**	30 **dreissig**	200 **zweihundert**	

EATING OUT

A table for ..., please **Einen Tisch für ... bitte**

We have/haven't booked **Wir haben/haben nicht reserviert**

I'd like to reserve a table for ... people at ... **Ich möchte einen Tisch für ... Personen um ... reservieren**

I am a vegetarian **Ich bin Vegetarier/in**

May I see the menu, please? **die Speisekarte bitte?**

Is there a dish of the day, please? **Gibt es einen Tagesgericht?**

We'd like something to drink **Wir möchten etwas zu trinken**

Do you have a wine list in English? **Haben Sie eine Weinkarte auf Englisch?**

This is not what I ordered **das habe ich nicht bestellt**

Could we sit there? **Können wir dort sitzen?**

When do you open/close? **Wann machen Sie auf/zu?**

The food is cold **das Essen ist kalt**

The food was excellent **das Essen war ausgezeichnet**

Can I have the bill, please? **Wir möchten zahlen, bitte**

Is service included? **Ist das mit Bedienung?**

Breakfast **das Frühstück**
Lunch **das Mittagessen**
Dinner **das Abendessen**

Starters **die Vorspeise**
Main course **das Hauptgericht**
Desserts **die Nachspeisen**

Fish dishes **Fischgerichte**
Meat dishes **Fleischgerichte**
Fruit **Obst**
Vegetables **Gemüse**
Dish of the day **das Tagesgericht**
Wine list **die Weinkarte**

Salt **das Salz**
Pepper **der Pfeffer**

Knife **das Messer**
Fork **die Gabel**
Spoon **der Löffel**

Waiter **der Kellner**
Waitress **die Kellnerin**

MENU A–Z

Äpfelstrudel Apple pudding
Apfelsaft Apple juice
Apfelsinen Oranges
Aufschnitt Sliced cold meat
Austern Oysters
Belegte Brote Sandwiches
Birnen Pears
Blumenkohl Cauliflower
Brathähnchen Roast chicken
Bratwurst Fried sausage
Brokkoli Broccoli
Brötchen Bread roll
Eintopf Casserole
Eisbein Knuckle of pork
Ente Duck
Erbsen Peas
Erdbeeren Strawberries
Fasan Pheasant
Fenchel Fennel
Flunder Flounder
Forelle Trout
Frittatensuppe Beef broth
Frühstücksspeck Grilled bacon
Gans Goose
Gekochtes Ei Boiled egg
Gulasch Goulash
Fisolen Green beans
Heilbutt Halibut
Hering Herring
Himbeeren Raspberries
Honig Honey
Hummer Lobster
Kabeljau Cod
Kaffee Coffee
Kalbsleber Calf's liver
Karotten Carrots
Erdäpfel Potatoes
Käse Cheese
Käsekuchen Cheesecake

Kasseler Smoked pork loin
Kirschen Cherries
Knödel Dumplings
Krabben Shrimps
Kohl Cabbage
Konfitüre Preserves
Lachs Salmon
Lammbraten Roast lamb
Lauch Leek
Mais Sweet corn
Milch Milk
Obsttorte Fruit tart
Obstsalat Fruit salad
Orangensaft Orange juice
Palatschinken Pancakes
Paprika Pepper
Pfirsiche Peaches
Pflaumen Plums
Pilze Mushrooms
Rinderbraten Roast beef
Rotkohl Red cabbage
Rührei Scrambled egg
Sachertorte Chocolate cake
Schinken Ham
Scholle Plaice
Schokoladentorte Chocolate cake
Schweinebraten Roast pork
Schweinekotelett Pork chop
Seezunge Sole
Spargel Asparagus
Spinat Spinach
Stelze Pork shanks
Tomaten Tomatoes
Topfenstrudel Cream cheese pastry
Wienerschnitzel Veal escalope
Wild Game
Zwiebeln Onions

Streetplan

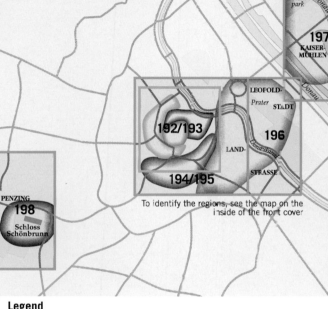

197 KAISER-MÜHLEN

Alte Donau
Donau-park
Donau

LEOPOLD-
Prater STADT

192/193

196
Donaukanal

LAND-

194/195

STRASSE

To identify the regions, see the map on the inside of the front cover

PENZING
198
Schloss
Schönbrunn

Legend

————	Main road		Park
═══	Other road		Important building
- - - -	Tunnel		Featured place of interest
══	Pedestrianised way	ⓤ	U-Bahn station
————	Rail line	ⓢ	S-Bahn (local rail) station
————	U-Bahn (underground) line		

192/193
0   100   200   300   400 metres
0   100   200   300   400 yards

194–196/198
0   100   200   300   400 metres
0   100   200   300   400 yards

197
0   100   200   300   400 metres
0   100   200   300   400 yards

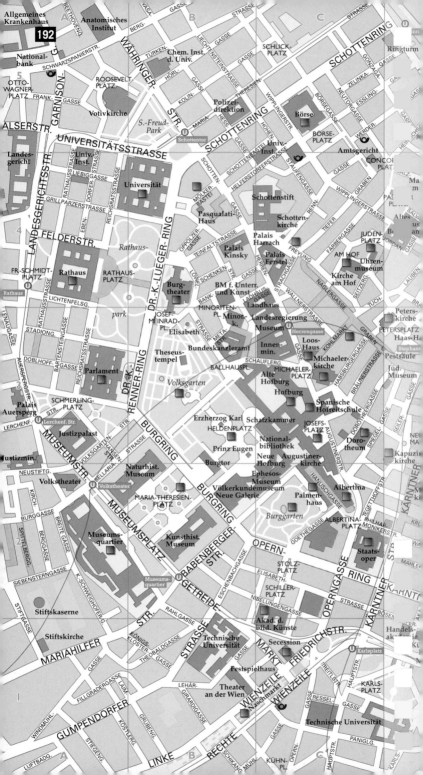

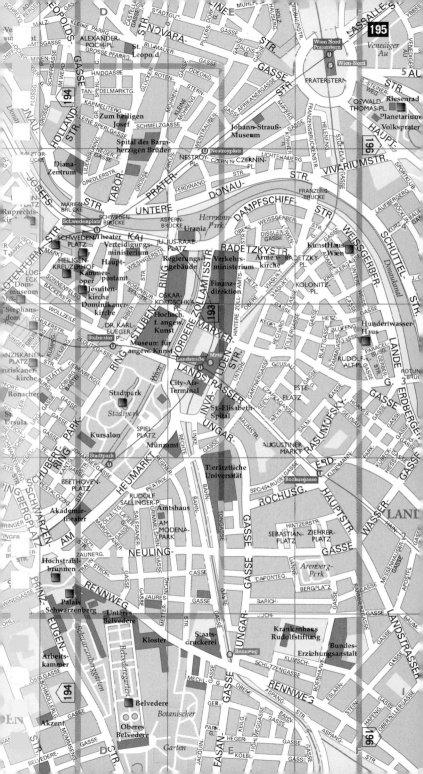

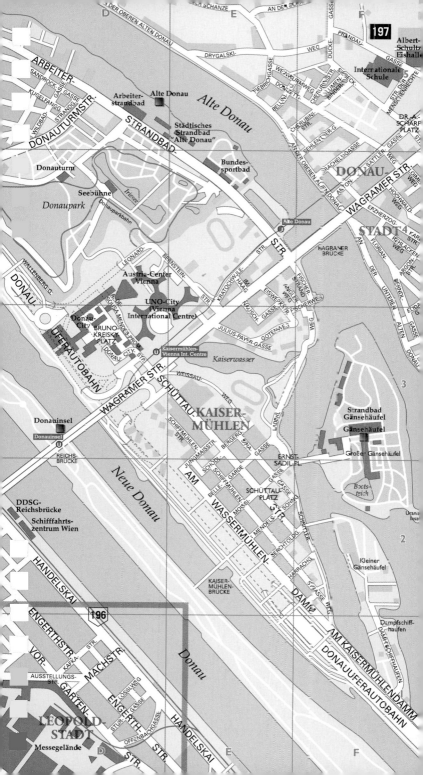

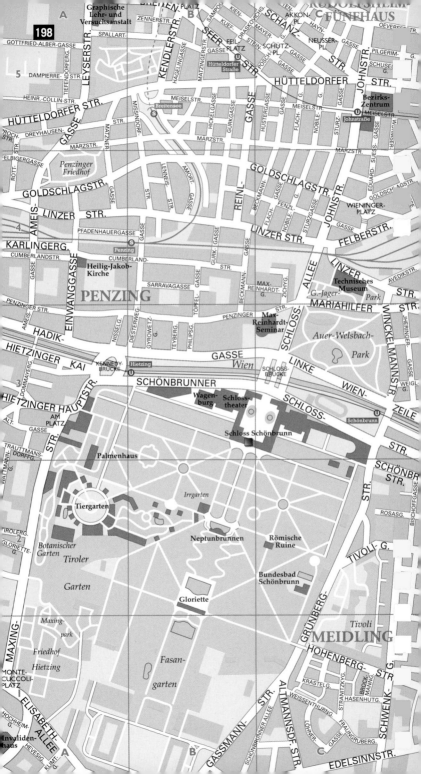

Streetplan Index

Index

Picture credits

SPIRAL GUIDES

Questionnaire

Dear Traveler

Your comments, opinions and recommendations are very important to us. So please help us to improve our travel guides by taking a few minutes to complete this simple questionnaire.

Send to: Spiral Guides, MailStop 66, 1000 AAA Drive, Heathrow, FL 32746–5063

Your recommendations...

We always encourage readers' recommendations for restaurants, nightlife or shopping – if your recommendation is added to the next edition of the guide, we will send you a FREE AAA Spiral Guide of your choice. Please state below the establishment name, location and your reasons for recommending it.

_____

_____

_____

_____

_____

Please send me AAA Spiral _____
(see list of titles inside the back cover)

About this guide...

Which title did you buy?

_____ **AAA Spiral**

Where did you buy it? _____

When? mm/ y y

Why did you choose a AAA Spiral Guide? _____

_____

_____

_____

_____

Did this guide meet your expectations?

Exceeded ☐   Met all ☐   Met most ☐   Fell below ☐

Please give your reasons _____

_____

_____

_____

_____

continued on next page...

Were there any aspects of this guide that you particularly liked?

_____

_____

_____

_____

_____

Is there anything we could have done better?

_____

_____

_____

_____

_____

About you...

Name (Mr/Mrs/Ms) _____

Address _____

_____

_____ Zip _____

Daytime tel nos. _____

Which age group are you in?

Under 25 ☐   25–34 ☐   35–44 ☐   45–54 ☐   55–64 ☐   65+ ☐

How many trips do you make a year?

Less than one ☐   One ☐   Two ☐   Three or more ☐

Are you a AAA member? Yes ☐   No ☐

Name of AAA club _____

About your trip...

When did you book? m m/ y y   When did you travel? m m/ y y

How long did you stay? _____

Was it for business or leisure? _____

Did you buy any other travel guides for your trip?   ☐ Yes   ☐ No

If yes, which ones? _____

_____

Thank you for taking the time to complete this questionnaire.